2

Vision and Rhetoric

edited by G. S. Fraser

*

POETRY NOW:
AN ANTHOLOGY

Vision and Rhetoric

STUDIES IN MODERN POETRY

***

by G. S. *Fraser*

BARNES & NOBLE INC.

NEW YORK

1960

Printed in Great Britain

Contents

❁

Preface

———————————— ✽ ————————————

Mr. David Wright, in a witty review of an anthology I had edited, once wrote that I seemed to have spent my whole adult life, with the exception of my years of war service, in writing, lecturing, broadcasting about modern poetry. I decided to collect some of my longer essays on this subject into a volume a couple of years ago, about the same time as, taking Mr. Wright's hint, I decided to give the subject, in my regular reviewing, a rest.

I have gathered the material in this book from an extraordinary variety of sources, and I only hope that the various manners lie fairly happily down on the page together: the 'God-gifted organ voice' of Printing House Square, the brisk, tangential informality of *The New Statesman*, the high jinks of *Partisan Review*, the patient expository tone of the British Council pamphleteer, the rambling digressiveness with which one sometimes rides a special hobby-horse in a 'little magazine'. I have to thank the periodicals I have alluded to, and the British Council, for permission to reprint much of the material and Professor Bonamy Dobrée, Mr. Alan Pryce-Jones, and Miss Janet Adam Smith both for putting work in my way and for helpful advice and criticism. Such merits as the pieces have also owe a great deal, I imagine, to what I have learned from the friendship and conversation of critics of poetry both older and younger than myself; Professor William Empson, Mr. John Hayward, Professor I. A. Richards, Professor R. P. Blackmur; Mr. Iain Fletcher, Mr. John Wain, Mr. A. Alvarez; to the early encouragement of Mr. T. Tambimuttu, who in *Poetry London* in the years of the Second World War published some of my first serious attempts at criticism; and to the many living English poets, mostly my good friends, who at all times have been genially ready to tell me where I get off.

I wondered, at first, whether essays written over so many years, and for such a variety of publics, written also mostly like Johnson's *Lives of the Poets*, 'with vigour and haste', the printer's devil waiting, would shake together in a book into any sort of consistent pattern. I have never had time to think out a theory of poetics, and, indeed, I doubt if my gifts lie that way. Jungian psychologists believe that there are four main faculties of the human mind, intuition, thinking, feeling, and sensation, and that no individual ever strongly exhibits more than two of them. A Jungian psychologist who is also a literary critic once told me, very gently, that I had no intuitions and that I could not think, but that my faculty of feeling was so strongly developed and, he flatteringly said, so nicely discriminative that it did duty for thinking, for all practical purposes. (My other, secondary faculty was an inward-turned responsiveness to sensation.) Certainly I would describe my primary approach to any work of literature as being made through a kind of groping tact; confronted with a new book, as with a new social atmosphere, I put out my hands and see what I can feel through my finger-tips.

Mr. F. W. Bateson was making the same sort of point as my Jungian psychologist when he described me once, with kindly humour, as the typical lively literary journalist who gets on very well without principles. Since I have been teaching the young, in a provincial university, over the last six months or so, I have learned to respect an approach to literature more slow, more patient, more hesitant than my own. Going over in detail with tutorial groups a poem like 'The Canonization' or 'The Wreck of the "Deutschland"', one realizes that much in English literature that one thinks one 'knows', one knows very superficially. And settling down in early middle age to the profession of an *universitaire*, I realize that, by what ought to be my present standards, much of the writing in this book is abominably cocksure, terribly smart and slick. Yet I comfort myself with the reflection that when I met a very distinguished university critic of poetry, Dr. Donald Davie, once, in London, he said that it was refreshing for a change to be able to talk in shorthand. And I think the trade of literary journalism teaches one to make points compactly, to treat the reader as an equal, and to try at least to entertain him if one cannot instruct or edify him.

I have obviously not only written too much about poetry, but read, perhaps too carefully and too respectfully, too many indifferent poems. What Mr. David L. Craig calls 'the omnivorous appetite of the reviewer' must have in some degree blunted my sensibilities; the hands of the priest become cauterized with holy things. But, reading over these essays, I do find in them an underlying consistency of attitude, and the first essay and the last do perhaps, in an indirect way, make explicit certain critical principles that I hold. The first essay is a consideration of the theory, stated in recent years in three successive books by Sir Herbert Read, Mr. John Bayley, and Mr. Frank Kermode, that what we call the 'modern movement in poetry', the movement we associate with the criticism of T. E. Hulme, with the Imagist movement, with the poetry and criticism of Mr. Pound and Mr. Eliot, is not a break-away from the romantic tradition but a continuation and completion of it; the reader will be able to watch me gradually being won over by this theory, grudgingly yielding to Sir Herbert, still keeping my distance with Mr. Bayley, but wholeheartedly on the side of Mr. Kermode.

The last essay in this book is on the theory of the poem as not an image elemented out of images but a mode of moral discourse, directed at the feelings, and providing rational motives for the feelings it seeks to evoke. By this theory, our final judgment on a poem ought to be a moral judgment on the poet's own judgment on the situation which his poem presents; poetry is not only an imitation of life, but an interpretation of life, a 'criticism of life'. This seems to be the theory of many of the younger poets in England today, and its emphasis is on the element of rational control in the composition of a poem, on the movement of a poem as a 'rational progression'; Dr. Donald Davie is going along this road when he advocates a 'rational conservatism' in poetry, emphasizes the binding function in a poem of syntax as opposed to the sometimes disruptive function of imagery, bids us, since the great romantic movement is now exhausted, go back and pick up the threads which the late Augustans dropped.

My objection to this theory, which is so much more easily defensible than any romantic theory of poetry, is both that in the end it does not wholly square with my personal experience of what writing a poem involves and that, if it does not produce so many bad poems as a romantic attitude does, it does not produce so many genuinely exciting poems either. There are many poems, for instance, of Dylan Thomas's which can hardly be defended as efficient communicative instruments and there is perhaps hardly any poem of his which could be put forward as a mature criticism of life. All Mr. Philip Larkin's poems are efficient communicative instruments; a poem like 'Church Going', of his, is an extremely sensitive, sane, and mature 'criticism of life'. It is relevant to the deep and central problems of contemporary life in a way in which Dylan Thomas's poetry is not. And yet Mr. Larkin's poetry lacks something which Thomas's poetry possesses, at its best, and that something I would call vision.

Gerard Manley Hopkins said that English poetry as a whole was very strong in vision, but weak in what he called rhetoric, 'the common teachable element in poetry'. It is the importance of rhetoric in this sense that the younger poets in England are today emphasizing, and they are thinking of rhetoric also as moral persuasion. And I would certainly agree that a great poem of moral persuasion, like Gray's 'Elegy', is a more impressive piece of work than a poem of genuine vision more or less unrelated to common moral experience, like, for instance, Thomas's 'In Country Sleep': but it is not more impressive than, it is not so impressive as, a poem like Yeats's 'Among School Children' in which a mature experience of life, a great man's awareness of the burden and the splendour of human existence, has its opposites resolved in vision. In that sense it will be found that, throughout this book, my religious temperament getting the better of my liberal and sceptical intellect, I come down in the end on the side of the romantic tradition, looking above all for concentrations and intensities. Yet I see that I have paid much more attention than a romantic critic like Sir Herbert Read, say, would to what poets say, to their judgments about life, and how far I agree with these. So far, I have my Augustan element, too, and indeed when I find myself reading a poet merely for pleasure, it is often Pope in his *Moral Epistles* or Byron in *Don Juan*. One has to say, finally, in criticism of poetry, how far one likes the man and approves of what he is getting at; though, as with Dr. Johnson and Mr. Eliot on Milton, one can dislike the one, disapprove of the other, and still, in the end, be bowled over by the poetry.

But in so far as I relate poetry to life it is not, I think, as a moralist. I have never cared greatly for merely moral men. I have loved people who have struck me as possessed of a quality almost like sanctity. And I have loved people who have combined sad weaknesses with an unusual vitality, with unusual generosity, warmth, charm. That taste for saints and for gay, sad dogs is reflected, I hope, in what I have to say about the deeper and wider human attitudes that lie under poetry. One looks in the greatest poetry not for the copy-book headings; but for either, or both, of two things: intense purity of vision: response to the fullness of life.

The Romantic Tradition and Modern Poetry

Among modern English critics of poetry, Sir Herbert Read is probably the most distinguished disciple of Coleridge. In a more apt sense than usual, Coleridge's revolution in criticism might be called a Copernican one. It involved even a double shift of centres; from particular poems and kinds of poetry, as a main topic of criticism, to the general poetic process; and from the tastes and expectations of the intelligent common reader, as a critical standard, to the experience of the poet. For Coleridge it was no longer, as it had been for Dr. Johnson, the business of the poet to produce a standard composite article that might be given, as it were, separate marks for judgment, wit, truth to natural feeling, invention and design; it was rather, the business of the reader to educate his sensibility until he could not only appreciate a poem but, at least in some degree, reproduce in himself the complex of feelings out of which it had arisen. He had to make himself, so far as he could, a poet. The justification for this novel demand was that poetry, for Coleridge, had a moral use that lay far beyond the sensitive appreciation of words on a page. A poem, in fact, might do its best work for the reader after, as a pattern of words, it had been forgotten. The poetic habit of mind, which the good reader should cultivate, could break down a crust of conventional associations that numbed men, living in an artificial society, to the deep springs of life. Thus for John

Stuart Mill, an admirer of Coleridge, Wordsworth's poetry became, during a crisis of depression, a substitute both for religion and for therapy; it became a source of moral health.

Sir Herbert Read, even today, when in criticism generally a kind of neo-Johnsonianism is becoming orthodox, continues to take this lofty view of the use of poetry; it is not, for him, merely one of the props and ornaments, one of the nobler and more necessary diversions of human life; in poetry, rather, a formative principle, which is broadly continuous throughout the universe, displays itself in one of its highest shapes. The process by which a poem takes form may be thought of as a model, or an example, of the larger process by which a human life integrates itself. For Sir Herbert, however, in spite of the general tendency of his philosophy towards an optimistic organic idealism, there are factors in life, art and society that thwart the formative principle; in particular, the imposed shape of 'rhetoric' is for him no more the true poetic shape than the 'normal' life imposed by social convention is the true shape of human potentiality. Poetry and life, at their best, are self-shaping.

Sir Herbert's general notion of organic form in poetry derives, of course, from Schelling and Coleridge (though some of his particular applications of it have roots as recent as the Imagist movement of 1912). Near the beginning of *The True Voice of Feeling* he restates the fundamental romantic insight, as he understands it, thus:

'The form of a work of art is inherent in the emotional situation of the artist; it proceeds from his apprehension of that situation (a situation that may involve either external objective phenomena or internal states of mind) and is the creation of a formal equivalence (i.e. a symbol) for that situation. It resists or rejects all attempts to fit the situation to a ready-made formula of expression, believing that to impose such a generalized shape on a unique emotion or intuition results in insincerity of feeling and artificiality of form.'

These are deceptively lucid and perhaps rather hastily

written words (it seems natural enough to say that a form resists or rejects something, but surprising to say that it believes anything). Nevertheless, few modern critics are willing to commit themselves to such large and bold statements of principle, and every phrase in the passage demands patient and respectful attention. Such attention may, perhaps, force us to qualify some of the things Sir Herbert says, and thus may modify the total impact of his words. He seems to give us a picture of the artist as a solitary individual, new to the world, re-creating the world for himself, and inventing a quite new language to express it in. In fact, however, the artist's emotional situation includes his general response to the tradition he is working in, and his particular response to the kind of work of art he is trying to produce. When we qualify the main position in this way, it becomes more plausible, but less exciting; and that perhaps tells us something both about the potentialities and the limitations of the romantic approach.

One point in this passage which perhaps deserves special attention is Sir Herbert's sharp and easy distinction (a traditional romantic one) between 'external objective phenomena' and 'internal states of mind'. To some modern philosophers (and especially to the phenomenologists) anything that can be the object of attention, including pain or worry, is, so far, an 'external objective phenomenon'; on the other hand, we habitually project our memories, desires, and expectations into the world beyond our bodies, and therefore any description of that world, other than a purely scientific one, is partly a description of an 'internal state of mind'. Sir Herbert, in fact, seems to postulate a simple division in experience, where what we are aware of is a unified complexity; and it is not mere metaphysical pedantry to make this point here, since the most important of Sir Herbert's purely critical distinctions—between 'organic forms' and 'rhetoric', as exemplified, for instance, respectively in Donne and Pope—seems to rest on a purely ideal disjunction of a similar sort.

The term 'rhetoric' has a great many meanings, from the art of persuasion to a too conscious and perhaps insincere deployment of that art; rhetoric can also be considered not as an art but a science, as that part of grammar which deals with metres, tropes, and elegances of style; in this sense, Hopkins called rhetoric 'the common teachable element' in poetry, as opposed to poetic vision, which must be thought of as innate. Still, there is a rough sense in ordinary usage in which most critics would probably say that *both* Donne and Pope are masterly rhetoricians, though of different schools, and also, great poets; their rhetoric sometimes hampers their poetry, is sometimes (and probably much more often) a support to it, but is in any case inextricably interwoven with it. For Sir Herbert, however, rhetoric is rhetoric, poetry is poetry, and never the twain shall meet. Now this is very like his too facile disjunction of external objective phenomena and internal states of mind. There is not in experience an inner world we can separate from the outer, nor an outer from the inner; every perception has some tinge of feeling, and every awareness is an awareness of something other than itself. We can nevertheless talk sensibly of 'inner' and 'outer' worlds. Similarly, we can talk sensibly of the poet's vision and his rhetoric; but there is no critical act by which we can, as it were, strip off the rhetoric and be left with the vision. Such communicative structure as a poem has is, in the widest sense of the term, rhetoric by definition.

It may be more important still, however, in examining Sir Herbert's statement of principles, to notice that if a genuinely 'unique emotion or intuition' ever did occur, it could never be communicated. All experiences are unique, of course, in the trivial sense that they only happen once; but we can talk about them because they have common or similar elements, and because we have 'ready-made' words for these. What Sir Herbert has in mind here, obviously, is complex and intense experiences which require for their 'formal equivalence' or (complex) 'symbol', for their adequate artistic expression, an equally complex and intense pattern of words. As unrecurring configurations, both experiences and patterns probably are, in more than a trivial if still not quite in an exact sense, 'unique'. They demand an enormous dual effort which is one both of grasping and shaping. Nevertheless, both experiences and patterns are built up of familiar elements and fall, as wholes, into classes. One love-affair, in other words, resembles in some ways other love-affairs; one love-poem other love-poems. The possibility, not merely of art, but of language itself, of any human system of signs or symbols, depends on our power of seeing similarities, abstracting structural elements, imposing a 'generalized shape' on the 'unique'. It is hard, in fact, to think of any artist who has not 'accepted a ready-made formula of expression' at least in the sense of making use of what communicative machinery lay handy. And when we recognize these facts, we may wonder whether a work of art need be 'artificial' in a bad sense because it is in the manner of a school, or 'insincere' because it expresses feeling according to some convention of decorum. These may all seem petty and quibbling points, and irrelevant to Sir Herbert's main, and justified, emphasis—and that of the romantic tradition generally—on the integrity and autonomy of the creative process. But a philosophical critic invites and probably desires even captiously detailed questioning of his broad statements of principle. And these observations may suggest at least one limitation of the romantic approach in criticism: in its much-needed emphasis on the idea of art as expression, it tends to ignore the historical and cultural conditions that make artistic expression possible, or, more broadly, to ignore the idea of art as communication.

In practice, of course, Sir Herbert's general principles are not so limiting as, applied with dogmatic literalness and without the safeguard of his fine sensibility, they might be. Poets whose verse and criticism seem to him alive, like T. E. Hulme and Mr. Eliot, are for him really in the great romantic tradition, though they consider themselves neo-classicists; and the great pre-romantic poets whom he admires—and, apart from a total rejection of the Augustans, his admirations are catholic—are in this large honorary sense, romantic, too. Rather similarly, in relation to verse technique, some of the best poets of the past can be considered as honorary adherents—particularly on its 'free verse' side—of the Imagist movement of 1912. By some ingenious but not convincing experiments in scansion, Sir Herbert persuades himself that Wordsworth's blank verse—perfectly orthodox blank verse as it seems to most of us, and very blank verse indeed as it seems to a few recalcitrant non-Wordsworthians —is so full of irregularities that it must be thought of as struggling towards the condition of *vers libre*. Here, Sir Herbert is simply not making sufficient allowances for conventions like that of the courtesy stress on light syllables, or for the substitutions which are common in the English iambic pentameter in every foot but the second and fifth. He is thinking of 'correct' metrics, as he thinks of 'correct' rhetoric, as consisting of the cruel imposition on what might have been living matter of a dead mechanical shape. No rhetorical and no metrical tradition has really such rigidity; no tradition of any sort can establish itself in practice (can, as it were, provide young artists with working models) unless it has in fact a great deal of that organic flexibility which Sir Herbert rightly admires.

A rather similar point might, more sharply, be made about Sir Herbert's attempt to improve Keats by eliminating rhetorical inversions: by substituting

> 'Then I saw a wan face,
> Not pin'd by human sorrows, but blanch'd bright
> By an immortal sickness which does not kill,'

for what Keats wrote,

> 'Then saw I a wan face,
> Not pin'd by human sorrows, but bright blanch'd
> By an immortal sickness which kills not. . . .'

There are reasons in the order of ideas (quite apart from

20

metrical points that might be made) for preferring 'saw I' to 'I saw' and 'bright blanch'd' to 'blanch'd bright'; it is the fact of the vision that needs salience, not *whose* vision it was; it is the splendour of the face that we are to become aware of, before we realize it is a splendour of sickness. Sir Herbert here seems himself to have become a rhetorician of the very sort he disapproves of, retrospectively imposing upon Keats a rule (that of avoiding inversion, even where it points an emphasis or aids condensation) that happens to be rigidly obeyed by most young modern poets.

It is not, perhaps, over such points of detail that Sir Herbert's real gifts as a critic best display themselves. An example of the value of his psychological approach to the general poetic process is his famous essay, the revised version of 'In Defence of Shelley'. Matthew Arnold and Mr. T. S. Eliot both attack Shelley for his immaturity, his apparent inability to learn from experience, or to make contact with 'real life'. Shelley is a shrill adolescent, and theirs is the voice of middle age, which 'knows better'. Sir Herbert's defence is highly ingenious. Certainly, he says, Shelley was immature; moreover, he was an unconscious and self-absorbed homosexual, who had fantasies about incest, and recurrent guilty delusions of persecution; he was incapable of taking a permanent interest in other people, or an objective view of the world; he lived in a universe of projections; and that is why he is such a good poet of his kind. Shelley's psychosis is, for Sir Herbert, the ground of his special gifts—his generality, his rapidity, his unifying sweep: '. . . in the case of the incompletely adapted individual, his essential sub-jectivity will demand a more generalized kind of unity, in which there is no separation of the individual from the world at large.' Thus when we know in one sense 'the worst' about Shelley, we are in a position to appreciate the best. Matthew Arnold's difficulties and Mr. Eliot's do not arise from Dr. Richards's famous problem of poetry and belief—which Sir Herbert considers a critical red herring—but simply from imperfect understanding and sympathy.

Nor can we reject the vision of a psychotic from the standpoint of 'normality'—which in any case is usually merely the standpoint of the obedient and uncreative philistine. Mental illnesses themselves can be processes of integration; they can enable the individual to reflect in himself, and if he is an artist to symbolize for others, processes of division, and attempts to transcend division, that are general in society.

Sir Herbert displays a similar acumen (and a similar gift for establishing fruitful connexions between purely critical ideas and the disciplines of psychology) in his essays on the other great romantics, Wordsworth, Coleridge, Keats, and even Byron. The tact and charity of the essay on Byron are particularly admirable, since *Don Juan*, for Sir Herbert, is great verse rather than great poetry; and since Byron, as a man, has a theatrical side; which his critic cannot find congenial. When Sir Herbert deals, however, with his own contemporaries, T. E. Hulme, Mr. Pound and Mr. Eliot, he very properly discards the psychological approach and writes, rather, as an expert verse craftsman. These essays, with their severely technical approach, will fascinate practising poets, but may disappoint the general reader. Even the practising poet, perhaps, may regret that, in his essay on Mr. Eliot, Sir Herbert concentrates on the plays rather than the poems and devotes so much of his energy to deciding where the stresses and caesuras come in a speech from *The Cocktail Party*. The truth is, probably, that like all effective verse for the theatre these long lines with their mobile stresses leave something to the choice of the actor. Yet these passages of scansion—like Sir Herbert's confident rejection, on technical grounds, of Walt Whitman and D. H. Lawrence from the 'true' free verse tradition—are extremely interesting in relation to Sir Herbert's always suggestive but always overstrained distinction between 'rhetoric' and 'organic form'. There are times in these later essays when he seems, without being aware of it, to be sketching out a rhetoric of organic form. The insights by the light of which he accepts and rejects could, often, be generalized as rules;

and the rules could then be consciously applied by young poets. For them there is much technical enlightenment in this book, as for their elders there is much human wisdom. Every reader will find something to disagree with; but the very act of disagreement should make us respect a critic who forces us to question our sensibility, to ask ourselves how many of our responses are a mere matter of fashion or habit, and to clarify, even if in opposition to his, our own fundamental principles.

II

The Romantic Revival can be seen as the grand formative influence upon the greater poetry of the Victorian age: even though Arnold consciously reacted against it, and even though, in Browning and Tennyson, the New Victorian themes—in a sense 'outer' and 'social' themes—of faith and doubt complicated the early Romantic mood of self-exploring aspiration and of direct response to the deep life of nature and of the mind. Similarly, at a certain distance, and with a certain complication, the greatest poet of our own age, Yeats, can be seen as coming out of the Romantic Revival. He comes immediately out of its decadent development, out of Pater and the Pre-Raphaelites; and as far as he comes out of its roots he comes out of Blake and Shelley, out of their mythomania, and out of the conscious stylishness of that 'Romantic classic' Landor, rather than out of the noble sobriety of Wordsworth, the careless dash of Byron, or the yielding, feminine richness of Keats. (The poet Dorothy Wellesley thought that in his character and the range of his interests Yeats a great deal resembled Coleridge, but it is hard to see that he at all resembled him as a poet.) Nevertheless, until quite recently critics have tended to consider the significantly 'modern' poetry of our own century, the innovating poetry, the poetry, for instance, of Mr. Eliot or Mr. Pound or Mr. Auden, as marking a decisive break with the Romantic tradition.

The Romantic Tradition and Modern Poetry

The centrality which the Romantic Revival enjoyed for Victorian critics has been usurped, gradually, over the past thirty or forty years, for many critics by the seventeenth century. The very special and local and peculiar virtues of poets like Donne are often, today, used as a kind of universal touchstone. So good a critic as Mr. John Speirs will eagerly comb out stray examples of metaphysical wit—phrases like 'gospel kail'—from so unmetaphysical a poet as Burns; so good a critic as Mr. Cleanth Brooks will go solemnly through a sonnet by Wordsworth looking for a latent, and fashionable, 'paradox' and 'irony'. And a poet like Shelley, who cannot be brought into line in this way, is dismissed because the logic of his poetic constructions is a large-scale, not a small-scale, logic; because the detail of his language has not that sinewy tightness, that ripple of sudden surprises, that we like in Marvell and Donne.

The great Romantics have not, of course, been exactly put on the shelf. And yet a phrase of Mr. Eliot's, about Wordsworth, about 'the still, sad music of senility' does suggest the kind of tone in which, until quite recently, they have often been talked about. (Is the phrase a fair description, for instance, of that very late, very moving, and certainly very unequal poem, the 'Extempore Effusion on the Death of James Hogg'?) This shyness about the great Romantics is, of course, partly due to the fact that they do not lend themselves to that most typical kind of modern criticism, the close examination of the texture of a poet's language. One of the best points made in Mr. John Bayley's lively book, *The Romantic Survival*, is that, in spite of Wordsworth's on the whole clumsy and unfortunate experiments with 'the real language of man', the great Romantics were not notable innovators in style. There is not a specifically Romantic style in poetry, as there is an Augustan style. Wordsworth's blank verse, in its movement and in its diction, is not so very unlike Cowper's or even Akenside's; it is his matter, it is the theme of the growth of a poet's mind, that is new.

The Romantic Tradition and Modern Poetry

There are, of course, other poets of the Romantic Revival who lend themselves more easily than Wordsworth or Shelley to close criticism, and who seem more certainly in some sense 'Romantic', in their essence, than Byron. If Byron wanted to consider himself, at his best, a belated Augustan, he may have had some reason on his side, though it has been pointed out that his characteristic easy, glancing tone is not very like Pope's but sometimes very like Cavalier poets', such as Lovelace (whom he had almost certainly never read); and when Mr. Bayley puts forward Mr. Auden as a modern Romantic poet, partly because of his obvious affinities with Byron, a critic must make the same reservation. Byron was a great poet of the Romantic period, and Mr. Auden owes a great deal to Byron, but neither, as Mr. Bayley admits, is in the least influenced by the theories of poetry held, for instance, by Coleridge, by Wordsworth, by Shelley, or by Keats. What, however, of Blake, or of Keats himself, two poets of the Romantic period who have, and very rewardingly, attracted modern close critics?

Blake is a special case. He was a transcendentalist, like Coleridge, but going, as Coleridge said, a good deal farther. Source-hunters like Miss Kathleen Raine are now busily at work relating him to English folk-song, to Swedenborg, to Lavater, to *Ossian*, to Tom Taylor's eccentric commentaries on Plato, to, at the commentators' most ambitious, a great tradition of religious wisdom—not orthodox Christian wisdom—to which it is claimed that Spenser and Milton and Shelley and Yeats also belong. It is safest, at the moment, to see him not as a Romantic somewhat out of step but as the founder of a school, including both painters and poets, of specifically English symbolists, visionaries, and makers or remakers of myth. He can certainly stand, he needs, the very closest analysis, but the analysis seems, as Mr. F. W. Bateson has pointed out in a recent small selection of Blake's poems, often to bring out an awkward gap between Blake's intentions and the effect on an ordinary sensitive reader of his poems. Deeper understanding of the intentions does not spoil the poems, but it does not necessarily make the shorter poems, at least, seem better.

Only Keats, of all the great Romantics, was consciously an artist first and foremost; and the great 'Odes' particularly repay the detailed attention which they have in recent years received. Keats is a poet who can be sampled, adequately, under the microscope. But, partly because the others cannot be sampled adequately in this way, many critics have liked to think that the best poetry of our own age marks a rejection of what they stood for. That is the thesis that Mr. Bayley is questioning. He points out that we *respond* to a phrase like Blake's 'dark Satanic mills' long before we have even a vague notion of what, in his environment or in his private mental world, Blake was referring to; he thinks that the habit of analysis is becoming so strong in us that in a modern poem we might praise a phrase like 'dense, ambitious mills'—even though it arouses no *frisson* whatsoever, —since it is the sort of phrase we could fit tidily into a context. We treat poems as machines, to be taken to pieces, and forget that there is a ghost—a *Geist*, a mind, a spirit—*in* the machine. It is something like the excitement and directness of the response of the early readers of the great Romantics to them that he wants to arouse in us, in our approach to modern poetry. (Like many people who attack analysis, he is, it might be said in passing, very good at analysis himself.)

The first part of Mr. Bayley's book is an extremely clear and compact summary of the evolution of the Romantic idea throughout the nineteenth century and after. It would require too much space to summarize his summary, and it may be more useful to make a few critical points. Throughout his book he gives the effect of sacrificing to clarity of outline, and to the ease of the general reader, qualifications which, in a work addressed primarily to scholars, he would no doubt have wished to make. (He uses once or twice, for instance, Mr. Eliot's phrase about the 'dissociation of sensibility' without giving any indication of from how many sides, recently, it has been shot at.) In his very first chapter, he much too simply equates the theories of Wordsworth and Coleridge about the poetic imagination—he more or less boils them down to 'the great "I am", "the dread watch-tower of man's absolute self",' to what Keats called 'the egotistical sublime'—and sets them in polarity with Keats's theory of 'negative capability'. But, of course, what Coleridge had to say about the imagination as a power that dissolves experience in order to re-create it might have been much more sympathetic to Keats than to Wordsworth.

When Wordsworth writes,

> 'but this I feel,
> That from thyself it comes, that thou must give
> Else never canst receive,'

and when Coleridge writes,

> 'O Lady, we receive but what we give,
> And in our life alone does Nature live,'

they seem, at a first glance, to be saying, in partly identical words, the same thing, but in fact they are saying things radically different. Wordsworth is saying that to receive an influx of life, which is immanently there in Nature, we must have in ourselves a pure and responsive spirit; Coleridge, going part of Blake's way, is saying that the influx of life we *think* we get from Nature is fed back to us from what we have projected into Nature of the life of the mind, which is also, in its true depths, the life of Mind as such. Immanentist and Transcendentalist Romanticism are, from the first, in polarity with each other. Coleridge's theory of the imagination is subjective but not egotistical; it throws doubt on the reality both of the phenomenal senser and the phenomenon sensed; whereas Wordsworth's mountains are as tough as his mind.

Keats's 'negative capability', if one were to attach a metaphysical principle to it, might be called a kind of monistic aesthetic phenomenalism, as Coleridge's theory of the imagination is a monistic transcendentalism; whereas what Wordsworth seems to believe in, when he is at his best as a poet, is a dualistic immanentism, a real interplay between a real Nature and a real Mind. Keats is unlike both Wordsworth and Coleridge in that he does not try to get *beyond* experience, he luxuriates in it: 'O for a life of sensations rather than thoughts!' He seeks to be at one with his sensations, to merge perceiver and perceived. His is the aesthetic life, in Kierkegaard's sense (pain is an element in a total hedonic composition). Thus, at the very roots of English Romanticism, there are three theoretical attitudes: out of Wordsworth's way of feeling and thinking Hardy could come; out of Coleridge's, Yeats; out of Keats's, Pater. By merely bifurcating his paths, from the start Mr. Bayley has his signposts wrong.

It is by such polarities, always suggestive and always oversimplified, that Mr. Bayley proceeds. It is very wrong, for instance, to say:

'Blake and Wordsworth had symbolized mystery and power by the simplest means—the grain of sand, the caterpillar on the leaf—universal order can be deduced from the smallest fragments of being.'

The grain of sand, the caterpillar on the leaf are Blake's properties, not Wordsworth's. They are not 'fragments of being', from which, in the fashion of Paley and his watch found in the desert, 'universal order' is to be coldly 'deduced'. They are order already. They are 'minute particulars' in which 'universal order', so to call it, is—so beautiful and complete is their organization—*exhibited*; and for Blake they are less natural objects than supernatural emblems or symbols. As for Wordsworth, he needs not a single emblematic object but a great stretch of *The Prelude* or the whole of 'Resolution and Independence', he needs a huge lump of experience and the digestion of it, to 'symbolize mystery and power'.

Mr. Bayley's sketch of the evolution of Romanticism is, then, excessively schematic; perpetually the reader is underlining what seem rash statements and putting queries in the margin. But its very schematism makes it perhaps a useful text for young readers, like Mr. Bayley's students at Oxford, to start from; if they do not take it as a final statement, but as a set of useful clues. The second, rather shorter, part of the book consists of essays on three modern poets, Yeats, Mr. Auden, and Dylan Thomas, who seem to Mr. Bayley to carry on the Romantic tradition. The essay on Yeats is sensitive and perceptive, particularly good on Yeats's gift of conversational self-dramatization and of ending a poem with an effective gesture rather than a clinching argument. It shows fine taste in its choice of quotations but it says, perhaps, little that is radically new.

The essay on Mr. Auden is, on the other hand, perhaps the most brilliant short study that has been made of that poet. It seeks very ingeniously to dispose of the notion that Mr. Auden was at any time a socially committed or propagandist or 'social realist' poet in any real sense. It claims that even in the 1930s Mr. Auden's ruined powerhouses and conspirators and explorers and 'ruined boys', like his use of ideas from Marx and Freud and Groddeck, were a set of gimmicks, no more, no less, exactly like Yeats's allusions to 'profound McTaggart', and his phases of the moon, his cones and his gyres. Mr. Auden, if Mr. Bayley is right, in those days took us all in by seeming to capture us with urgent topical journalism, when in fact he was captivating us with poetry; what we took for parts of a message were elements in a composition.

'Auden [says Mr. Bayley] has followed Yeats in showing how the intense private world of symbolism can be brought right out into the open, eclecticized, and pegged down to every point of contemporary interest and everyday life, while remaining none the less a private and even a *substitute* world.'

The italics are mine; Mr. Bayley demonstrates brilliantly both Mr. Auden's mastery of what he calls 'the sung short story' and the asymptotic relation of his 'poetic' world with the 'real' world. Mr. Bayley notes, also, that whereas Mr. Eliot's poems 'even at their most exploratory and personal retain a public susceptibility . . . to straightforward explanatory gloss', Mr. Auden's 'apparently public, outgoing themes are in fact self-contained'.

The essay on Dylan Thomas is, perhaps, a little less satisfactory. The emphasis is on the 'thinginess' of Thomas's language, his use of the word *as* the thing, or as the magic equivalent of the thing, and attempts at exegesis of what might be called Thomas's prose sense—or even Thomas's broad drift in a particular poem—are perhaps excessively deprecated. For the critic of Thomas, Mr. Bayley thinks, 'indication of the types of linguistic experience we encounter in his work, and of how we may best enjoy them, remains the most constructive critical approach'. The few poems that have an easily get-at-able 'sense' (as Dr. Richards uses that word) rather disconcert Mr. Bayley: was all that effort only to say *that*? He is right, however, to insist on the remarkable concreteness of Thomas's poetic statements, or presentations, and on the danger of trying to 'explain' the poems by relating the concreteness to vague generalities. Yet a reader who has lived patiently with Thomas's best poems for some time may feel that, after all, they are *about* something, they have both themes and subjects, and that it is often possible to say, though no doubt in a cumbrous and hesitant way, what one thinks they are about. Yet, all in all, this is an exceedingly stimulating book; what it loses in authoritativeness, sometimes, by making a shockingly complicated subject seem deceptively simple, it may gain in useful immediacy of impact.

III

Let a poet explain.

'But it has often happened in the past, as we learn from the history of literature, that poetry has been used to enunciate arguments or hypotheses: that the *complete* language

which is peculiarly its own, the language in which the *form*
—that is to say, the active element and the sense of *Voice*—
is of equal value with the substance—that is, with the
ultimate modification of the *mental* content—has been used
to communicate "abstract" ideas, which are (or seem to be)
independent of their form. Very great poets have sometimes made this attempt. But no matter how great the talent
employed on such noble enterprises, the attention needed to
follow the ideas cannot help but be out of step with that
which follows the music. The *De Natura Rerum* is here in
conflict with the Nature of Things. The state of mind
in which we read a poem is not the same state of mind in
which we follow the development of pure thought. The
state of mind of a man engaged in dancing is not the same
as the state of mind of the man who walks through a difficult stretch of country intent on making a topographical
map or a geological survey.'

These lucid sentences by Paul Valéry, in Mr. Gerard
Hopkins's excellent translation of his essay on 'Poetry and
Abstract Thought', provide a useful lead-in to Mr. Frank
Kermode's extremely important book of speculative and
scholarly criticism, *Romantic Image*. They announce, as Mr.
Kermode himself never quite does in such a bald and
abstract way, or with such deceptive simplicity, his main
theme. Like so many recent English critics of poetry, Sir
Herbert Read and Mr. John Bayley among them, Mr. Kermode is setting out to re-define the notion of the Romantic
tradition, especially in its relation to English poetry and
criticism; and like Sir Herbert, and in some degree Mr.
Bayley, he is anxious to assert that the modern movement
in English poetry, the movement of revolt which we associate with the names of T. E. Hulme, Mr. Ezra Pound, Mr.
T. S. Eliot, the later work of Yeats, is not a reversal of the
Romantic tradition, but, like that French Symbolist tradition of which Valéry was the last great ornament, the
logical continuer of it.

His central theme is the contrast between the poem as an

image made of images—for which Yeats's great image was the dancer—and the world of discourse. Discourse conveys, or seeks out, information. Images joyously or terrifyingly reveal. In modern society, the conveying or the seeking out of information, communication with an ultimately practical purpose, is increasingly our main social nexus. Pragmatic curiosities draw men together. Privileged revelations tend, on the whole, to isolate men from each other; they are also, even in the greatest of poets, intermittent, and no moment of revelation guarantees that any other will ever succeed it. The Romantic view of the poet's fate tends, therefore, to be a tragical one:

> 'We Poets in our youth begin in gladness;
> But thereof come in the end despondency and madness.'

And the Romantic view of the poem, refusing to consider the language of poetry as in any sense a kind of discourse, makes discursive criticism of poetry, in theory, irrelevant. The Romantic poem is not a statement about life, but, like a plant, an expression of life. As critics, 'we murder to dissect'. As Yeats wrote in his old age:

'I am happy, and I think full of an energy, an energy I had despaired of. It seems to me that I have found what I have wanted. When I try to put it all in a phrase I say, "Man can embody truth but he cannot know it. . . ." '

Three concepts, in fact, for Mr. Kermode are central to the notion of Romanticism. One of these is the concept of the poet as an alienated man, cut off from the common life of action or routine, isolated in a society whose values he cannot accept; of the poet as *different*. Even poets like Goethe or Wordsworth, who insist on the poet's normality, who insist that he is an ordinary man, with greater moral strength, intellectual insight, and organic sensibility, are in the end insisting on the poet's difference; such normality as theirs is an ideal normality, something which in actual life is very uncommon. A second concept is that of the poetic imagination as giving access, through 'a translucency of the intelligible in the real', to a world which may or may not be thought of as real and transcendent, which may be thought of as a supernatural world, or a dream world, or a world that only exists in art, but which is not the common world and not within reach of the common operations of reason. It is not an empirical world, but one to which even the poet's own privileged access is extremely precarious. The third concept is that a poem is not to be thought of, for instance, on the analogy of a mathematical construction or even on the nobler analogy of a house built from traditional materials, in a traditional style; it is to be thought of on the analogy of a plant that has its own dumb principles of growth. This aesthetic biologism has its roots in the late eighteenth century in Germany, and its great English exemplar is Coleridge. Mr. Kermode quotes some witty sentences by Mr. M. H. Abrams: 'It is astonishing how much of Coleridge's critical writing is couched in terms that are metaphorical for art and literal for a plant; if Plato's dialectic is a wilderness of mirrors, Coleridge's is a jungle of vegetation.' And he quotes Goethe's great sentences about *Hamlet*, which seem to foreshadow the splendid last stanza of Yeats's 'Among School Children': 'It is a trunk with boughs, leaves, blossoms, and fruit. Are they not all one, and there by means of each other?'

From these three basic concepts of the poet's difference or isolation, of the image as the instrument of poetic revelation, and of the organic nature of the poetic process, there can be derived, as Mr. Kermode shows in his brilliant third chapter, a very elaborate set of criteria for what a true Romantic poem should be. It has organic form, not mechanical shape. It has a unity of symbolic meaning which is independent both of the poet's conscious intentions (we build better than we know) and of the response of any particular set of readers. It has a paradoxical relationship to life. In one sense, as an image made of images, it is something snatched from the flow of space and time, beyond life, and so dead; in another sense it is more living than life, in that it gives access to a higher order of being, and in that it is itself, like the highest living organisms, a beautiful example of complex organization. It draws on the Great Memory or the Book of the People, on an underground tradition of a shared language of symbols, and thus, though obscure, it is not private; it never, at least ideally, passes over into sheer uncommunication.

Its form and its content are at one, it does not 'communicate "abstract" ideas, which are (or seem to be) independent of their form'. The poet plans and thinks but the planning and thinking are not something which the poem 'puts over', but something which is used up in the making of the poem. It is concrete. Mr. Kermode quotes Oscar Wilde (it is one of the great merits of his book that it places Yeats's 'tragic generation', one of the few groups of important Victorian writers not yet revived in the schools, squarely in the tradition): 'Like Aristotle, like Goethe after he had read Kant, we desire the concrete, and nothing but the concrete can satisfy us.' Yet such concreteness does not imply a limited fixity, an exhaustibility of aspects. The same poem, at different times, can say different things to us. Mr. Kermode quotes Wilde again: 'When the work is finished it has, as it were, an independent life of its own and may deliver a message far other than that which was put into its lips to say.'

For all these metaphors of life and growth, there is a sense also in which, especially for the later poets of the Romantic tradition, the poem as something completed, rounded, finished, stands in an antithetical relationship to Nature. Mr. Kermode quotes Wallace Stevens on the jar set in the Tennessee wilderness:

> 'It took dominion everywhere,
> The jar was grey and bare.
> It did not give of bird or bush,
> Like nothing else in Tennessee.'

The Romantic poem is like a tree or a dancer, in one set of

analogies, but in another it is, like Yeats's clockwork Byzantine golden bird, 'an artifice of Eternity'. That it should be in some sense a *living* artifice is the paradox about it. It is in another sense an irruption, an epiphany, a revelation, for Yeats as for Blake, from the Other Side to the 'vegetative universe'. And if what Romantic poetry celebrates is the organic, the instinctive, the gay and thoughtless springs of life, the soul become body, 'Unity of Being', a paradisal state that precedes discursive thought, the poet, *as* celebrating that state, is set apart from it. *He* is under Adam's curse, *he* has to earn his poetic bread by the sweat of his brow. From this paradox springs the Romantic sense of the poet's vocation as a tragic one; of all his achievements as a set of Pyrrhic victories, to be terminated only by his final defeat (which is also, however, his final release) in death.

The theme of the fate of the Romantic poet Mr. Kermode finds perfectly stated in one of Yeats's greatest poems, 'In Memory of Major Robert Gregory'. He quotes a very interesting obituary notice which Yeats wrote on Gregory's death in action in the First World War. Yeats, as Mr. Kermode puts it, is in this obituary 'already systematizing Gregory, making his memory the node of much complicated speculation'. Gregory is set in a tradition, the tradition of English symbolism, of Blake and Calvert and Palmer, which is a subjective tradition, and has deep affinities with the lyrical Romantic tradition of Wordsworth. It is Gregory's fate to be a great poetic painter (and therefore to suffer the rending isolation of the Romantic artist), but his aristocratic accomplishments, the ease and gaiety of the social life open to him, fight against his fate; but unlike Synge, unlike Lionel Johnson, unlike the other friends whom Yeats names in his elegy, Gregory is able to escape the fate of the Romantic artist, to die, still 'our Sidney and our perfect man', in battle: 'Gregory alone of them all found a definitive joy in abandoning the pain and delight of the dream for self-destructive action.'

Mr. Kermode then goes on to show how this tragic concept of the artist's fate affected Yeats's symbol, or image, of the work of art. The poet is divided, and the poem must be undivided. An obvious symbol for such undivision is the body of a beautiful woman whose thought is in her movements, who has been taught 'the heroic discipline of the looking glass'. As early as 1900, Yeats was writing: 'You cannot give a body to something that moves beyond the senses, unless your words are as subtle, as complex, as full of mysterious life, as the body of a flower or of a woman.' The image of the woman, with her beautiful expressionless face and inward-turned dreamy gaze, gradually developed, because of the cruelty of the poet's fate, into the image of Salome, dancing before, or dancing holding in her hands, John the Baptist's head. The image of the dance itself became an image of poised unity of being moving between dividing extremes. The organic image of the flower becomes, in 'Among School Children', the image of the Tree of Life, the tree Adam ought to have robbed instead of the Tree of the Knowledge of Good and Evil. Mr. Kermode traces the development of such images in Yeats's work, and sources for them in Blake, in the French Symbolists, in minor writers of the 1890s, with fascinating scholarship. His chapters on Yeats are among the best pages that have ever been devoted to that great poet. They set him in a context, they make many opacities apprehensible.

The second part of Mr. Kermode's book is devoted to the development of the Romantic idea first of all in Arthur Symons's work on the French Symbolists and later in the criticism of T. E. Hulme and the early criticism of Mr. T. S. Eliot. Here his purposes are, more than in the chapters on Yeats as a great Romantic, controversial and polemical. He wishes to show that a great deal of what we think of as typically 'modern' critical theory, and which we associate particularly with Hulme and Mr. Eliot, and in a lesser degree Wyndham Lewis and Mr. Pound, is firmly rooted in the late Victorian age. Victorian editors of Donne, for instance, were already using phrases not wholly unlike Mr. Eliot's 'fusion of thought and feeling'. Arthur Symons, like Mr. Eliot, arrived at an appreciation of Donne and the Jacobean dramatists (and to some extent therefore at a misinterpretation of them) partly through an appreciation of the Symbolists. Wyndham Lewis's Vortex, the Image of the Imagists and Mr. Ezra Pound's later more dynamic ideogrammatic Image, Hulme's 'intensive manifold', Professor Lehmann's 'aesthetic monad', are all, under new verbal disguises, much the same sort of thing that the young Yeats had in mind when he said: 'A symbol is indeed the only possible expression of some invisible essence, a transparent lamp about a spiritual flame. . . .'

Hulme, blasting and bombardiering against the whole Romantic tradition, was nevertheless speaking in language that Coleridge would have understood when he said: 'Images in verse are not mere decoration, but the very essence of an intuitive language.' Similarly, Mr. Kermode thinks that Mr. Eliot's famous phrase about the 'dissociation of sensibility' is not a useful historical instrument but a brilliant subjective expression of the traditional Romantic myth of the poet's alienation. The historian can find no period of history, at least no period of literary interest, in which the language of feeling was really at one with the language of thought, in which men were not divided against themselves. Mr. Kermode points out that the idea of 'dissociation of sensibility' which was used by Mr. Eliot to boost Donne and deprecate Milton could—or a rough equivalent to it could—be used by Mr. Pound to boost Cavalcanti and deprecate Petrarch, or by some critic more or less of Mr. Pound's school to boost Catullus and deprecate Virgil. This makes it, for him, a merely subjective notion.

Yet it might be said that the language of Donne, Cavalcanti and Catullus has a fresh and struggling quality, a raw, new quality, and that of Milton, Petrarch and Virgil a settled, elaborate quality; and another pair of whom the

37

same observation might be made are Keats and Tennyson. If there are never, in literary history, exactly periods of un-dissociated sensibility, are there not periods about which we feel, in retrospect, 'bliss was it in that dawn to be alive'; and other periods of which the heavier atmosphere is more that of a long autumn afternoon? Mr. Eliot was not—he never has done so—putting a finger on *nothing*. But this is a minor criticism of a rich, packed, suggestive book. Mr. Kermode makes us realize the extraordinary strength of the prolonged trajectory of the Romantic Movement; it is only quite recently that poets and critics have been asking themselves whether perhaps the connective and persuasive powers of the mind, whether the disciplines of logic and rhetoric, may not, after all, as well as the 'image-making powers', have an important part to play in the creation of great poetry.

W. B. Yeats

I

For just over ten years before he died in a hotel in the south of France, at the beginning of 1939, William Butler Yeats had been universally recognized by his peers as the greatest poet, writing in the English language, of this century. The recognition dates from the publication, in 1928, of his finest volume, *The Tower*. In June of 1939, he would have been seventy-four. He had been writing verses since his 'teens and had been a poet of some reputation since his twenties. Since the turn of the century, he would probably have been mentioned by any critic in a list of the four or five most distinguished English poets, and, in any consideration of Irish poetry, he would have been head of the list. He had won the Nobel Prize for literature, he had done more than any other man to bring about the birth of the Irish theatre, and he had sat in the Senate of the Irish Free State. Yet every critic knows that these public honours are never the full measure of a poet's reputation. At regular intervals during his long life, shrewd critics had been convinced that Yeats was finished. To George Moore, in the Edwardian decade, it seemed that all Yeats's best poems had been inspired by his hopeless love for Maude Gonne; that love was never to find physical fulfilment, and Moore thought that Yeats's lyrical gift would wither, like cut flowers in a glass. To the young Mr. T. S. Eliot, in the early Georgian era, Yeats seemed not much more than an interesting survival from the 1890s. The young Mr. Pound, sending some of Yeats's poems to an American magazine, took it upon himself to polish and improve them. The young Mr. Middleton Murry, one of the best critics of poetry of his period, dismissed *The Wild Swans at Coole*, which came out in 1919, as the work of a used-up aesthete. The interesting generation of writers who came to Oxford after the First World War thought little of Yeats. 'Surely', wrote T. E. Lawrence to Ezra Pound, 'Yeats is no good?' Mr. Robert Graves, in the *Pamphlet Against Anthologies* which he wrote with Miss Laura Riding, made jovial hay of 'The Lake Isle of Innisfree'. Thus, though Yeats had never been neglected, the full recognition of his greatness, like its full flowering, came very tardily.

To many critics, almost up to the last ten years of his life, it seemed that Yeats, wonderful as his gifts were, did not live wholly in the real world. Thus Dr. I. A. Richards, in *Science and Poetry*, 1925, commenting on Yeats's interest in magic, wrote:

'Now he turns to a world of symbolic phantasmagoria about which he is desperately uncertain. He is uncertain because he has adopted as a technique of inspiration the use of trance, of dissociated phases of consciousness, and the revelations given in these dissociated states are insufficiently connected with normal experience.'

Quoting this comment, Mr. T. S. Eliot, in *After Strange Gods*, had even more severe things to say as late as 1934:

'. . . Mr. Yeats's "supernatural world" was the wrong supernatural world. It was not a world of spiritual significance, not a world of real Good and Evil, of holiness and sin, but a highly sophisticated lower mythology summoned, like a physician, to supply the fading pulse of poetry with some transient stimulant, so that the dying patient may utter his last words.'

The centrally important critical problem about Yeats becomes clear if we contrast these passages with the noble tribute which Mr. Eliot paid to Yeats on his death:

'There are some poets whose poems can be considered more or less in isolation, for experience and delight. There

W. B. Yeats

are others whose poetry, though giving equally experience and delight, has a larger historical importance. Yeats was one of the latter. He was one of the few whose history was the history of our own time, who are part of the consciousness of our age, which cannot be understood without them.'[1]

How are these pertinent strictures to be reconciled with this deserved praise? In what sense was the mental history of Yeats, which from a superficial point of view was so odd and eccentric, more profoundly 'the history of our own time'? Was Mr. Eliot, feeling that every truly great poet must in some sense be representative of his time, and feeling intuitively sure of Yeats's major qualities, merely making a formal claim that Yeats *must* be representative. Or can Yeats's representative quality be illustrated in detail?

II

When Dr. Richards, in *Science and Poetry*, suggested that a poet like Yeats, who took ghosts and fairies seriously, could hardly have anything quite centrally significant to say to the modern mind, he was making a crude but sensible point. The main debate of that mind, in this country, in the last eighty years, has been between an orthodox religious and an orthodox scientific attitude. Yeats was neither orthodoxly religious nor orthodoxly scientific; he had his own science, which was an occult one, and his own religion or 'sophisticated lower mythology', and in prose he sometimes reconciled them at the level of magic. In his better poetry, on the other hand, he often quietly jettisons both of them. The scientific attitude leads, in practice, to a kind of democratic humanitarianism. Yeats believed in aristocracy and, though his humane and fastidious temperament made him recoil from violence, he often allowed himself to

[1] See 'The Poetry of W. B. Yeats' in *Purpose XII* (1940), reprinted in *Southern Review*: Yeats Memorial Issue, April 1941; and in *Selected Prose* (1953).

41

romanticize violence, when it was safely set in a mythological past. The modern Christian attitude tends to lead to
a preoccupation with sin. From this, Yeats was quite free.
In the last ten years of Yeats's life, these two contrasting
attitudes were well represented in this country by the work
of Mr. Auden and Mr. Eliot. Mr. Auden, in the 1930s, was
a kind of liberal semi-Marxist, profoundly but not always
obviously affected by a Christian upbringing; Mr. Eliot was
a Christian conservative, profoundly but not always obviously affected, particularly in his concern with social questions, by a liberal upbringing. These two poets, in fact, had
much more in common with each other than either had
with Yeats. Yet Mr. Auden, like Mr. Eliot, nobly saluted
Yeats's passing:

> 'Earth, receive an honoured guest;
> William Yeats is laid to rest.
> Let the Irish vessel lie
> Emptied of its poetry. . . .'[1]

In saluting Yeats, neither Mr. Auden nor Mr. Eliot can
have been merely saluting a great artist in verse. Both, in
Yeats's work, given the deep seriousness of their critical
attitudes, must have found a kind of wisdom, even though
that expressed itself through ideas and gestures of which they
disapproved. Yeats was as firmly set against Mr. Auden's
attitude of the 1930s, which he symbolically described as
'Moscow', as against Mr. Eliot's, which he symbolically
described as 'Rome'. Just as he was never a political demo-
crat, never at all sympathetic with the

> 'levelling, rancorous, rational sort of mind
> That never looked out of the eye of a saint
> Or out of a drunkard's eye,'

so he was very much further, also, from any traditional
Christian attitudes than many scientifically-minded agnos-
tics are. What may be called his morality was neither that

[1] W. H. Auden, *Collected Shorter Poems* (1950).

of a diluted and imperfect Christianity, nor that of a progressive humanitarianism. It could be better described as a
morality of 'style'. It very much resembled (given that
Yeats had a more genial and generous temperament) the
morality of Nietzsche. Yeats's instinctive sympathies were
with the strong and proud, not with the weak and humble;
with the brilliant rather than the stupid, with the exceptional rather than the average. They were not, however,
like those of Nietzsche, with the oppressor rather than the
oppressed. Yet, as an Irish nationalist, Yeats identified himself with the liberal wing of the Protestant Ascendancy, with
those, like Swift and Grattan, 'who gave though free to
refuse', rather than with the masses of the Irish people.
Yeats's frank admiration for qualities like strength, beauty,
recklessness, a dominating spirit, a 'proper pride', set him
against the obvious superficial currents of our age. If he
does, indeed, have the central representativeness that Mr.
Eliot claims for him, one reason may be that this aristocratic or 'natural' morality—which is the morality of schoolboys, of film-fans, of soldiers, a morality based on the
instinctive admiration we feel for those who excel us—is
more firmly rooted in us than we think, and that when we
find it nobly expressed we instinctively respond to it. More
broadly, for all our preoccupation today with 'security', we
still have hankerings after the heroic.

III

The case, however, for Yeats's representativeness has
never been properly argued. The mere exposition of the
meaning of many of Yeats's poems, as related to his personal history, to his social background, and to his philosophical opinions, is in itself such a complicated task that
very little that can properly be called 'criticism' of his poems
—criticism in the sense of concrete evaluation, of 'distancing' and 'placing'—has been written. Maud Gonne and
Madame Blavatsky and the Abbey Theatre and Irish politics

and the esoteric symbolism of *A Vision* tend to bulk so large
in accounts of Yeats that they crowd out any consideration
of his diction, his rhythms, his way of constructing a poem,
the coherence and sensitivity of his responses. What Mr.
John Wain wittily calls 'the Gypsy Petulengro approach'—
the painstaking exposition, with diagrams, of what Yeats
meant by gyres and cones and 'phases of the moon'—
becomes so absorbing in itself, that mere literary criticism
no doubt seems, by comparison, dull. This sketch is not
primarily concerned with Yeats as a magician or a mystic.
Miss Margaret Rudd may be perfectly right when, in a
recent book about Yeats, she says that he is a rather inferior
mystic, if we compare him with Blake. What is also true is
that the Blake of the prophetic books is a rather inferior
artist if we compare him with Yeats—these have to be
approached, as even Yeats's book of occult philosophy, *A
Vision*, need not be, with a primarily extra-literary interest.
'Willie,' Mrs. Yeats is reported once to have wisely said,
'you are a great poet, but you are no saint.' The great poet
is our subject. He was, of course, no saint; but we may
make out a case in passing that he had many of the virtues
of Aristotle's 'magnanimous man' or of the *honnête homme*
of the French seventeenth century. His representativeness
for our own age does, as I have suggested, largely depend
on the fact that he both possessed and praised what we think
of as archaic virtues. He was the last quite whole-hearted
spokesman of the aristocratic idea.

IV

Yeats came from the outer fringe of the Irish Protestant
Ascendancy, from a rather better family than Shaw's, and
perhaps from not quite such a good family as Wilde's. He
spent his childhood between London and Ireland, and
though in Ireland his family counted as minor gentry, in
London, in so far as London bothers about such things, they
probably counted as shabby-genteel bohemians. Yeats's

father, J. B. Yeats, was an unsuccessful painter who wrote brilliant letters and had a genius for friendship. As a painter, he was influenced by the Pre-Raphaelites and he handed down to his son the idea of a 'religion of beauty', and a romantic taste, that even in Yeats's youth was a slightly old-fashioned one, in art and literature. There are certain great writers, of the type of Ibsen, whom the young Yeats could never absorb; to the end of his days his attitude towards Degas and Manet was rather like that of Sir Alfred Munnings towards Picasso. J. B. Yeats was also influenced in his ideas by the agnostic rationalism of Huxley and Tyndall, and against this side of his father the young Yeats violently reacted. As a boy, Yeats was dreamy and backward, fond of long solitary walks. To his dying day, he never learned to spell properly and diffidence about his scholarship prevented him from going to Trinity College, Dublin. This lack of a formal education is important in Yeats's development. He read very widely, but never systematically. He was bad at languages; in so far as the French symbolist movement influenced him at all, it was through translations made by his friend, Arthur Symons, and when in later life he said that he had 'almost forgotten his Hebrew', he meant that at one period, for some occult purpose, he had memorized a few words of that language. Even for himself, the map of what he knew and did not know can never have had very firm outlines. The young Yeats began writing verses very early. This early work shows much vividness of imagery, but it was some time before Yeats learned to write in regular stanzas or even to make all his lines scan. The first drafts of his poems to the end often show a surprising technical hesitancy—a trite choice of words, a flat shaping of the line; the poems were perfected by a habit, early acquired, of endlessly patient revision. The young Yeats was lucky in that his father encouraged him to go on with his poetry and even actively discouraged him from tying himself down to the drudgery of regular newspaper work. Yeats, however, soon became a fluent free-lance journalist, chiefly on topics of Irish folklore. By his early twenties, he had begun to make a reputation. In London, he became one of a group of minor poets, among them Arthur Symons, Lionel Johnson, and Ernest Dowson, whom today we tend to dismiss as 'decadents'.

If we compare the young Yeats carefully, however, with these friends of his of the 1890s, we notice important differences. Lionel Johnson and Ernest Dowson and Aubrey Beardsley were men of weak will, whom weakness drove to dissipation or perversity. They were men of essentially religious natures, hovering on the edge of conversion or despair. The possibility, ever present in their minds, of being damned gave them not a relish but a momentousness to sin. They tended to lack self-control (Dowson and Johnson were alcoholics). They did lack practical capacity. Yeats's early poems are full of melancholy, but they have little to say about sin. The young Irishman was not haunted by the fear of damnation. He was chaste and temperate—the greatest love of his life, that for Maud Gonne, was a wholly chaste one, and his failure to win her did not drive him to prostitutes or drink. Shy and dreamy though he was, he was fundamentally a masterful man. Maud Gonne, dragging him at her heels on nationalist agitations, soon found that he was a natural orator and could easily dominate committees. His religion was, far more than that of his companions, genuinely a religion of poetry. Reacting against agnostic rationalism, he had not reacted in the direction of orthodoxy:

'I was unlike others of my generation in one thing only. I am very religious, and deprived by Huxley and Tyndall of the simple-minded religion of my childhood, I had made a new religion, almost an infallible church of poetic tradition, of a fardel of stories, and of personages, and of emotions, inseparable from their first expression, passed on from generation to generation by poets and painters with some help from philosophers and theologians.'[1]

[1] *The Trembling of the Veil* (1922).

46

How far there, one wonders, was he right about himself?
Was he really 'very religious'? We wonder both about the
word 'fardel' with its dandified air—the faded elegance of
the 1890s—and about the word 'stories', which brackets off
the question whether the 'stories' are true. The attitude is
aesthetic rather than ethical or religious; in a sophisticated
way, the young Yeats is playing a child's game of 'Let's
pretend!' There are late poems of his, like 'Among School
Children', that do express a properly religious attitude, one
of mystical acceptance of a world experienced as contradictory; but the properly religious attitude that is often to
be found in Yeats's poetry has little to do with—even tugs
against—the pseudo-religious notions. It is not a playing
with fantasies, but a response to the whole. The very fact
that the young man could so easily concoct a 'new religion'
for himself—out of Irish folklore and Blake and Madame
Blavatsky and anything that came handy—is evidence of a
rather unreligious nature; evidence of a blithe and irresponsible temperament, that of a young man sure of his genius,
and unconvicted of sin. The note of the 1890s, the genuinely
religious note, that is not to be found in Yeats's early poems
is that of Lionel Johnson's 'The Dark Angel':

> 'Dark Angel, with thine aching lust!
> Of two defeats, of two despairs:
> Less dread, a change to drifting dust,
> Than thine eternity of cares.'

Yeats's early religion, if it was properly a religion at all,
was one without anguish or dread.

The charm of much of Yeats's early poetry is thus
slightly equivocal—dreamy and melancholy, passive and
self-indulgent, as indeed from this account of his poetical
religion we might expect it to be. Mr. Robert Graves's
attack on 'The Lake Isle of Innisfree' is, in fact, an attack on
a poet for not being properly awake. In a poem from
Yeats's volume of 1893, *The Rose*, a poem called 'A Faery
Song', a modern reader is embarrassed by the monotonous

doleful music, by the yearning that neither seems to have nor to seek for an object:

> 'We who are old, old and gay,
> O so old!
> Thousands of years, thousands of years
> If all were told:
>
> Give to these children, new from the world,
> Silence and love;
> And the long dew-dropping hours of the night,
> And the stars above. . . .'

Even throughout the 1890s, however, there was a constant slow hidden growth in another direction. In *The Wind Among the Reeds*, the volume of 1899, the diction does indeed seem on the surface as formal and faded, the cadences as mechanically 'beautiful', as ever; and the symbolism also, growingly intricate but not growingly vivid,

> '. . . a coat
> Covered with embroideries,'

hangs now like a rich worn tapestry between the poet and the hard stone walls of the world. But the yearning has now an object, Maud Gonne. The individual words clutch more at particular objects. There is a movement towards active feeling, positive grasp:

> 'I became a man, a hater of the wind,
> Knowing one, out of all things, alone, that his head
> May not lie on the breast or his lips on the hair
> Of the woman that he loves, until he dies;
> Although the rushes and the fowl of the air
> Cry of his love with their pitiful cries.'

Yeats, at some time after 1909, changed the 'dreamy Celtic dying fall of the last two lines there to an arrogant rhetorical question:

W. B. Yeats

'O beast of the wilderness, bird of the air,
Must I endure your amorous cries?'

The poem had enough latent strength to stand the change.
We should look, in the early poems, for that latent
strength. Their weary, withdrawn note is a kind of protective colouring which Yeats has taken from his friends of the
1890s. (He was often, throughout his life, ready admiringly
to imitate his minor, but never his major contemporaries.
A natural leader, he liked to disguise himself as a follower
even of small men.) There is, of course, a paradox here.
Yeats made himself a major poet, starting with the equip-
ment and apparently the tastes of a good minor one—with a
chaste but excessively 'poetic' diction, with exquisite but
trite cadences, with a tendency to use symbols in a way that
was decorative, and even fussily so, rather than deeply exploratory, with a narrow and rather wilfully sad range of
moods, always just on the verge of the literary pose or the
'stock response'. He started, also, without much grasp of
the outer world; his early poems rarely make us *see* anything; we can weave our own day-dreams round them,
which is another matter. And though he acquired unique
rank, among his contemporaries, as a visionary poet, it is
probable that the merely *visible* world left him, to the last,
rather cold. Usually he evokes it for us by a kind of trick,
not describing the thing, but reminding us of our feelings
about it:

'A sycamore and lime-tree lost in night
Although that western cloud is luminous . . .

Back turned upon the brightness of the sun
And all the sensuality of the shade. . . .'

We remember our feelings about staring towards a fading
distance at sunset, about sharp contrasts in a garden of light
and shade. We ourselves, most of the time, *make* Yeats's
physical world for him. We believe in it, because we be-

lieve in Yeats, and rather as we believe in a painted Elsinore
when Hamlet is talking. We can, in fact, think perhaps most
fruitfully of Yeats's poems as speeches made by him at
crucial moments in a long noble drama. No poet lends
himself so little to the cold-blooded examination of his
poems as isolated objects; no poet gains more from being
read as a whole, with a full knowledge of life. Yeats, as he
grows older, acts, with growing assurance and spontaneity
the difficult part of himself. The acting in the end, having
gone through the stages of lyrical mime and heroic and
satirical tirade, becomes almost naturalistic.

V

The Edwardian decade saw the masterful side of Yeats's
nature coming to the surface. By 1908, when the first collected edition of his works came out, he had made a reputation not only as a poet and a dramatist, but as the man who
had put the Abbey Theatre on its feet, who kept it going,
and who had bravely defended Synge against local preju-
dice. Through Lady Gregory, who had become his patron,
Yeats was now accepted by that 'Big House' society of
which, in his childhood, he had only touched the fringes.
He was becoming self-conscious about his ancestry. Some
of the younger men in Dublin, and some older contemporaries like George Moore, thought him conceited and
arrogant; but nobody any longer thought him a mere shy,
ineffectual dreamer. He had resigned himself to unfulfilled
love, and found public activity a distraction. Maud Gonne
had made an unfortunate marriage, and though she was
separated from her husband, she had become a Roman
Catholic, so there was no prospect of her divorcing her husband and marrying Yeats. He and she, in any case, were
becoming estranged in a deeper sense. She felt that the
Abbey Theatre had tempted Yeats away from the national
cause. She would have liked cheaper seats and plays that
were straight nationalistic propaganda. Yeats, in fact, in the

Edwardian decade, had become more concerned with the bigotry and bad taste, as he considered it, of his Dublin audience than with Ireland's wrongs.

The Great War, apart from the deaths of friends like Major Robert Gregory, hardly touched Yeats emotionally. But the Easter Rebellion of 1916, which took him by surprise (he was not in the confidence of any of the more extreme nationalists), made him regret his growing aloofness from the Irish cause. He remained a very moderate nationalist—he felt that England might still 'keep faith'—and indeed the 'troubles' of 1919 and after gave him a vivid sense of how violence can in a short time destroy values that it has taken law centuries to build up;

> 'We had fed the heart on fantasies,
> The heart's grown brutal from the fare;
> More substance in our enmities
> Than in our love; O honey-bees
> Come build in the empty house of the stare.'

Yet he felt himself more profoundly identified with the Irish people than he had been for many years.

Yeats's long romance with Maud Gonne had meanwhile ended in a kind of comic fantasy. Her husband, one of the rebels of 1916, had been shot. Yeats felt he ought to ask her to marry him again, but was probably relieved when she refused. At the same time, he fell in love with her beautiful adopted daughter, who as a young girl had been half in love with him. The adopted daughter could not make up her mind. Yeats gave her a date by which to do so, and when her final decision was against marrying him, suddenly married another young lady, Miss Hyde-Lees. Not unnaturally, after such a complication of emotions, he was in a state of depression and anxiety after his marriage—even if there had not been the business of Maud Gonne and her daughter, he was a man in his fifties, weighed down by anxiety for his country, and marrying, after an unusually chaste bachelor existence, somebody much younger than himself—and it was partly to distract him that Mrs. Yeats started the experiments in automatic writing that ultimately gave him the material for *A Vision*. In judging Yeats's occult philosophy, we should always ask ourselves how far, at a fundamental level, he himself took it seriously; and how far it was a necessary plaything for a powerful and distressed creative mind.

VI

Many critics agree that it is on the volumes published in the last twenty years of his life, from *The Wild Swans at Coole* of 1919 to the posthumous *Last Poems and Plays* of 1939, that Yeats's future fame will mainly rest. The sharpening and hardening of his attitudes, the development of the tough, complex, and ironical 'later style' can, in fact, be traced further back, to the significantly named *Responsibilities* of 1914. There is even a hint of the new style in 'Adam's Curse' from a volume of 1904, *In The Seven Woods*:

> 'I said, "It's certain there is no fine thing
> Since Adam's fall but needs much labouring.
> There have been lovers who thought love should be
> So much compounded of high courtesy
> That they would sigh and quote with learned looks
> Precedents out of beautiful old books;
> Yet now it seems an idle trade enough." '

It can, however, be agreed that there is a remarkable new maturity, a new 'realism', in the work of Yeats's last twenty years; and this can be traced to several sources.

Yeats was now writing as a married man, a man with a house and children of his own, more rooted in everyday life than he had previously been. He was writing also as a man who had seen the dream of his youth, Irish independence, come true; and who was becoming aware of certain ironies, for him tragic ironies, involved in its coming true. His own personal dream had been of a free Ireland that would be a kind of replica, without the tensions or troubles, without the injustice to the majority, of the Ireland of Grattan's Parliament.[1] He wanted to go back to the eighteenth century rather than on into the twentieth. He hoped that the 'Big Houses' would survive, that the Protestant Ascendancy would still, because of their wealth, their wit, and their manners, constitute a dominant group. He thought of the local grandees patronizing poets and the peasants touching their hats. He was romantically innocent about politics. He found, of course, that what had come into existence was not a Protestant-dominated aristocratic Republic but a Roman Catholic farmers' democracy; and the farmers did not want to touch their hats to anybody. Some of the 'Big Houses' were burned in the 'troubles', others were deserted because they cost too much to keep up and because they, like even the nationalistic aristocracy, had outlived their social function. Yeats had hoped that Dublin, as the capital of a free Ireland, would become a great cultural centre; he saw the

---

[1] Until 1780, the Irish Parliament could reject or accept, but not amend, laws relating to Irish matters passed by the British Parliament. Irish patriots like Flood and Grattan took advantage of the American Revolutionary War (which involved war with France) to claim and secure legislative independence for the Irish Parliament. The Volunteer Movement—a kind of unofficial defence militia—ostensibly raised to resist invasion was in fact used to put moral pressure on the Viceregal Government. The Viceroy and his staff, however, retained practical control of Irish affairs by offering honours and sinecures to the pro-Government Parliamentary majority. The new Parliament did not represent the Roman Catholic masses of the people, or even their wealthier elements. Thus the short period of Irish Parliamentary independence—or really, of independence for the Protestant Ascendancy —ended in the bloody 'troubles' of 1798 and a little later in the Union secured partly by lavish bribery, of the Irish with the Imperial Parliament. Nevertheless, the short period of Grattan's Parliament was marked both by splendid oratory and by a gay and brilliant social life in Dublin; and was thus often remembered nostalgically in the nineteenth century by Irishmen who saw Dublin, both socially and culturally, becoming more and more of a 'provincial' city.

'blind, bitter town' becoming more rather than less provincial. The Dublin City Fathers gave the freedom of the city to a retired Tammany boss, a Mr. Croker, but rejected the suggestion of Dr. Oliver St. John Gogarty that they should also give it to Yeats. Sean O'Casey's tragic masterpiece, *The Plough and the Stars*, aroused as passionate an opposition from the Abbey Theatre audience as *The Playboy* had done. Yeats's growing bitterness comes out as early as *The Wild Swans at Coole* in one of his most powerfully sustained shorter poems, 'The Fisherman':

'All day I'd looked in the face
What I had hoped 'twould be
To write for my own race
And the reality;
The living men that I hate,
The dead man that I loved,
The craven man in his seat,
The insolent unreproved,
And no knave brought to book
Who has won a drunken cheer,
The witty man and his joke
Aimed at the commonest ear,
The clever man who cries
The catch-cries of the clown,
The beating down of the wise
And great Art beaten down.'

Yeats, in this new Ireland, was not, in spite of the prestige that the Nobel Prize brought him, a centrally representative figure. He became a Senator, but found himself allied in the Senate, a little unromantically, with rich bankers and brewers; a speech which he made protesting, on behalf of the religious minority, against a proposal to make divorce illegal made him unpopular. The esoteric philosophy of *A Vision* is partly to be understood, as we have suggested already, in terms of Yeats's need for distraction. We should not take that book more seriously than Yeats took it. He had a long philosophical correspondence with Sturge Moore about hallucinatory cats, and other visions of this sort: are they real beings to which we have access only at privileged moments (Yeats would have liked to think so), or are they, on the other hand—hallucinations? It is interesting that in this correspondence he never refers to either the 'facts' or the 'arguments' of *A Vision* as having any relevant authority. He explicitly stated elsewhere that it was not very profitable to discuss the theories of *A Vision* in terms of 'belief'. Many of the ideas in the book, like that of eternal recurrence, are not new; they are in Vico and Nietzsche. Yeats, after he had written the first draft of *A Vision*, also found them in Spengler. Their truth, or otherwise, cannot be discussed here. They provided props for Yeats's attitude to life, which was becoming a kind of tragic stoicism. He sees life as tragic, but feels that it can be acted with the style of a tragedy. We can embrace our destiny joyfully: 'Hamlet and Lear are gay.'

It should be particularly noticed, however, that Yeats's attitude towards the supernatural was a profoundly ambiguous one. He wanted, from a world beyond ours, in contrasting moods, two apparently quite contradictory kinds of assurance; one that we are, in fact, bound, as the Buddhists tell us we are, to the 'great wheel of existence' and shall reappear upon this stage, in various roles, again and again; the other that, as the Buddhists also tell us, we can escape ultimately from 'the great wheel'—but not to non-being, a concept which never attracted Yeats, but to some kind of finite timeless perfection. He was not sure (as perhaps no Western man who studies Eastern thought ever is) that he really wanted to escape from the wheel. Thus in the face of the 'symbolic phantasmagoria', he retains the freedom of inconsistency. His images of a Byzantine heaven in which he would be transformed into a golden bird (the artist becoming an eternal work of art) symbolized his desire to escape from the disorder, the irony, the failure of life; but so also other symbols—as when he says he would like to live again, even in a 'foul ditch', as a 'blind man battering blind men'—stand for a craving for life, at any level, the 'lust and rage' of which he speaks in his *Last Poems*, that grew stronger in him as he grew older. Often he hated life for not being perfection. Sometimes, also, he feared perfection for not being life.

VII

Yeats's early love poems are dreamily erotic, without being in the least consciously sexual; some of his later poems are so harshly sexual that they cease, in effect, to be erotic:

> 'From pleasure of the bed,
> Dull as a worm,
> His rod and its butting head
> Limp as a worm,
> His spirit that has fled
> Blind as a worm.'

A glandular operation that Yeats underwent in his last years no doubt accentuated this tendency, but it was already there. It is best considered, however, as part of a more general tendency in his latest poems towards self-questioning, self-stripping:

> 'These masterful images because complete
> Grew in pure mind, but out of what began?
> A mound of refuse or the sweepings of a street,
> Old kettles, old bottles, and a broken can,
> Old iron, old bones, old rags, that raving slut
> Who keeps the till. Now that my ladder's gone
> I must lie down where all the ladders start
> In the foul rag-and-bone shop of the heart.'

The man who wrote that stanza also wrote:

> 'We were the last romantics—chose for theme
> Traditional sanctity and loveliness. . . .'

Anybody who wants to get the full range of Yeats must be able to respond to both kinds of statement—must be able to accept the tautness of a terrible great poet's sincerity. In that stanza from 'The Circus Animals' Desertion', Yeats has become aware that the symbols of his poetry have a Freudian meaning of which for most of his life he has been unconscious. But we should notice also that this stanza which bids farewell to the symbolist method is a triumphant example of it; for we 'know what the poet is saying' here, but we cannot 'say it in our own words'. A merely clinical interpretation will not work. Is, for instance, 'the raving slut/ Who keeps the till' the Freudian Censor—is the money she will give us in return for old rubbish a release of Libido? Are the 'old iron, old bones, old rags' and the 'mound of refuse' symbols for the Freudian anal-erotic hoarding instinct? Is the 'foul rag-and-bone shop of the heart' merely the sexual imagination, with its accumulated scraps of lustful memory? Quite obviously not, and quite obviously what Yeats is saying here is something more general and profound. There is something basically blind, grasping, insensate in all of us; something that hoards rubbish, that shuts doors, that hides away from the light. We climb up, but we never wholly get away. All that is still under our feet, in the cellarage. And the 'heart' is what grasps and is insensate, but also what loves and suffers, and the 'ladders'—the ways upwards and outwards, to the free air and the life of the spirit—do start there. And when we have said all this, of course, the stanza still retains, as all great symbolist poetry does, its eternal residue of mysterious suggestiveness.

The bare honesty of such poems, even more than the rich, dark mysteriousness of 'Byzantium' or 'The Statues', may partly account for Yeats's hold on the young. In his last volume he asks himself more frankly than most poets have done whether he may not have done as much harm as good:

> 'Did that play of mine send out
> Certain men the English shot?'

Yet he can still strike a last grand attitude:

> 'Cast a cold eye
> On life, on death.
> Horseman, pass by!'

He would not, like Rilke (these lines were written out of irritation with Rilke) accept death as a final dark consummation. He would not accept life itself uncritically. And in the last thing he was working on, *The Death of Cuchulain*, the harlot (an eternal harlot, who has slept with 'Conall, Cuchulain, Usna's boys') speaks of the polarities and antinomies, of disgust and delight in physical love, of dread and delight in battle; speaks also of the Irish patriots of 1916, delighting in what they dreaded, who were always in Yeats's heart; speaks of gods and heroes whom we seem to embody, or who seem to stand behind us, in the crucial moments of our lives:

> 'That there are still some living
> That do my limbs unclothe,
> But that the flesh my flesh has gripped
> I both adore and loathe.
> *(Pipe and drum music)*
> Are those things that men adore and loathe
> Their sole reality?
> What stood in the Post Office
> With Pearse and Connolly?
> What comes out of the mountain
> When men first shed their blood?
> Who thought Cuchulain till it seemed
> He stood where they had stood?'

VIII

Yeats felt that there was a tension between his life and his poetry. He thought sometimes of the poem as a kind of anti-personality which the poet builds up to compensate for or conceal personal weaknesses, of the poem as a 'mask'. This idea has something in common with Mr. Ezra Pound's idea of the poem as a *persona*. Mr. Pound is a poet who, according to one of his most appreciative but also harshest critics, Mr. Percy Wyndham Lewis, has no 'personality' of his own worth speaking of; he can function only by pretending to be somebody else, a Provençal troubadour or a Chinese sage. Yeats's masks in poetry are not of this sort; even in his earliest work his own personality seems to me to come over, or at least an important aspect of it, the 'poetic' aspect. Similarly, no doubt, at meetings of the Rhymers' Club in the 1890s, Yeats, fundamentally a very shy and diffident young man, put on a suitable 'literary dandy' or perhaps sometimes a 'dreamy Celt' personality. As Yeats's poetry matures, one of the things that happens is not so much that it becomes more 'personal', less of a 'mask', as that he gets more of his personality into it. He gets in things like irony, humour, arrogant irascibility, the coaxing manners of the professional Irish conversationalist, which in the 1890s he would probably have considered 'anti-poetic'; he gets in more of the prosaic detail of life, transformed by a poetic apprehension of it.

We might compare, even from *Responsibilities*, the generalized evocation of Maud Gonne,

'A crowd
Will gather, and not know it walks the very street
Whereon a thing once walked that seemed a burning
  cloud,'

with the prose bareness of a line and a half from 'Beautiful Lofty Things' in *Last Poems*:

'. . . Maud Gonne at Howth Station waiting a train,
Pallas Athene in that straight back and arrogant head.'

That line and a half evoke Maud Gonne, her setting, her bearing, her character (Pallas Athene, the goddess of wisdom, was severe and virginal). The more conventionally 'poetic' phrase about 'a burning cloud' tells us much about Yeats's feeling but does not evoke any image of a woman at all.

Often the force of the later poetry comes largely from this directness, like that of speech:

> 'And here's John Synge himself, that rooted man,
> "Forgetting human words", a grave deep face. . . .
>
> Before a woman's portrait suddenly I stand,
> Beautiful and gentle in her Venetian way.
> I met her all but fifty years ago
> For twenty minutes in some studio. . . .
>
> Does the imagination dwell the most
> Upon a woman won or woman lost?
> If on the lost, admit you turned aside
> From a great labyrinth out of pride,
> Cowardice, some silly over-subtle thought
> Or anything called conscience once;
> And that if memory recur, the sun's
> Under eclipse and the moon blotted out.'

There is no rhetoric in these passages; only in the last of them any figures of speech, and these so commonplace (a human relationship as a labyrinth, the sense of loss seeming to blot out the sun and moon) that they could occur un-affectedly in ordinary conversation. Common turns of speech are also sometimes exploited for irony. In *The Tower* we are told the story of Mrs. French (it is in Sir Jonah Barrington's memoirs, 1833) and how a footman at dinner one day clipped off the ears of a farmer who was behaving boorishly and brought them to her in a little covered dish. It is with a delighted shock that we meet the lady again, in a summary of the characters in the poem, as

> 'Mrs. French,
> Gifted with so fine an ear. . . .'

Critics who have discussed to the verge of tedium Yeats's more obscure occult fancies might have discussed with more advantage this strong simplicity of his later style. Behind the strength is honesty of statement. The lines quoted above,

> Does the imagination dwell the most,

express a complex of feelings which most of us have experienced but which few of us have the courage to put on record: a complex of feelings that might be called remorse for compunction. Yeats speaks for what he calls, in a poem addressed to Von Hugel, the 'unchristened heart'; but with a dignity and passion that make it very unlikely that his words should ever cause scandal to Christians.

Yet if there were only pride and pagan courage and high art, only contempt for 'this filthy modern tide', only the obstinate 'lust and rage' of a 'wild, wicked old man' in Yeats, should we turn to him as we do, not only for distraction, not only for stimulus, but for wisdom and consolation? We look in poetry for love. All great poets are more profoundly capable of love than common men, and they may be terrifyingly more capable of hate, too. Yeats's capacity for hate distressed even close friends of his, like the Duchess of Wellington. It was there to the last, as in the poem, 'A Bronze Head':

> 'Or else I thought her supernatural;
> As though a sterner eye looked through her eye
> On this foul world in its decline and fall;
> On gangling stocks grown great, great stocks run dry,
> Ancestral pearls all pitched into a sty,
> Heroic reverie mocked by clown and knave,
> And wondered what was left for massacre to save.'

But he could hate like that *because* he could love. And the 'touchstones' that I would choose from his poetry, to persuade an unsympathetic reader to reconsider it, all speak of love. I would choose these stanzas from 'A Prayer for My Daughter':

'An intellectual hatred is the worst,
So let her think opinions are accursed.
Have I not seen the loveliest woman born
Out of the mouth of Plenty's horn,
Because of her opinionated mind
Barter that horn and every good
By quiet natures understood
For an old bellows full of angry wind?

Considering that, all hatred driven hence,
The soul recovers radical innocence
And learns that it is self-delighting,
Self-appeasing, self-affrighting,
And that its own sweet will is Heaven's will;
She can, though every face should scowl
And every windy quarter howl
Or every bellows burst, be happy still.'

I would choose a line or two from the gentle minor elegy
for Eva Gore-Booth and Con Markiewicz:

'Dear shadows, now you know it all,
All the folly of a fight
With a common wrong or right.
The innocent and the beautiful
Have no enemy but time. . . .'

I would choose the magnificent two last stanzas of
'Among School Children':

'Both nuns and mothers worship images,
But those the candles light are not as those
That animate a mother's reveries,
But keep a marble or a bronze repose.
And yet they too break hearts—O Presences
That passion, piety, or affection knows,
And that all heavenly glory symbolize—
O self-born mockers of man's enterprise;

W. B. Yeats

Labour is blossoming or dancing where
The body is not bruised to pleasure soul,
Nor beauty born out of its own despair,
Nor blear-eyed wisdom out of midnight oil.
O chestnut-tree, great-rooted blossomer,
Are you the leaf, the blossom, or the bole?
O body swayed to music, O brightening glance,
How can we know the dancer from the dance?'

And (though Yeats is not on the whole a poet of striking single lines, of lines that impress us out of their setting) I might choose a line and a half from 'Nineteen Hundred and Nineteen':

'Man is in love and loves what vanishes,
What more is there to say? . . .'

Yeats's poetry I believe to be the centrally important part of his work. His two best plays, *Purgatory* and *The Words Upon The Window-Pane* are magnificently successful, but minor in scale; his longer plays seem to me all to dilute his art. He wrote very delightful prose and his reminiscences of the 1890s in particular, are a primary document for a fascinating period. He was not a good literary critic. His introduction to *The Oxford Book of Modern Verse*, like his selection of poems in that book, is strikingly odd and eccentric; but it has the wit and charm of everything he wrote, and here and there, among statements that seem quite absurd, it has extremely penetrating paragraphs—particularly, perhaps, about his friend Mr. Ezra Pound, whose qualities and weaknesses no subsequent critic has estimated so justly. But it was into his poetry that he put himself most completely. The poetry, however, is better poetry because he gave himself to so many other things. His patriotism, his public spirit, his capacity for staunch friendship and passionate love all enrich it. The sense, which grew so strong in him in later life, that every victory he had worked for implied a defeat of something he perhaps cared about more, lends almost all his later work a poise of complex irony. The characteristics which some of his contemporaries disliked, such as his arrogance or 'proper pride', are in his poems, too. Yet all true poets are fundamentally humble. Yeats was humble before the mystery of life. He never took either himself or his systems quite so seriously as some of his disciples have done. He was the last great poet in the English romantic tradition; and the only poet in that tradition, except Byron, with a genuine sense of humour and gift of wit. The true man, with the modesty and the generosity that underlay all his poses, comes out in the letters to Sturge Moore. Yeats is writing about the Nobel Prize:

'Yes, it will be a great help to me in several ways. Here especially it will help. I will find it easier to get the Government to listen to me on artistic things. I look upon it as a recognition of the Free State, and of Irish literature, and it is a very great help. People here are grateful because I have won them this recognition, and that is the distinction I want. If I thought it a tribute to my own capacity alone I, being a very social man, would be far less pleased.'

All great poets tend to overawe us. They speak with 'something above a mortal mouth'. And they need their solitudes to withdraw into. But it is as a lover, as a friend, and as a patriot, as 'a very social man', that Yeats would like us to remember him. It is his broad and deep humanity that provides the substance of his art.

Yeats and 'The New Criticism'

I regret having to make a good book the peg on which to hang a largely polemical article. *The Permanence of Yeats*, recently published by the Macmillan Company of America, is a most admirably representative selection of some of the best critical studies written in the last thirty years about a great poet. My polemical concern is not with the book itself, but with some of the essays in it by younger men: and not so much with the essays as with a method used in them, and not even so much with the method itself as with what seems to me a flat-footed application of it. The method is what is called in America that of the New Criticism. It derives very largely from Cambridge—from that close examination of texts by Dr. Richards, Dr. Leavis, and Mr. Empson, to which all people who care seriously for poetry must be grateful, whatever reserves they may have about some of the general standpoints and particular judgments of these fine critics. I do not say that any one of them has what one can call a *method*: one might rather say that each has a recognizable *approach*, and that a common admirable quality of all of them is a patient attention to the words on the page rather than to an idea of a poem in one's head, arrived at after a few hasty readings. What one has to complain about in the New Criticism is precisely that it does seem to substitute a *method* for an *approach*—that it seems to assure American undergraduates that, though sweeping and summary judgments will probably be wrong, the young critic is safe if he plods through a poem line by line and writes down a prose paraphrase of what he thinks it says. The *approach*, in fact, when it becomes a *method*, becomes a *method of analysis*. Now analysis is an admirable way of testing, and of reinforcing, summary judgments arrived at by ordinary literary tact and sensibility. It is not a substitute for tact and sensibility; it is not, and cannot be, the *primary* instrument of literary appreciation. To sort out and order your impressions of a poem usefully, you must first of all have a fairly massive and coherent body of impressions to sort out: I would even say that you must have 'lived with' the poem in question, been on intimate terms with it, for a long time, perhaps even for years. If your *first* reading of a poem has analysis primarily in mind, you are likely to fall into one of two traps. You will substitute for the poem, in your mind, your own over-simple account of what it says; or if it is a really difficult poem, you will add to your account of its difficulties, accounts of your own difficulties of apprehension. I propose, by examining passages from two essays in *The Permanence of Yeats*, to illustrate these twin dangers of a too brashly intellectualistic approach to the mystery of poetry.

II

My first example is one of gross over-simplification, which, if taken seriously, would impoverish one's appreciation of a subtle and complex poem. It is from an otherwise stimulating essay by Mr. Walter E. Houghton, on Yeats's 'Crazy Jane' poems.

Mr. Houghton is commenting on this famous lyric:

> ' "*I am of Ireland,*
> *And the Holy Land of Ireland,*
> *And time runs on,*" *cried she.*
> "*Come out of charity,*
> *Come dance with me in Ireland.*"

One man, one man alone
In that outlandish gear,
One solitary man
Of all that rambled there
Had turned his stately head.
"That is a long way off,
And time runs on," he said,
"And the night grows rough."

"I am of Ireland,
And the Holy Land of Ireland,
And time runs on," cried she.
"Come out of charity
And dance with me in Ireland."

"The fiddlers are all thumbs,
Or the fiddle-strings accursed,
The drums and the kettledrums
And the trumpets all are burst,
And the trombone," cried he,
"The trumpet and the trombone,"
And cocked a malicious eye,
"But time runs on, runs on."

"I am of Ireland,
And the Holy Land of Ireland,
And time runs on," cries she.
"Come out of charity,
And dance with me in Ireland." '

Mr. Houghton notes (though he makes no critical use of the fact) that the chorus there is adapted from a medieval fragment, which is to be found in Mr. Kenneth Sisam's well-known anthology of fourteenth-century verse and prose:

'Icham of Irlaunde,
And of the holy londe
Of Irlande.

Gode sir, pray ich thee,
For of saynte charité,
Come ant daunce wyt me
In Irlaunde.'

The rhythm, however, has been transformed: and the phrase, 'And time runs on', is something added by Yeats.

Mr. Houghton says about this poem: 'Granting that any explanation of a poem so delicate must be too literal and crude, let us say that a woman very like Crazy Jane is in a pub somewhere outside of Ireland. As she looks at the rowdy scene (even the orchestra is drunk—the fiddlers are all thumbs), suddenly she thinks of Ireland, of everything romantic that the name can suggest, its heroic past, its holy miracles, its national aspiration, its beauty—everything which Yeats has captured in her song. No one pays any attention except one man, another Jack the Journeyman ("stately" in line 10 means "showing a sense of superiority, repellently dignified; not affable or approachable"—N.E.D., 2.b.), who first pretends to take her literally ("that's a long way off and it's getting late") and then when she repeats her appeal, he "cocks a malicious eye"—gives her the wink, and agrees there's no more time to lose: *they better get going.*' (The italics are mine, and the phrase is an example of the odd vulgarity that jars on one, from time to time, even in literate and sensitive American prose.) 'On which the woman sings her romantic vision all the more fiercely in the face of this coarse and common reduction of the ideal. Technically, the reduction is brilliantly made by having the man pick up the phrase about running on and twisting it to his own meaning: so that we feel at once, intuitively, the contrast between two very different dances, holy and unholy, between charity and lust. In short, the greatness of the poem lies in its simple statement of tragic contrast.'

Let me put my cards on the table at once, and say that I think the greatness of the poem lies in no such matter: but in its complex statement of ironic contrast. Moreover, it must be obvious to most readers of Yeats that this contrast between charity and lust, however 'tragic' or 'simple' (and it is certainly among other things a fairly *trite* contrast), is not a very probable theme for him to take up. He is a poet of 'romantic love' in which 'lust' is keyed up to the pitch of nobility.

> 'Yet always when I look death in the face,
> When I clamber to the heights of sleep,
> Or when I grow excited with wine,
> Suddenly I meet your face.'

and of an aristocratic morality in which the impact of 'charity' is severely restricted to the people one actually cares for: and in which 'uncharity' has a critical function,

> 'The living men that I hate,
> The dead man that I loved,
> The craven man in his seat,
> The insolent unreproved,
> And no knave brought to book
> Who has won a drunken cheer,
> The witty man and his joke
> Aimed at the commonest ear,
> The clever man who cries
> The catch-cries of the clown,
> The beating down of the wise
> And great Art beaten down.'

It is relevant that these lines are about the actual new Ireland which Yeats helped to bring into existence, as opposed to the visionary 'Holy Land of Ireland' of our poem. The sort of moral which Mr. Houghton sees Yeats as pointing would have struck him, wrongly of course from a Christian point of view, as slack and sentimental. Yeats was not a great Christian poet *manqué*. He was a great un-Christian poet who succeeded. And if one tries, with all the goodwill in the world, to read Mr. Houghton's interpretation back into this poem, one feels its inadequacy.

But if it feels inadequate as a whole, it also looks implausible in detail. The pub and the drunken orchestra in the pub, which Mr. Houghton talks about, exist in his imagination, not in the text. He must have an odd idea indeed of English pubs if he thinks they run to large brassy bands, allow mysterious Irishwomen to sing their songs in competition with these bands, and are roomy enough for crowds of people to ramble in. Yeats gives us very few stage-directions for this essentially dramatic little poem: we are told that the place is not Ireland, and that the time is night, that the weather is rough, that people are wandering to and fro, and that only one of them turns to listen to the singing woman. I do not think that we are intended to envisage the scene with any particularity, but we can set it if we like in an English or Scottish seaport on the Irish Channel, late at night, with the streets thronging after the pubs have closed, and only one of the passers-by turning to listen to the song of an Irish beggar-woman. Even this is quite unnecessarily detailed, but, unlike the scene imagined by Mr. Houghton, it at least does not conflict with anything in the text.

No, the logical connection obviously enough of the unsatisfactory band with the woman's words in the chorus about Ireland, is that she asks the protagonist of the poem (or he chooses to take her song as addressed to him personally) to come and *dance* with her in Ireland: and he replies that they will not find very pleasant music to dance to. (That he, not she, is the protagonist of the poem, is a point worth insisting on. What happens in the poem takes place in the stanzas. The woman's words which are a chorus to the stanzas in the sense of a refrain are also a chorus to the action of the poem in the sense of a formal commentary on it.) But before he tells her that, the protagonist tells her that the Ireland she is singing about is a 'long way off'. I think he means in time as well as in space—that it is back in the fourteenth century, where her words came from, and not merely across the sea on a rough night. She is speaking for, and from a lost Ireland of saints and scholars, and far from being Crazy Jane, she is, I think, a late version in Yeats's work of Kathleen ni Houlihan. 'Time runs on,' then, in the poem, in a more subtle and ambiguous set of senses than Mr. Houghton has imagined. It is as if the woman and the man were both saying to each other, 'It is later than you think,' but at cross-purposes. She is speaking with a sense of urgency: the man must come back to Ireland and help to save, or re-create, the old legendary 'holy land of Ireland' before it is too late: he is saying that she is a voice from the past, a ghost from the dead, that the Ireland she is talking of is dead and gone, with O'Leary in the grave. The dream with which she tempts him is only a dream. The reality which he will find is something inexpressibly vulgar, a brassy band, and even at that out of tune: (it is not to trumpets, drums, and trombones, even in the best of condition, that we can imagine the dance she speaks of being danced). The lovely things she speaks of have gone for good. If the man (and, as I shall suggest, it is not wholly fantastic to identify him with Yeats himself) goes back to Ireland, his life will be a tragic or absurd attempt to make a dream come true. But the fascination of the dream overbears the coherency of the argument:

> 'Man is in love and loves what vanishes,
> What more is there to say?'

The refrain is repeated a third time and this time the man has no answer.

Let us note, in passing, some other dubious details in Mr. Houghton's interpretation. 'Stately' here may imply something like 'lofty' or 'arrogant' but it will not imply '*repellently* lofty and arrogant', for loftiness and arrogance were qualities Yeats liked and admired. And 'cocked a malicious eye' in the second stanza simply cannot, cannot be the equivalent of Mr. Houghton's vulgar 'gives her the wink'. It represents rather that note of sardonic mockery which for Yeats, as for most Irishmen, was something positively valuable in itself, a necessary preservative against the softness that turns the romantic attitude into the sentimental one. The man in the poem is meant to be an attractive and even heroic figure. This is clinched, if something is still needed to clinch it, by the phrase 'one *solitary* man'—solitude, for Yeats, is always the companion of dignity. (There is a faint and trembling ambiguity here—the possibility of 'solitary' being used facetiously as it is in Ireland and Scotland for 'single'—'Not a solitary sixpence among us'—but even there the facetiousness comes from conferring a mock-dignity. 'One solitary man' I think *functionally* in the sentence means 'only one man' or 'one man alone' but if this causes a certain ironical questioning of the usual dignified associations of 'solitary', it does not lead to their disappearance. We also think of the man as having naturally a solitary nature, and not being the type to mingle with crowds.)

I suggest that it would be plausible to see the man in the poem as Yeats himself, in the London of the 1890s, in his 'first hard springtime', called back to Ireland away from his friends of the Theosophist Circles and the Cheshire Cheese by the 'romance' of the Irish past (and if the woman in the song can be thought of as a final version of Kathleen ni Houlihan, she might also be thought of as a symbolic transformation of the masterful Lady Gregory): he yields finally to the call but he does not delude himself at all about what he will find in the Irish *present*—the brassy band playing patriotic music out of tune, the bad poetry and bad rhetoric that so abundantly accompanied the Irish as they accompany all young nationalist movements: 'great hatred, little room', bigotry and provincialism that will howl down in turn, having learned nothing by the twenty-year interval between them, the two masterpieces of the Irish prose theatre, *The Playboy of the Western World* and *The Plough and the Stars*. He will find the ignorance and self-sufficiency that lost for Dublin Sir Hugh Lane's magnificent collection of pictures. Most bitter of all, he will find the very dream that lures him back being used to justify fanaticism and cruelty.

Yeats and 'The New Criticism'

'We had fed the heart on fantasies,
The heart's grown brutal from the fare;
More substance in our enmities
Than in our love. . . .'

Yeats was a great romantic poet, the last of these, precisely *because* he never confused the romantic dream with reality.

It might be objected that I am using, for the interpretation of this poem, details from the poet's biography and fragments from his other poems. Mr. Houghton is taking the text by itself. But Yeats's poems, impressive individually, are even more impressive as a coherent and continuous body of work: and the subject-matter of many of them comes directly, of many more indirectly, from his own biography. We cannot really import into the appreciation of poetry the strict isolating methods of mathematical, logical, or grammatical analysis—of the working out of the structure of an equation, a propositional function, a sentence—and there is no reason really, other than a pedantic self-conceit, why we should wish to do so. It may well be that without a knowledge of Yeats's life and work a reader would miss many of the implications of this short poem: but the proper reader will have acquired such knowledge, or be patient to acquire it. Even a sensitive reader new to Yeats would, I hope, see that the poem is *not* about the simple tragic contrast between charity and love but about the ironic interrelations of the realistic and romantic attitudes.

III

My second example is one of portentous muddle, masking a gross failure to understand. In an essay by Mr. Delmore Schwartz in *The Permanence of Yeats* there is a quite astonishing passage about this certainly rather difficult stanza from Yeats's 'Among School Children' (I have italicized certain key words, as they seem to me, for the understanding of the stanza, though I should add that they

73

are not, except one of them, words that have caught Mr. Schwartz's attention):

> 'Plato thought nature but a spume that plays
> Upon a *ghostly* paradigm of things;
> *Solider* Aristotle played the taws
> Upon the bottom of a king of kings;
> *World-famous* golden-thighed Pythagoras
> Fingered upon a fiddle-stick or strings
> What a star sang and careless Muses heard;
> *Old clothes upon old sticks to scare a bird.*'

Mr. Schwartz's muddles in examining this passage are, to be sure, partly the fault of American printers and dictionaries. The only meaning he could find for 'taws' was *marbles,* such as schoolboys play with; and Aristotle in his American edition of Yeats's *Collected Poems* is described as 'soldier Aristotle'—the sort of irritating misprint that makes a kind of defensible sense, though it makes a lame scansion. I don't know if the word 'taws' is still current in England, but in Scotland in my childhood it meant the teacher's strap and it formerly, when such barbarous instruments were in use, meant his birch. But if Mr. Schwartz is not to be blamed because dictionaries and printers create unreal problems of interpretation for him, he is to be blamed when, having with considerable acumen arrived at both a correct reading and a correct interpretation—having guessed that Aristotle after all must be 'solider' and that the taws is some instrument of chastisement—he harks back mournfully to a completely fancy meaning, which he has invented himself and which he says is much better than the meaning Yeats put into the Poem.

This is his fancy meaning: 'Given the first two lines of the stanza, which are certainly an effort to describe Plato's view of nature, suppose one takes the next two lines as a description of Aristotle's cosmology. "A king of kings" would thus be Aristotle's Prime Mover or God: the taws or marbles would be the concentric spheres which constitute the world for Aristotle and to which the Prime Mover gives impetus or movement. The reference is playful and ironic and also exact in saying that the taws or celestial spheres were played *against*' (my italics: Yeats's word is *'upon'*) 'the bottom of the Prime Mover, since he is, in Aristotle's description of his life turned away from all nature and wholly engaged in eternal thought about himself. And the whole sense of the passage, taken in this way, is a good extension by example, of the contempt for nature which Yeats is trying to state. The succeeding four lines . . . help this interpretation by their reference to Pythagoras on the same level of discourse, namely different philosophies of nature expressed in concrete figures.'

All this sounds so learned and plausible that at a first reading one almost begins to wonder whether, in accepting what seems to be the obvious sense of the lines most in question (that Aristotle, a character of an earthier disposition than Plato, assuaged his *angst* or soothed his pride by using his birch on the bottom of his royal pupil, Alexander, the future conqueror of the world) one has been obtuse. But, in detail, Mr. Schwartz's interpretation simply will not do. To begin with, Yeats's subject in this stanza, as a reading of it in its context will make clear, is not the recapitulation of early Greek philosophies but a sardonic consideration of the futility of 'the consolations of philosophy' in the face of old age and death: it is not the doctrines, so much as the personalities, and especially the personal weakness, of the three philosophers, that are engaging his attention. Secondly, marbles, small hard globes colliding against each other, might provide an excellent illustration for the atomic universe of Epicurus, but they provide the worst possible illustration for Aristotle's universe of concentric spheres. Thirdly, Aristotle's Prime Mover is surely a concept of metaphysics not a mystery of religion: a concept that is not intended to be figured anthropomorphically in a refined, let alone in this gross and heathenish fashion: an It rather than a He. Fourthly, Yeats's imagery is sometimes fantastic, but never merely grotesque, as the image of small boys playing marbles against the back parts of a Graecized Jehovah surely is. Yeats's great precision of language would not allow him to talk of playing marbles 'upon' somebody's bottom when he meant playing marbles 'against' it. Sixthly, so far does it seem from being the case that Yeats, in this poem, is trying to state any 'contempt for nature', that the poem concludes with one of the most beautiful of all his organic metaphors. Mr. Schwartz, in fact, is himself in the end forced to reject his own fantasies, but he does so reluctantly and churlishly: 'This historical-biographical interpretation' (that Aristotle was only, after all, tanning the hide of the youthful Alexander) 'seems to me obviously inferior, in terms of the poem itself, so far as significance goes: *they*'— i.e. 'the lines', for Mr. Schwartz's disappointment has affected his grammar—'seem to stick out wrongly from the rest of the stanza: what has Aristotle's whipping of his noble pupil to do with contempt for nature. It would seem rather *to be*'—i.e. 'to have to do with'—'contempt for monarchy.'

What, however, has Yeats's poem as a whole or this stanza in particular to do with contempt for nature, or for monarchy either? In what sense is it even his intention in this stanza to give us a rhymed summary of Greek cosmologies? 'Among School Children' is about a more human and interesting subject, the hollowness of greatness, especially for the great themselves, as they grow old. The poet, visiting school-children at an Irish convent, in his capacity probably not only of famous man of letters but Irish Senator, is reminded by the sight of them of the stories told to him in his youth by a beautiful woman he loved of her own childhood. He imagines that in her childhood she may have looked like one of these young girls in front of him, and the thought fills him with a sudden ardent excitement. But then he recalls her present appearance, an elderly woman as he is an elderly man—still beautiful in a sense, but gaunt and hollow-cheeked, as if she drank nothing but wind and ate nothing but shadows. And he thinks bitterly also of his own lost youth, good looks, sexual vitality—but puts the thought aside as inappropriate to the occasion.

> 'Better to smile on all that smile, and show
> There is a comfortable kind of old scarecrow.'

But his bitter thoughts cannot leave him. Is the effort of keeping up appearances as 'a sixty-year-old smiling public man' worth it? Would any mother if she could see her son at sixty, weakening towards the grave, think the sight of him

> 'A compensation for the pang of his birth
> Or the uncertainty of his setting forth?'

That is the question which the stanza under consideration is asking, and the answer has nothing at all to do with 'contempt for nature'. It would be truer to say that the stanza expresses something like 'contempt for mind'. Plato and Aristotle and Pythagoras could impress the world, but they do not impress Yeats: for he sees them evading a problem— the problem of the growing hollowness of greatness and wisdom, the growing unconvincingness of 'all these large dreams by which men long live well', with the approach of old age and death—which he himself, in this poem, is facing squarely and honestly. Plato tries to pretend that his decaying natural body is something illusory, that reality is spiritual, but Yeats's use of 'ghostly' (with its connotations here of spectral, phantasmal, unreal) puts Plato's heaven of bodiless abstractions in its place. In case the overtones of scorn should not be caught, Yeats makes them much more obvious when he talks of 'solider' Aristotle—solider than Plato in the sense of shrewder, more down-to-earth, more acute by the world's standards and also in the sense of, by other standards, grosser, more earthy, more obtuse. The 'realistic' nature of Aristotle's consolations—the tangible birch on the tangible royal bottom—are mocked at brilliantly. The lines are, what they are meant to be, broadly and cruelly funny. Nor is Pythagoras, though he is perhaps a philosopher more to Yeats's taste, exempt from mockery —he is 'world-famous', the epithet which journalists reserve for film-stars and politicians, and obviously he loves his fame: he allows lies to be spread about him, such as that he has a golden thigh. With a genuine interest in mathematics and music, he nevertheless, in a brilliant charlatan's fashion, puts his philosophy together out of any bits and pieces that are handy.

'What a star sang and careless Muses heard.'

Perhaps the tone about Pythagoras is a little less harsh than about the other two. But the continuing note of scorn is unmistakable, and the last line clinches it:

'Old clothes upon old sticks to scare a bird.'

Crudely, 'With all their fine talk, they were a set of old scarecrows!' But I think that one is possibly not being too ingenious (and the syntax at least doesn't contradict the interpretation) in taking the lines to refer to the philosopher's *speculations* as well as to their ageing *selves*. The old clothes are man's most ambitious metaphysical speculations. The sticks are the actual nakedness of human existence. The bird that, if it is not scared away, will eat up all the seeds of human culture is, let us say, the awareness of that nakedness: of man as merely another appetitive animal, given over to death. The philosophers can scare that bird away from the common fields but not, perhaps, from their own private gardens. The name of the bird is despair.

This is only one moment, the negative moment, of a poem which closes, as we have seen, on a note of rich acceptance. But this negative moment is not itself an acceptance of despair. It is a rejection of false consolations—of the claim of any system of concepts, soulful, tough, or fantastic, to protect us from despair. But Yeats rejects the 'consolations of philosophy', or of systematic abstraction, only to turn immediately to the consolation of what in the widest sense can be called religion. He turns from the concept,

78

which is always abstract, to the image, which is always concrete:

> 'Both nuns and mothers worship images,
> But those the candles light are not as those
> That animate a mother's reveries,
> But keep a marble or a bronze repose.
> And yet they too break hearts—O Presences
> That passion, piety or affection knows,
> And that all heavenly glory symbolize—
> O self-born mockers of man's enterprise;
>
> Labour is blossoming or dancing where
> The body is not bruised to pleasure soul,
> Nor beauty born out of its own despair,
> Nor blear-eyed wisdom out of midnight oil.
> O chestnut tree, great-rooted blossomer,
> Are you the leaf, the blossom or the bole?
> O body swayed to music, O brightening glance,
> How can we know the dancer from the dance?'

These three kinds of image—that of a 'Ledaean body' known by the lover's 'passion', that of a saint's or Christ's or the Virgin's 'marble or . . . bronze repose' known by the nuns' 'piety', that of the restless and lively growing child known by the mother's 'affection'—are not to be equated with the *actual* lover, or carved figure, or child. They are 'Presences' which project themselves from or around these, they are archetypes to which we try to make particular experience conform. They are 'self-born' (perhaps) in that we do not feel the need to justify them, explain them, relate them to anything else: to give anything else meaning, we relate it to *them*. They 'break hearts' because what nun, lover, and mother dream of *is* a dream, to which actual experience or achievement will never more than sketchily or approximately correspond. They are 'mockers of man's enterprise' because it is in these moments of awareness of the concrete mystery of life, in all its intensity and beauty,

79

that we see most clearly how much of what we call our lives is mere routine and abstraction. Yeats having invoked these 'Presences', which give human life its worth and dignity, one expects him in the last stanza to pray to them. Instead, surprisingly, he instructs them—he tells them about the ideal conditions under which they would not 'break hearts' and 'man's enterprise' or woman's childbed pains, her 'labour' would not be mocked by them. Man's enterprise and woman's labour have the naturalness of flowers and the harmony of the dance when the body is not sacrificed to the soul, when beauty, like the beauty of the ageing woman in an earlier stanza, does not express the soul's despair because of the decay of the body, when wisdom does not come from reading that ruins our eyes. (There is so little 'contempt for nature' here that Yeats does not even envisage the opposite case of the soul being sacrificed to the body.) To think of soul and body apart (or to make similar abstractions, for instances of the individual and society, or, as Yeats himself did in one of his poems, of perfection of the 'life' or of the 'work') is in any case the fallacy of the philosophers, the fallacy of mistaking notions for realities. What is needed—and also what, in some ultimate and mysterious sense, is the actual truth about the universe, if we could see it—is harmony. And Yeats's two images for this are (*a*) from nature, and (*b*) from art.

> (*a*) 'O chestnut tree, great-rooted blossomer,
> Are you the leaf, the blossom, or the bole?'

We can take the 'bole' as the human body and as the body of society and as any time-honoured institution: 'the leaf' as whatever recurrently shelters and protects these—habits, customs, traditions, repeated ceremonies: the 'blossom' as their flowering in great art, or deeds of individual heroism, or ardours of romantic love.

> (*b*) 'O body swayed to music, O brightening glance,
> How can we know the dancer from the dance?'

There again the 'dancer' could be taken as the existence, the 'dance' as the function of human society, and the 'brightening glance' is just like 'the blossom'—it is the overflow of organic harmony in almost arbitrary, almost superfluous beauty. It is the *expression* of the life of the dance, as the blossom is the *expression* of the life of the tree. We are, indeed, though we are certainly expressing no 'contempt for nature', to think of something more than mere nature here: of a cosmic dance, from which all the abstractions of our thinking—i.e. 'mind' and 'nature', 'mind' and 'body', my death and other continuing lives—are in some sense wrong and false abstractions. The blossom falls but new blossoms will spring next year: one dancer tires, but another takes his place in the continuing dance. Thus the final mood of the great and difficult poem is one of mystical acceptance: but Yeats is able to make this gesture of acceptance adequately only because earlier, and particularly in the stanza about which Mr. Schwartz made so many blunders, he has honestly faced the worst that can be said about the human condition.

Though this is a difficult poem, its difficulties do not come, as in so much of Yeats's work, from the use of a private system of references. It is, as some other critic shrewdly notes in *The Permanence of Yeats*, 'classical' rather than 'symbolist' in method. There is no use of private mythology and the kinds of experience referred to in the poem, and the kinds of meditation about such experience, should be familiar to most mature and sensitive readers. I know few of Yeats's poems in which the general line of argument is at once so rational and so massive, or in which there is so much that the sensitive common reader can at once accept. I hope these considerations excuse my carping tone about Mr. Schwartz. The difficulties of the poem are all what I would call legitimate difficulties, and it is the business of the critic to help the sensitive common reader to get over them: it is anything but his business to put up new and artificial barriers between that reader and a great poem.

F
81

IV

It may be said that in attacking certain injudicious applications of the method of analysis, I have had to rely chiefly on that method myself: I have merely substituted longer for shorter, or fuller for skimpier, analyses. But what has been at the back of my mind all along is that it is the business of a poem primarily to be understood and enjoyed, not primarily to be talked about. One uses the method of analysis didactically or controversially; I had lived with the two poems we have been considering for years, and it is only my irritation at Mr. Houghton's and Mr. Schwartz's treatment of them that has goaded me into making these cumbrous paraphrases of Yeats's perfectly adequate verse. I had the *feeling* that I understood these poems (I *knew* I enjoyed them) and I had sufficient confidence in myself as a reader not to feel it necessary to test this feeling, as I have been testing it now. Now, of course, in young and untrained readers this feeling that one understands may, in very many cases, be a delusion; it ought to be tested. That was Dr. Richards's point in 'Practical Criticism'. The exercise of giving a coherent prose account of the sense of a poem, prevents a greedy and impatient reader from making a snap judgment about the poem before he has, in any proper sense, 'experienced' it. Laziness and self-conceit are the commonest faults of the immature reader, and Dr. Richards's approach did much to correct these. But there is a certain sense in which they are ingrained and inescapable faults: there is a lazy and self-conceited way of 'closely examining' a text as well as a lazy and self-conceited way of making a 'summary judgment' on it. If the obvious danger of the Old Criticism was a mere parroting of received opinions by young men, can we not also envisage the young New Critic flipping rapidly through a book of poems, saying, 'Ah, here is what looks like a difficult passage! Can I say something clever about it?' (I find it extremely difficult, for instance, to believe that Mr. Schwartz has really patiently lived with 'Among School Children', *as a total composition.*)

Perhaps one should be a little suspicious of all attempts to make too much of 'method' in criticism. A method is, almost by definition, something fool-proof; and every critic, who is not always a fool, knows that he is sometimes a fool. On his off-days, perhaps a 'method' can prevent him from going too far astray: but even from this point of view the method of the New Criticism is still obviously in need of refinement. There ought to be some, so to say, almots mechanical safeguards against Mr. Schwartz's kind of irrelevance. But, to sum up, criticism does remain in the end one of the liberal, not one of the mechanical, arts. The critic may *apply* certain methods. But he does not, in the end, rely on his methods. He relies on himself.

Pound: Masks, Myth, Man [1]

———————————— ❈ ————————————

I

This will not be the kind of essay that Ezra Pound himself
would approve of. I am writing on the passenger deck of a
vessel bound for Japan, the books I want to quote from are
in the hold, and so I shall have to talk around him, and
around him, digging up what illustrative tags I can from
my memory. That is not his own way of criticizing. It is
perhaps not quite true of him, as John Crowe Ransom says
it is of Eliot, that he 'never lifts his nose from the page'; he
has forcible opinions on a hundred subjects, and his critical
essays are full of all sorts of pungent 'asides'; but on the
whole he is at his best as a critic when he opens a book,
thrusts it at you, and says 'See for yourself'. What you have
to *see*, generally, is not an illustration of some favourite
thesis but a poem on a page, worth looking at for its own
sake. He exposes you to impacts. Some of his best critical
essays—that on French poetry, for instance—are not so
much even close examinations of texts as little anthologies,
with just enough commentary to let the reader get to grips
on his own. And in the essays illustrated by translations,
those on Provençal poets or on Cavalcanti's *Donna mi prega*,
the prose setting of the translations has often the air of acute,
but disconnected, notebook jottings. And Pound's best
criticism, no doubt, *is* in his translations. He makes ghosts
walk again, in their habit, as they lived; yet his ghosts,
paradoxically enough, have a common aspect; we know

[1] This was first published in 1950, in a volume of tributes to Mr.
Pound on his sixty-fifth birthday, assembled by Mr. Peter Russell.

them by their gait, and the gait is Pound's. *Homage to Sextus Propertius*, for instance, will send you (if you have the kind of schoolboy smattering of Latin I have) to Propertius, looking for a wry humour, which is perhaps only Pound's, or which anyway no one would have seen in Propertius until Pound had read it into him. He gives things his own flavour; but I am not, in this essay, attempting to give him *my* flavour. I am trying to arrive at a tentative judgment of him as he is in himself.

Such versions, or such handlings, rather, as *Homage to Sextus Propertius*, are what Pound calls *personae*, as he might say masks or maybe roles. But the puzzle for his readers is, of, say, Pound and Propertius, which is the actor and which is the part: is it a question of Garrick as Hamlet, or Hamlet as Garrick? Perhaps we should think of neither of these simple alternatives; Pound's Propertius is more an antique Roman than a Yank, but just sufficiently a Yank to be not too stuffily an antique Roman. This is perhaps Pound's great gift as a poet of roles—his power of forcefully combining partial inadequacies into a not at all inadequate whole. Propertius, for instance, needs re-interpretation, even distortion, to bring him within our own framework; but we must also re-interpret and distort that framework (we must correlate two variables, in fact) to come to terms with *him*. This is why both Pound's rage against academic scholars, and the rage of academic scholars against Pound, are largely critically irrelevant. Academic scholars are able to get an objective view of a text by dissociating it as far as possible from their own contemporary sensibility, which is what the poetic critic and translator—who for that very reason can never get a wholly objective view—dare not do. The scholar must not, and the poet must, project himself into the text. A kind of amateur scholarship has, perhaps, been a stumbling-block to Pound. It is right for a poet, making the first draft of a translation, to guess, guess all the way—to use his intuition about how a poem of a certain kind *must* be built up—but I think he should then check his guesses with a good dictionary or a reliable crib. His guesses will be brilliant but not necessarily accurate. Pound, I feel, has too often omitted this checking; he has more of the spirit of scholarship than many scholars, but, after all, the letter counts too. On the other hand, it is this schoolboy eagerness that has kept him, for so many years, so wonderfully fresh as a man and a poet.

The sensibility, then, of Propertius, or Li Po, or Bertrans de Born, is one variable that Pound has had to adjust in shaping his masks; another variable has been his own raw, quick, exceedingly American sensibility. That, in isolation, has its inadequacies, too. Pound's emphasis, for instance, on the notion of 'culture' is very American, and there is that little early poem (not one of his best) where he imagines American life strangely transformed by a general study of 'the Classics'. I think that for the intelligent American reader today—for the intelligent reader almost everywhere, for that matter—one trouble is that there are too many 'Classics' altogether. The point about somebody like Jefferson was not that he had read a great deal (the eighteenth-century novel, for instance, which for us is a 'classic', for him was an unwholesome distraction), but that what he had read was what most educated gentlemen of his time, in England and France as well as in Virginia, would have read too. That age demanded of a gentleman a wide, clear, and superficial range of knowledge over a known range of subjects; Lord Chesterfield, for instance, told his son that a young man should know about architectural styles, but not about building materials, for the latter kind of knowledge was not 'liberal' but 'mechanical'.

A great deal of what was once liberal knowledge has today become mechanical in that sense; even literary criticism has today its quite elaborate technical jargon. But our liberal knowledge, the part of our knowledge that is still genuinely liberal, has no longer the cohesion that it had in Jefferson's day. There are more books worth reading than we shall ever read, and more arguable points of view than

we shall ever come to terms with. Let us imagine that
Pound could dictate a course of reading in 'general literature' for the leading American universities; it would be a
drop in the bucket, it would leave the general cultural con-
fusion richer, perhaps, but also more thick and sticky than
ever. Our reading today is rather, in fact, like an American
salad—cheese, gherkins, nuts, lettuces, pears, endives, perhaps a slice of pineapple and a rub of garlic—and one needs
a bottle of thick mayonnaise to mask the contrasting
flavours, and the name of the mayonnaise, in the United
States, is 'culture'.

'Culture', as most Americans use the word, covers anything that is not obviously practical or pleasurable; like
visiting, for instance, Stratford-on-Avon. In this sense, the
notion of culture can become a blanket smothering individual taste and discrimination—and this, of course, is not,
one would never dare hint it, exactly Pound's sense of culture. But his sense has something, at least, in common with
what the American humanists, Irving Babbitt and Paul
Elmer More, understood by culture; and what they understood was in a sense the opposite of what an anthropologist
understands by *a* culture; they understood not something
that could be encouraged to grow out of the habits and
perceptions of daily American life, but something that had
to be protected from these. Their humanism was an admirable notion, but it had no roots in the American soil, and so
produced no flowers or fruits there. On the contrary, one
would be tempted to say that some of the best and most
racy American writing (*Huckleberry Finn, Fiesta, Soldiers'
Pay, The Thin Man*) springs from the soil of a sensitive
philistinism; poetry, too, William Carlos Williams's poetry
of red brick houses, suburban wives, cheerful standardized
interiors. It was a weakness, an amiable and typically
American weakness in Pound, that he was too eager to make
everybody else read his own favourite authors and too
hopeful about the changes that would spring from such a
reading. It is not so much *what* people read, as *how* they

87

read, that can make them startlingly and pleasantly different.

Our point, however, is the poetry. In these masks or roles of Pound's, the inadequacies of an eager American eclecticism, and of various primitive or archaic attitudes, not easily revivable in contemporary terms, do seem to combine, after all, as something poetically adequate. This whole question of the triumphant combination of inadequacies becomes peculiarly fascinating in the unique case, before *The Cantos—Hugh Selwyn Mauberley—*where the *persona*, the mask, the role, is not the old empty armour that begins to shape, and clank, and move as if it had life in it, as Pound's swan passes on the stream—I am making an allusion, there, to the opening of one of the early Cantos—but, on the contrary, a role, a contemporary role, rather like Pound's own. I say 'rather like' for *Mauberley* is not *exactly* Pound. He is, one gathers, a minor poet of genuine talent, high, frail ambition, and classical tastes: a sort of Landor *de ses jours*, but with a wistfulness and an irony that are more like Laforgue. The poem has the smell of its time. When we read, for instance, of Mr. Nixon advising the poet to 'take a column', and 'butter reviewers', warning him that the 'nineties tried your game, but died of it', we cannot help thinking of Arnold Bennett, playing the part of the Card in life as in literature.

In such a discouraging atmosphere, Mauberley can only drift, collect fugitive impressions, remember the 'nineties and the pre-Raphaelites, bitterly note decay.

> 'In that thoroughfare
> The sale of half-hose has
> Long since superseded the cultivation
> Of Pierian roses.'

In the end he vanishes to a euphoric death in the South Seas:

> 'I was
> And I no more exist;
> Here drifted
> An Hedonist.'

Mauberley, in his passivity, is in some degree inadequate as a person, though not in the least so as a *persona* (Dr. Leavis, if I remember rightly, though a passionate admirer of this poem, has something sniffy to say about the 'merely aesthetic' attitude implied in it). Pound himself was made of tougher stuff. He did not drift to the South Seas, but instead started to study economics and to write the longest readable poem of our time, *The Cantos*. This was a move from the lyrical scale to the epical; and it implied, at the same time, a move from the lyric mask to the epic myth.

II

The nature of the underlying myth in *The Cantos* begins to become really clear about half-way through, in the two long sections where the anecdotes, of which the poem is largely composed, are no longer broken off in the middle to be taken up, in a different setting, several Cantos further on. Of these two large monolithic chunks, intruding so strangely into a kaleidoscopic poem, one is about John Adams, the second President of the United States; it consists largely of extracts from letters by him or about him, of documentation. For most readers, just as poetry, it is one of the least successful sections; it presupposes, for the English reader at least, a grounding in the early history of the United States which few English readers are likely to have. The other section is a condensed version of the history of China; and on the whole most readers, I imagine, will find this one of the most wonderful sections of the poem—it is, perhaps more than any other part, properly epical. But, failures or successes, these two sections give the key to the myth.

It is the myth of the noble leader and the stable community, of the good society which has been, and can be again, and which wicked men seek to destroy. The good society, for Pound, is stable rather than changing; the only natural kind of change is deterioration, and therefore to preserve the stability of society a constant, daily effort of *renewal* is required. Certain sacred exemplars of stability must be kept in mind, figures like Confucius and Adams, documents like the Confucian writings and the American Constitution. The noble leader, like Adams, and the stable society, like China, have qualities in common. Their stability is preserved by the exercise of an acute but severely practical intelligence. They both respect tradition, but by that they mean the cultural inheritance of skills and insights and wisdom; not merely anything at all that has come down from the past. There are times when a break must be made,[1] but when the break has been made, it has something of finality about it—just as for Burke, for instance, the 'Glorious Revolution' of 1688 was, among other things, a kind of sacred barrier against any subsequent revolutions whatever. Stability has two enemies besides its own natural tendency to decay. One is the activity of the moneylender, the tax-gatherer, the banker, the great financial combine; the other is the otherworldliness—like Taoism in China—which treats life as a vain dream.

Pound thus thinks of certain purposes as valid throughout history, but as constantly thwarted. He thinks it possible to separate the wheat of history from the chaff; and this distinguishes him from historicists in the strict sense like Hegel, Marx, Croce, or Collingwood, for whom such a distinction is untenable, for whom everything that happens in history is necessary, and reasonable, and therefore right. To separate the wheat from the chaff, Pound must feel sure that he has a stance *outside* history; or access to certain permanent values.

What set? Partly those of the artist who keeps his eyes open. 'By their fruits ye shall know them.' There must be something right about the society that produces Chartres and something wrong about the society that produces, say,

[1] But those making the break—Confucius, the Whigs of 1688, the American Founding Fathers, Pound himself as a poetic innovator—will claim always to be going back to an earlier and sounder tradition.

London south of the river. Men like Adams and Jefferson
respect the arts, but they are not in Mauberley's sense
'aesthetes', and indeed throughout *The Cantos* Pound seems
to be moving away from Mauberley's still faintly ninetyish
attitude towards one more like Ruskin's in *Unto This Last*;
it must be good men, in a good society, who build a good
cathedral.

The odd thing is that in religion Pound is a kind of
eighteenth-century deist (one of his literary heroes, and an
oddly assorted set they are, is Voltaire), and there must be a
sense in which the cathedral, and the whole outer fabric of
medieval life that he loves so passionately, is nothing for
him but an adorable mockery or a beautiful empty shell.
Critics have noted, and very rightly, the new and very
moving note of religious humility in the 'Pull down thy
vanity' passage in *The Pisan Cantos*; but none of them have
noted that the divinity not exactly invoked but hinted at
there—the deity that sheathes a blade of grass more elegantly
than a Parisian dressmaker sheathes a beautiful woman—is
just the divinity of the Deists: 'Nature', or 'Nature's God',
it hardly matters which one calls it, for it is just enough of a
God to keep Nature running smoothly. The *feeling* of the
passage is anything but Voltairean, but the *notion* is quite
Voltaire's: the God envisaged is wholly immanent. There
is a good deal of disquiet and horror at odd moments in
The Cantos, but so far as I can see there is no sense of the
transcendental, no awareness of the great gulf that separates
finite existence from the mystery of nothing or the mystery
of being. These ultimate questions are for Pound, as for
Confucius or William James, vain distractions from the
immediate business of living. There is work to be done,
danger to be met; do not let us, Pound seems to be saying,
vainly sit and brood, in solitary uselessness.

The anguish that Pound feels most acutely is not about
eternity, but about time. 'Time is evil. Evil.' That couple of
tiny sentences comes in a passage where Pound is describing
how Ignez da Castro, who has been murdered because the

old King of Portugal did not want her to be the wife of the young Crown Prince, was dug up from her grave when the Prince ascended the throne, how she sat crowned with 'the King still young beside her', and how 'a day, and a day, all the Lords of Lisboa' filed past her to kiss her hand. Time is evil that has corrupted her beauty in the grave, that has left of the young King's love only pride and bitterness and a dry ache for revenge. Such are among the most moving moments in *The Cantos* and they break through the sturdy and enclosed optimism which is (surprisingly, when one considers the violence and cruelty of so many of the incidents related) the prevailing mood of the myth. The *myth* of *The Cantos* is that of the stable society, the good society, which has been and which, if only men will let themselves be guided by the sacred exemplars, can be again. The *truth* of *The Cantos* which comes out very often, for instance, in *The Pisan Cantos*, is that of a total waste, bitterness, and loss, which it is not really within human power to compensate or repair. It is something other than man himself that gives him strength to recognize, and to outface, the worst. 'It was not man/Made courage, or made order, or made grace.' Who was it then? This question, in *The Cantos* that are still to come, seems to demand a more positive answer. There is something in the whole pattern of the poem that demands an encounter with the transcendental at a culminating point.

The Cantos started off with a Homeric sea voyage (significantly enough from Circe's island, where Mauberley perhaps, like poor Elpenor, might have been glad enough to linger), and with a visit to hell-mouth, the sacrifice of a sheep, and a raising of the spirits of the mighty dead; while another sort of hell, the hell, as some critic has acutely said, of *others*—of newspaper proprietors, war profiteers, puritan bishops, and those who think of sex in terms of rubber goods, but certainly not of 'ole Ez' himself—plays a prominent, if jarring, part in the earlier Cantos. There are glimpses, too, of a kind of earthly paradise, sea and sun dazzle, nymphs, Bacchus transforming pirates into furry animals, masts into trees, of troubadours, of Renaissance soldiers, of American pioneers, of the Cid—a great froth and flurry of everything that is lively in Pound's memory or imagination; a great invocation, with sidelong snarling glances at the present, of everything that seems splendid in the real or legendary past. The effect is wonderful, but would be bewildering if the pattern—of interweaving stories started, dropped, taken up again at random—were continued indefinitely. The first thirty or so Cantos state a 'matter' one might say, in the medieval sense, the 'matter of Europe'. The American episodes there come in with a strange, disquieting gritty effect, more 'realistic' but less 'poetic'; the Chinese allusions with an effect of remote, grave, and not immediately relevant wisdom.

Then come, soberly, the great exemplars: the poem touches, if sometimes a little leadenly, the ground of China and America. We know where we are, we have a clearer sense of direction. After all, against brilliant and unstable Europe—and the European ghosts have all been called up from Hell, after all—some more stolid but safer concept of society is to be justified. Then, with *The Pisan Cantos*, there is a change again; we have left hell, and the heavenly phantasmagorias that a classic hell affords, the

> 'hero's iron shade
> Glittering through the gloomy glade,'

and we have ascended from the broad plains of earth, of America and China, to the mountain of purgatory.

The poet moves for the first time mainly through his *own* past, recalling dead or distant or estranged friends—Yeats, Hueffer, Jepson, Newbolt, Nancy Cunard—with a new tenderness; expressing his personal feelings more frankly and on the whole with less toughness than in the past—there are no just wars in spring or autumn (ancient Chinese wisdom, but he feels it personally, the sacredness of sowing and harvest), and, however unpractical and sentimental such

93

a view is, he has learned, from his own sad experience, that
he does not like the idea of either animals or men being in
cages. Things have not worked out either as he had hoped
or as he had calculated. His poem itself, which was to be an
impersonal epic, is taking an unexpected direction. He must
cast down his vanity. . . .

There are, I believe, about eighteen Cantos still to come.
It would be rash to make any predictions about them, but
we have had a long sea journey and we must have a return
to Ithaca; we have had a raising of many ghosts, and they
must be ceremoniously laid; we have had the gods of
Greece, and the sacred human wisdom of Confucius and
Adams, and the *Deus sive Natura* of Spinoza or Voltaire; it
is time, as I have already suggested, for us to confront the
Transcendent. We have had hell, and earth, and the earthly
paradise, and a personal purgatory; of a truly supernatural
paradise (not necessarily or very probably a Christian one)
we must also have a glimpse.

But these are abstract formal demands, and about abstract
form in this sense, a preconceived form into which whatever matter immediately available must be moulded, Pound
has never cared much. All these prophecies may be wrong.
What does seem certain is that, in *The Pisan Cantos*, he has
been forced for the first time to come to grips in poetry
with *himself*; to recognize to what great extent the whole
pattern of his long poem is, as it were, not objectively read
off from history, but projected from his own inner being.
If one takes them as an objective statement about history,
The Cantos are, one must recognize, a failure; a great deal
of evidence is presented but in the nature of the case it is
not, and cannot be, exhaustive; and even if one accepts it as
tendentiously selected, it is not certain that it will prove
what Pound wants it to prove. Even as a special pleader, he
does not quite make out his case.

He will be forced, I think, in the Cantos that are to come,
to recognize that *The Cantos* are an objective failure (that
flattened and smoothed into prose, so to say, they would

94

not make a convincing thesis about history), but at another level, which one cannot call a merely subjective level, this recognition might set the seal on the poem's success. Pound might recognize that, like Langland, he has written a *vision*. And it is a much more personal vision than Langland's. Pound is free, certainly, of the shadows of Freud and Proust, but we are none of us free of the shadow of Rousseau. The structure of *The Cantos* has in fact no exact analogy in previous literature, but if it is in some sense epical, it is also in some sense confessional. Pound is quite without *introspective* interest in himself, yet perhaps the clearest concrete impression *The Cantos* leave with us, after we have rejected their myth, and accepted their truth, is one of Pound the man. It is perhaps Pound the man at the centre of *The Cantos* that prevents them falling apart into mere fragmentary chaos.

III

Yet about the man himself, apart from his poetry, it is perhaps not critically proper to say very much. I shall merely say one word about what I think is the main error in his thinking; an error responsible for flaws in his work and also, of course, for his personal misfortunes. It is a very common error, especially among loyal, active, passionate, and courageous men. It has to do with his ideal of stability. I am not writing as an irresponsible advocate of change for its own sake. We are creatures of habit and, though some changes are always necessary, change in itself is always disagreeable to us. Like Ezra Pound, I too think we should aim at stability in society. But I do not really think that we shall get it, ever, in any permanent sense. We are aiming at something ideal: we have no models of a really stable society in history (certainly neither China nor medieval Christendom is such a model, if one looks into its history in any detail, since the one society stagnated and rendered itself vulnerable to outer pressure and inner upheaval, and the other, a society of perpetual war and debate, was shaken to pieces by its own inner strife). We have only models of more or less striking and ambitious failures to achieve stability.

We seek society's stability, by a kind of instinct, as we seek our own health; though we know that in the long run we shall fall ill and die. It is this instinct, or this impulse, to stabilize that seems permanent in history. There are probably also permanent *elements* of human behaviour; but there are no permanent stable social forms. Every social form is at the best showily, and imperfectibly, stable; it will be broken down in time, and a new form (still imperfect, but more suited to new times and circumstances) will take its place. Politics is a heroic activity just because, almost by definition, it is bound to fail.

It is Pound's error, it seems to me, not to recognize this; to believe in stable forms that have been destroyed by malice, and to believe in the possibility of reinstating them, and of curbing the malice that would destroy them. Malice, certainly I would agree, is something that works permanently for the destruction of stability. But whose malice? That, for instance, as Pound sometimes suggests, of those who sell armaments? What about the malice of those who buy? We are *all*, in fact, malicious, and must curb our malice (or seek divine or scientific help to curb it) as well as we can. The human race cannot be divided into the many simple, innocent good and the few cunning wicked. That way lie persecution and death-camps. It is Pound's weakness, as a man and a poet, to be able to spot evil in his enemies and not in himself and his friends. The problem of evil, or of innate human self-centredness and aggressiveness, is the one problem with which his life, his poetry, and his politics, have never come to grips. He has been right to stand up, indeed, for human dignity in an age in which there has been an almost hysterical cult of guilt.[1] But there

[1] By talking loudly about *universal* guilt one intends, generally, to assuage an uneasy sense of *individual* guilt. 'You are, at least potentially, as bad as me.' True, but not *actually* so bad, and this is resented.

96

is a sense, and perhaps he has failed to recognize this, in which human dignity is itself a *persona*, a mask, a role. I would rather read Pound any day than Kafka; but there is a sense, after all, in which Kafka goes more deep.

We should think not of this error and these misfortunes but of the man himself, as his works and his friends present him to us, the most generous and impulsive and unworldly of men; devoting two or three hours every day to his poetry and the rest to helping and encouraging younger friends. The evocation of comradeship in *The Pisan Cantos* has a peculiarly touching and genuine quality, and my own feeling, for what it is worth, is that there is more natural goodness in Pound than in half a dozen of his distinguished contemporaries who have had enough common sense— Pound has no common sense at all, I would say, he is a kind of eternal schoolboy, or magnificent *naïf*—never to put a foot wrong. Where he yields himself to blind and stupid hate, or to harsh, uncharitable, destructive anger, I shudder; but whether or not we can hold him fully responsible for such outbursts (and it seems clear that he is the victim of certain compulsive obsessions), it is clear also that they are not *central* to what he has to say. In the perspective of history, his errors will seem incidental; his epic, his vision, his confession, his discovery of himself through his exploration of history, of humility through the assertion of pride, of truth through persistence in error, these will seem typically and broadly human, and in their pathos noble and profound.

The Waste Land Revisited

Thirty years after its first appearance, three facts about *The Waste Land*, two of which could not be foreseen, and one of which was not known, by contemporary critics, are of peculiar interest. The first fact is that, though perhaps no contemporary poem has had through its mood, its imagery, and its diction—and through some but not all of its technical devices—a more striking influence on a subsequent generation of poets, no subsequent poet has written a successful poem which imitates or adapts the *form* of *The Waste Land*. It might be said that even the influence of the mood and imagery of the poem has been though a powerful, a rather oblique one. A younger poet like Mr. Louis Mac-Neice found, as he has told us, in his university days a romantic excitement in Mr. Eliot's metropolitan imagery which Mr. Eliot did not consciously intend to put there. When he read such lines as

'On a winter evening round behind the gashouse
Musing upon the king my brother's wreck
And on the king my father's death before him,'

his youthful reaction was not so much a perception of ironic contrast as a feeling that it would be rather fun to play Hamlet beside the gasworks. (Mr. Eliot might have murmured, like Mr. Prufrock, 'That is not what I meant at all. That is not it, at all.') The history of literary influences is full of such paradoxes. 'Prufrock' has similarly given a glamour for many of us to the idea of 'one-night cheap hotels' and, by the play he makes with the idea of 'seediness', Mr. Graham Greene has given us a romantic interest in dim and flavourless interiors, and the Tottenham Court Road. Any good writer injects by his skill a positive quality even into scenes and episodes of which he may consciously merely intend to emphasize the negative value. There is no doubt that one of Mr. Eliot's purposes in *The Waste Land* was to point a contrast, as in the lines quoted above, between the splendour and dignity of some aspects of the past and the sordidness of some aspects of the present. What younger poets learned from him, however, was that the sordidness could have its own tang. They had enough sense, in the early 1930s, to see that a complexity and elaboration of form like that of *The Waste Land* were beyond their youthful scope. They could, however, appropriate the gashouse, and note, as Mr. Eliot did, the run of the contemporary speaking voice. It is rather as if young admirers of Braque had decided that fish on a kitchen table make a first-rate subject for a painting, but that the way to paint them is not as Braque does, but in a traditional naturalistic manner.

The second fact has some relation to the first. No contemporary poem has been subjected to more detailed and laborious analysis than *The Waste Land*, yet no critic has either confidently assigned it to one of the traditional kinds of poetry or, if he considers it as the invention of a quite new kind of poem, has invented a new name for that kind. In conversation, indeed, such names may be sometimes thrown out. An enthusiastic young man may describe *The Waste Land* as a condensed epic; a stubborn traditionalist may call it a cento[1]. But obviously neither of these names fits. The third fact has perhaps again some connection with the second. Mr. Eliot very largely left the final decisions about the form of *The Waste Land* to his friend, Mr. Ezra Pound. The fact that he sought and welcomed such advice (it might even be correct to say, such instructions) suggests that there must have been a stage in the composition of the

[1] A cento is a poem made up of lines and phrases appropriated from other poems.

poem when he found its matter so disturbing that he could not take a detached view of its form. He had been exploring, as an early reviewer of *The Waste Land* shrewdly noticed, 'the limits of coherency'. On Mr. Pound's advice, he very drastically cut and rearranged his first version. (The manuscript showing the cuts and alterations, which would be of inestimable critical value, is now unfortunately lost.) For a generation that has grown up with *The Waste Land*, it is hard to imagine the poem as having any other shape. Mr. Eliot was obviously right to trust to Mr. Pound's technical judgment. But at the same time, if we consider the history of the poem's composition, it is clear that its form falls between two stools. It is not a traditional form, imposed on poetic matter, planned in advance. Neither, on the other hand, is it Sir Herbert Read's 'organic form' which naturally grows out of poetic matter—though the form of the first, uncut version of the poem may have been so. It is to some degree at least an *ad hoc* contrivance—a deliberately devised scheme for holding together in a coherent shape an already existing body of poetry.

The existence of Mr. Pound's own Cantos may seem to some readers to contradict the statement made above that no other living poet has written a successful poem which imitates or adapts the *form* of *The Waste Land*. But *The Cantos* were begun earlier. Full though they are of magnificent poetry, few critics would be willing to say that as a whole they *are* a formal success. The difference in scale in any case makes any very general comparison unprofitable. And the similarity of technical devices is rather superficial. Mr. Blackmur has described the main narrative device of *The Cantos* as that of the interrupted anecdote. A story is begun, broken off, and taken up in a new setting later on. The main narrative device of *The Waste Land*, on the other hand, is that of cinematic cutting between various more or less self-enclosed scenes and episodes. Again, a single implicit theme—that of drifting barrenness in a world in-

capable of self-sacrificing devotion and no longer held together by the bonds of love and faith—unifies *The Waste
Land*. *The Cantos* have several themes, economic, political,
artistic, and personal; they are a panorama of one man's
view, at once more scrappy and more various than Mr.
Eliot's, of the significance of history; and the themes, or the
moral lessons which Mr. Pound deduces from them, are
often stated with didactic explicitness. If we were to compare these poems with two important works of a former
age, we might see *The Cantos* as having something of the
wide, rambling range of *The Ring and the Book*, and *The
Waste Land* as having something of the unified tone and
concentration on a single problem of *In Memoriam*.

Is it possible, in fact, now that we have lived with it for
thirty-one years, to say what sort of a poem *The Waste Land*
is? It is not in any plain traditional sense a lyrical, a meditative, a descriptive, a didactic, a satirical, a narrative, or a
dramatic poem, though there are elements in it that link it
with all these broad kinds. Mr. Lawrence Durrell has noted
that it would be easy to arrange it as a radio feature with the
voice of a male commentator taking the narrative and
meditative portions of the poem and actors and actresses the
various 'speaking parts'.[1] Mr. Eliot, in his own reading of
the poem, suggests magnificently the variations of pace, but
does not very strikingly dramatize the separate voices. Mr.
Robert Speaight, on the other hand, in a recent recording,
not only effectively mimics these voices but actually sings
both the fragment of an Australian ballad about Mrs. Porter
and her daughter and the line or two of 1920-ish jazz:

> 'O O O O that Shakespeherian rag—
> It's so elegant
> So intelligent. . . .'

It is clear from any hearing of the poem that the narrative
and dramatic elements in it are of primary importance; but

[1] It *was* broadcast as a wireless 'feature' before the 1939–45 war.

it is clear from any reading of it that what may be called a covert didacticism is an element of primary importance, too. It is tempting, in fact, to think of *The Waste Land* as a narrative poem of covert didacticism, introducing speaking characters who represent virtues and vices, like the medieval allegory. It is not, of course, an allegory in any strict sense, but it has much in common with a vision-poem like *Piers Plowman* in which the abstract framework of allegory tends to crumple under the weight of the poet's concrete apprehension of contemporary life.

The human figures in *The Waste Land* do not, to be sure, to any notable extent, represent virtues. But they do represent vices, and like the figures in *Piers Plowman* they also represent different estates of the realm (the rich couple, the clerk and the typist, the false friend of Lil and Albert in the public bar, the humble people with dirty hands and broken finger-nails on Margate Sands). They also represent the sterile constriction or the pointless loosening of traditional social bonds in a society whose order is being undermined. The scale of the two poems is, of course, quite different, and where the author of *Piers Plowman* can deal with social bonds of every sort Mr. Eliot has to concentrate on those of love and marriage. And there is a broader and more significant general resemblance. Both poems make an immediate appeal to the radical temperament; they both vividly call attention to breakdowns of various sorts in a contemporary society. They both take a rather desperate view of the seriousness of these breakdowns. Nevertheless, neither Mr. Eliot nor the author of *Piers Plowman* is what Marxists call a progressive. Both are what Marxists call reactionaries. The author of *Piers Plowman* criticized a rapidly changing late medieval society by the rigid standards of an early feudalism, which retrospectively he somewhat idealized. Similarly, Mr. Eliot was a man of his age in illustrating what he regarded as the failure of society by examples of the failure of love between men and women. This was a favourite theme both of good and bad novels in the 1920s. But the progressive solution for the problem was more emancipation, not less; it was hygiene, broad-mindedness, and common sense, the gospel according to Havelock Ellis. *The Waste Land* does not in any explicit way put forward a solution for this problem; but the reader of today, in the light of Mr. Eliot's subsequent development, is likely to see the failure of all the levels of human love that are evoked in the poem as arising from a failure of the typical modern metropolitan man to consider chastity a virtue, compunction a necessary persistent check in all human relationships, and marriage a sacramental bond.

But this comparison should not be pushed too far. The characters in *The Waste Land* are perhaps not more real than those in *Piers Plowman*, but for a modern reader they are more actual. They adorn a possible tale (some of Mr. Eliot's earlier poems, 'Prufrock' and 'Portrait of a Lady', had resembled more than anything else poetic condensations of themes for a Henry James short story); they do not merely point a moral. They have the ambiguity of actual human existence; and this, moreover, is combined with a fluid vagueness, a shifting of outlines, which allows us to recognize in them also the indefinable human essence—or, in other words, our own deeper self. All the men in the poem, as Mr. Eliot has told us, are really one man, all the women really one woman; and the figure of Tiresias stands for the terrifyingly plastic poetic imagination, the imagination for which even that barrier between the sexes is a vague one. Tiresias (who is the poet and the reader) can identify himself with all levels of human experience. He has been male and female. He has argued with the gods and paid for it, but he has also 'slept among the lowest of the dead'. Thus the human essence with which the poem puts us in touch is not that merely of archetypal maleness and femaleness, in various social disguises. It is not even some permanent image of man as a wanderer in a desert, a knight on a quest, a dry soul looking for living waters, a prisoner in a tower.

Each of these images may be here and there relevant, but the essence we are put in touch with is something more concrete, less describable, above all more intimate. It is our own terrible plasticity, which is also at the root of our deepest *rapport* with others—a *rapport* that can exist without conscious sympathy, approval or even understanding. We not only know Madame Sosostris, we know what it is to be she. We not only watch the crowd flow over London Bridge, we are part of it.

The abrupt transitions of the poem give it, in fact, the effect not only of a vision but of a dream. One of the most alarming aspects of dreams is the ability of the dreamer to identify himself in turn with everybody he is dreaming about. He dreams about the pursuit of a criminal. He perhaps dreams that he joins the chase. He is even the great detective leading it. Then, suddenly, it is he himself who is being pursued. And has he not known obscurely from the beginning of the dream that the great detective and the criminal were two alternating disguises for the same inescapable identity? A kind of phantasmagoric shifting of roles and merging of sympathies of this sort accompanies every really sensitive and absorbed reading of *The Waste Land*. A reader has not really become soaked in the poem until he knows even what it was like to be the carbuncular young man on whom assurance sat like a silk hat on a Bradford millionaire. There is a contrary sense, of course, in which the isolation of the individual—the 'horrible tower'—is a main theme of the poem. But there is another, everyday isolation, in which we are comfortable enough; that of our habits, our hobbies, our routine. *The Waste Land* awakens us from that. It makes us intimately aware of a general human condition in which we participate.

If we are to think of *The Waste Land* in this way, however, as not only a vision-poem but a dream-poem, it is as well to bear in mind a remark of Pascal's: 'Life is a slightly less inconsistent dream.' For the subject-matter of *The*

Waste Land is life, not fantasy; paradoxically, it seeks to awaken us to, and to awaken us from, life's actual dream-like quality—life's inconsistency, to which religion and philosophy and high poetry all in their different ways seek to call our attention—by presenting waking perceptions to us in a dream pattern. Thus the London of the opening section of the poem is an 'unreal city' at several levels. It is unreal precisely as a dream is unreal. It is unreal also in the more noble sense in which a poetic vision is unreal—in the sense in which Wordsworth glimpsed a London from Westminster Bridge in the early morning, which few of the rest of us are likely to glimpse except at highly privileged moments. But though these implications are there for us now, and must have been there for sensitive readers from the beginning, they cannot have been consciously uppermost in Mr. Eliot's own mind. London, at that level, for Mr. Eliot, must have been unreal though actual; unreal like the top-story of Dante's Hell, the place of the drifters, whose lives had been without coherence, without tension or purpose, without noble endeavour or tragic failure, 'without infamy or glory'. It is of Dante's Hell, the weak scum floating on the top of it, that he is thinking when he presents to us the London crowd:

> 'A crowd flowed over London Bridge, so many
> I had not thought death had undone so many,
> Sighs, short and infrequent, were exhaled,
> And each man fixed his eyes before his feet.
> Flowed up the hill and down King William Street
> To where Saint Mary Woolnoth kept the hours
> With a dead sound on the final stroke of nine.'

The bell with its dead sound has begun to toll in the first lines there,

> '. . . so *many*,
> I had not thought death had un*done* so *many*,

and the words themselves, 'dead sound' (with the thick

dentals and the long dark diphthong) actualize what they allude to. The church bell, with its dulled note, is like a warning bell not heard by ships drifting at sea. The dead-and-alive crowd, not looking up, or around, or very far ahead, will flow on, not seeking a safe harbour, nor feeling any need for prayer. Yet there is something else. The melancholy clangour of the lines gives the dead-and-alive the dignity of real death. They are not the lost, but the allusion to Dante compares them to the lost, and the lost have their own very terrible dignity. The crowd has suddenly, when we feel this, the black grandeur of some great funeral procession. If we remember Langland, once more, the crowd also takes on yet another significance. Langland started off with 'a field full of folk'. When we think of his world we think of town and country growing into each other, booths and apprentices, open stalls, varieties of bright costume, chattering groups, rich merchants, poor scholars, priests and friars, women going to market, strong men on horseback. The amorphous, undifferentiated, well-disciplined 'crowd' is a quite modern conception. It does not divide easily up into 'folk'. It typifies the sameness-in-diversity of our world, its organization and loneliness, its patient law-abidingness and its inhuman unawareness of its neighbour. It stands for drift, incoherence, merging. Yet by seeing how good a symbol it is for death, for the acquiescent and patient flowing, the failure to notice and protest, that are as near as we can get in life to the feeling of death, we lend it a kind of life, the compelling life and the power over the imagination that the idea of death has.

The Waste Land has been examined in detail by several sensitive and thorough critics. A conducted tour of the whole poem, on the scale of these prolix remarks on a single short passage, would obviously at this stage be wearisome. Yet it is worth making the general point that the kind of ambiguity that pervades both the idea of unreality and the idea of death in the first passage tends to pervade the whole

poem. Negative ideas accrete a positive glamour round
them, through the poet's phantasmagoric art; and positive
ideas tend to have their basis undermined through his
abrupt irony. Thus the main human episodes of the poem,
those in the second and third sections, are concerned, as we
have noticed, with various kinds of failure in human love.
Mr. Eliot is dealing in these sections with what happens to
romantic love, to sexual urgency and passion and to marriage as an institution, outside the Christian sacramental
tradition. The element of covert didacticism is very important here. For, if we were reading *The Waste Land* not as a
poem but as a tract or a sermon we might be inclined to
accuse him of rigging his evidence.

Thus, the neurotic upper middle-class couple who appear
at the beginning of 'A Game of Chess' are not, as a recent
writer in *Essays in Criticism* has pointed out, really at all
centrally typical of either legal or irregular relationships
between wealthy and cultivated people, even in our own
troubled times. They belong to a very special Eliotic world
that echoes the tones of Jacobean drama:

> ' "My nerves are bad to-night. Yes, bad.
> Stay with me.
> "Speak to me. Why do you never speak?
> Speak.
> "What are you thinking of? What think-
> ing? What?
> "I never know what you are thinking.
> Think."
> I think we are in rats' alley
> Where the dead men lost their bones. . . .'

The episode is so magnificently put over that we do not
pause to criticize it. But in 'real life' he would stay, he would
speak, or there would be a divorce or a separation or, if the
relation was an irregular one, the woman would find a
slightly less unnerving lover. However rich, bored, sophisticated and unhappy our friends may be, few of us really

know a couple like this. We do, on the other hand, accept without question the social reality, and the reasonably central social significance, of the disloyal friend of Lil and Albert in the pub, of the typist who smooths her hair and puts a record on the gramophone, of the girl who raised her knees supine on the floor of a narrow canoe, and of the weeping young man who promised a 'new start'. Yet we may still feel that the instances have been rather carefully chosen to buttress a rather doubtful case. People do certainly pay for their pleasures and suffer for their passions, but in these two central sections of *The Waste Land* we may feel that the poet has not made it sufficiently clear—and perhaps does not himself imaginatively realize—that pleasure and passion may be, to the ordinary human creature at most times, worth paying and suffering for. Do sexual relationships, even in a period of fundamental social crisis, consist *essentially* of nervous exasperation, coveting your neighbour's husband, pawing, disgusted acquiescence and a humble making-do with second—or third—bests?

'He wept. He promised a "new start".
I made no comment. What should I resent?'

Mr. Eliot is a great and profound poet, but it might be suggested—on the evidence not only of these sections of *The Waste Land* but of the rather glum and limited, though common-sensical and moral, view of the possibilities of marriage put forward in *The Cocktail Party*—that there is a range of human experience he has never adequately explored. What it is can be perhaps best suggested by a quotation from Yeats:

'That there are still some living
That do my limbs unclothe.
But that the flesh my flesh has gripped
I both adore and loathe.
                    (*Pipe and drum music*)

Are those things that men adore and loathe
Their sole reality?
What stood in the Post Office
With Pearse and Connolly?'

It might be said that the sexual episodes in *The Waste Land* make it clear enough that lovers can loathe each other and the act of love, but not that they can alternately or even almost simultaneously adore each other and it. 'Pipe and drum' music, moreover, would be appropriate at no moment in *The Waste Land*; nor, in spite of all the poem's abrupt transitions, is there room in it for a transition so very abrupt and yet so very natural as that from the harlot's loathing and adoration of her trade to Pearse's and Connolly's loathing and adoration of the violent death they heroically faced in 1916 in the Dublin Post Office. For all Mr. Eliot's devotion to the seventeenth century, there is one trite comparison of that age which he has never appropriated —the thought that love is like war, as terrifying and exciting.

Thus in these two sections of *The Waste Land* there is something that may strike us at first as a captious and arbitrary destructiveness, as an analysis of a polar experience ('We hate what we love, we are disgusted with what we desire') too much in terms of the secondary and uncreative pole. Yet in the end, in the total pattern, this is not seen as a flaw. The reader out of his own experience can make actual these positive values of human passion which Mr. Eliot himself does not choose to actualize; and, resolving his negative responses in a higher complex of feelings, Mr. Eliot does actualize for us humility, compassion and compunction:

' "On Margate Sands,
I can connect
Nothing with nothing.
The broken fingernails of dirty hands.
My people humble people who expect
Nothing." '

'Nothing with nothing' there, is a 'breakdown', a final analysis of human existence in terms of the meaningless. 'The broken fingernails of dirty hands' begins, however, to mingle compassion with distaste. And if the 'humble people who expect/Nothing' are at one level still being destructively analysed—if the statement that they 'expect nothing' means at that level that they lack culture, faith, hope, purpose and money—at another level to be humble and expect nothing is a condition at which saints might aim. The people on Margate Sands are the wretched debris of an industrial civilization, but they are also the meek who shall inherit the earth.

About the splendid fifth section of *The Waste Land* there is, at this stage, nothing new to say. But one observation about the fourth and shortest section of the poem, 'Death by Water', may be new. This section has sometimes a very odd effect on the listener when the poem is read aloud. It can, like nothing else in *The Waste Land*, directly induce tears. This effect of pathos is partly from contrast. The other sections of the poem are, or seem, long: And they are complex. Their images come home to us with a familiar but sometimes shocking immediacy. Their technique is partly impressionistic and partly dramatic. Their cinematic cutting from episode to episode keeps us anxiously alert. We may be anxious also to spot allusions to the Grail story and to the sacrificed gods in *The Golden Bough*. 'Death by Water' is short, simple, unallusive—except in so far as Madame Sosostris had told us to fear death by water, and death by water is the polar opposite of death by hanging, and death by hanging stands for crucifixion, and taking up one's cross means following in the footsteps of Christ, and offering up one's life and witness as a sacrifice, so that death by water would mean the dissolution of the natural once-born man into the eternal flux—and classical, and remote. But it moves us also because it states more directly than any other part of the poem the essential pathos of the human condition. We are mortal. We are young and grow old. When we hear that somebody else has died, we remember that we shall die. The differences of class, of culture, of creed, of historical period, with which the rest of the poem makes so much play, do not after all affect the general and fundamental pathos of our lot:

> 'Gentile or Jew
> O you who turn the wheel and look to windward,
> Consider Phlebas, who was once handsome and tall
> as you.'

Such a cursory re-exploration of some selected aspects of *The Waste Land* will have added little, if anything, to the ordinary sensitive reader's understanding of the poem. Yet it may help us to answer some of the questions with which we started off. It seems clear that *The Waste Land* will remain a unique successful example of its form, whatever that form may be called. It was a form specially suited to an exploration of the 'limits of coherency' (both in the poet's inner responses, and in his outer world) and it performed that task of exploration in a final fashion, not only for Mr. Eliot's contemporaries in the 1920s, but for his successors in the 1930s, and for ourselves today. Mr. Eliot himself, with his usual scrupulous and ironical self-criticism, described it as expressing not a generation's disillusionment, but its illusion of being disillusioned. Another very fine critic described it, when it was new in the world, as a 'music of ideas', divorced from any kind of belief. Still another fine critic thought that it exhibited no progression, that it ended, morally, where it began. Time makes many things clearer, even to minor commentators. Far from being a 'music of ideas'—in the abstract sense in which some of Paul Valéry's poems might be thus described—*The Waste Land* seems to a modern reader to be, quite apart from its poetic value, an extremely significant document about London life in the 1920s. Far from being divorced from any kind of belief, it seems to express what might be called a radical and reactionary, as opposed to a liberal and progressive, attitude towards the disorders of modern society. Far from exhibiting no progression, it seems to progress towards the expression, in the fifth section, of very definite moral and religious aspirations. If it ends on a subdued and ironical note, it is because the poet is sanely aware that there is a difference between expressing aspirations and having them realized. And the reason why the poem's form has still no exact parallels is fairly clear. Mr. Eliot was immersing himself in 'the destructive element'. He managed to express perfectly, for his own generation and for all its successors till now, a sense of the disintegration of modern society, of our world's being, in a phrase of M. Gabriel Marcel's, 'a broken world'. The natural human response to a vivid awareness of 'a broken world' is an attempt to mend it. That was Mr. Eliot's response in his own later prose and poetry, and it was certainly the response of the young poets of the 1930s.

A Language by Itself [1]

———————————❋———————————

I would like to express the gratitude which, like every poet of my generation, I feel towards Eliot in language worthy of himself. I feel, of course, that this is beyond me: as Lord Herbert of Cherbury, struggling to express a similar gratitude towards John Donne, said, I could do it

> '. . . did I not need
> *A language by itself*, which would exceed
> All those which are in use; for while I take
> These common words which men may even rake
> From dunghill-wits, I find them so defil'd,
> Slubber'd, and false, as if they had exiled
> Truth and propriety, such as do tell
> So little other things, they hardly spell
> Their proper meaning, and therefore unfit
> To blazon forth thy merits, or thy wit.'

That quotation, besides expressing one's sense of embarrassed inadequacy on an occasion like this, suggests something else: Eliot resembles Donne in having given the more sensitive spirits of his time a new, a critical awareness of language. That is what Lord Herbert intends to suggest, and that also is what Thomas Carew suggests in his more famous, more brilliant elegy, which is, indeed, perhaps the best piece of criticism in verse in the English language

[1] This essay originally came out in 1948, in an anthology of tributes for Mr. Eliot's sixtieth birthday.

'The Muses' garden, with pedantic weeds
O'erspread, was purged by thee; the lazy seeds
Of servile imitation thrown away,
And fresh invention planted. . . .'

That is as true of Eliot in his time, as of Donne in his. Donne, like Eliot, had refreshed the language, and in every innovator and renovator there is a certain quality of harshness; the classics of an age of experiment may be thrown somewhat into the shade in a succeeding age of established convention. They are likely, however, to reassert themselves as soon as convention has exhausted itself. Such, as Carew foresaw, was to be the fate of Donne; such perhaps may be the fate of Eliot.

'Thou shalt yield no precedence, but of time,
And the blind fate of language whose tun'd chime
More charms the outward sense: yet thou mayst claim
From so great disadvantage greater fame,
Since to the awe of they imperious wit
Our stubborn language bends, made only fit
With her tough thick-ribbed hoops to gird about
Thy giant fancy, which had proved too stout
For their soft melting phrases.'

Their soft melting phrases: there was a difficulty, as Carew saw, in keeping up along 'the line of masculine expression' opened up by Donne—there was a counter-attraction, against his harsh genius, of the mild, the gentle, the soothing cadence; against his precise and passionate thought, of a noble and vague eloquence. Therefore, Carew thought

'. . . thy strict laws will be
Too hard for libertines in poetry.
They will repeal the goodly exil'd train
Of gods and goddesses, which in thy just reign
Were banished nobler poems; now, with these,
The silenced tales o' th' *Metamorphoses*
Shall stuff their lines, and swell the windy page,

Till verse, refin'd by thee, in this last age
Turn ballad-rhyme, or those old idols be
Adored again with new apostcay.'

These passages have a certain relevance, also, to Mr. Eliot's
position today. They cannot, of course, be applied to him
literally. Unlike Donne, he is not a writer who is ever
likely, in any age, to seem metrically harsh to any educated
ear. Unlike Donne, he cannot be said exactly to have banished 'the silenced tales o' th' *Metamorphoses*' from his verse;
classical mythology, but understood with a historical
breadth of view and a religious depth of feeling, is one of
his main sources of allusions. But, like Donne, he came on
his age with a peculiar shock of immediacy. Extremely
learned, as Donne was extremely learned, he nevertheless,
like Donne, was to bring poetry almost uncomfortably
close to the language and the feelings of common life. For
our age, like Donne for his, he has been a salutary disturbing
factor. He is also, like Donne, an eminently masculine
writer and a writer who sets standards both of aim and
execution which are hard for weaklings to follow. We have
only to open, today, the latest anthology of work by young
Oxford or Cambridge poets, we have only to look, even,
at the accomplished but, in comparison to Eliot, quite
academic diction of such a promising and regretted young
poet as Sidney Keyes, to realize that Eliot's laws are, indeed,
'too hard for libertines in poetry': and we have only to read
the critical attack by a contemporary of Eliot's, like Herbert
Read, on the 'line of wit' in poetry—on the tradition, that
is, which Eliot has drawn onwards to fresh triumphs—to
realize that wit, like Eliot's or Donne's, is not at every man's
fingertips, and that for those who lack it, it is hard to
admit that it is an essential ingredient of the highest poetry.
Why is it, for instance, that in spite of the enormous talent,
the enormous industry, of Browning and Tennyson, a
faintly musty odour still hangs about their work? Dr.
Johnson's answer, in another connection, will tell us. It had

not enough vitality to preserve it from putrefaction. It had not enough wit to keep it sweet.

I am talking, then, of Mr. Eliot especially as a poet (not as a critic, as a teacher, or as a representative of any particular beliefs) and from the point of view, especially, of what other poets of his time have got from him. He has, I am suggesting, for all of us, refreshed the language of poetry. I first read him myself when I was about fifteen or sixteen. Much of what he was talking about was beyond my experience or above my head. I found myself, nevertheless, reading him with tingling excitement, and pausing, with absorbed delight, on, for instance, such lines as these:

'In the mountains, there you feel free.
I read, much of the night, and go south in winter'

or these:

'. . . turning
Wearily, as one would turn to nod good-bye to
                                        Rochefoucauld
If the street were time and he at the end of the street'

or these:

'Would she not have the advantage, after all?
This music is successful with a "dying fall"
Now that we talk of dying.'

lines which, for the ordinary reader, may well seem not among his most absorbing or most exciting. They are transitional not climactic passages. For the reader, on the other hand, who is beginning to write poems, such lines are absorbing and exciting; he thinks he knows how to manage climaxes, but transitions are what stump him.

A struggling young poet, coming for the first time on Mr. Eliot's work, is struck by such transitional passages because they reveal to him the possibility of conveying in verse, with exactness, an equivalent of his passing moods and of the tone, and even of the shades of tone, of his individual speaking voice. Such lines reveal to such a young man a new possibility in verse as an instrument. Donne, of course, reveals the same possibility; but still, his voice, though still a living and individual one, is the voice of another age; and his metric meets the demands not only, one might say, of a special rhetoric but of a special physique. It is the metric of a preacher, who has learnt to cast his voice to the back of the hall; the metric is successful, but behind the success there is strain, and the voice, loud, slow, harsh, resonating—with what Saintsbury called its 'sad clangor'— is not a voice for most young poets to imitate. Eliot's voice in verse, in spite of a certain dryness, is much nearer to the common tone, the common cadence of poetry. It is an easy and graceful voice, and it could have revealed to us, if his interests had been other than they were, the possibility of combining that 'natural, easy' manner with a highly wrought artificial form. The poem which, as a boy, I knew by heart of Eliot's was *La Figlia che Piange*. It is one of his slightest poems; perhaps his only strictly conventional one; and certainly one of his most purely beautiful:

'So I would have had him leave,
So I would have had her stand and grieve,
So he would have left
As the soul leaves the body torn and bruised,
As the mind deserts the body it has used.
I should find
Some way incomparably light and deft,
Some way we both should understand,
Simple and faithless as a smile and shake of the hand.'

Such a passage is not typical of Mr. Eliot, and yet I felt it to be typical of something. In its simplicity, its transparency, its lack of larger implications, it has its equivalent in a famous passage in Donne, where he, too, for the moment lays aside his usual apparatus of scorn and irony:

'Sweetest love, I do not goe
For weariness of thee,
  Nor in hope the world can show
A fitter love for mee . . .

  Yesternight the Sunne went hence,
And yet is here to-day,
  He hath no desire nor sense
Nor halfe so short a way. . . .'

It is a mark of some very fine poets that, even in slight, occasional pieces, outside the main line of their development, they can suggest new lines of development to others. In an essay of Ezra Pound's, I was to discover what *La Figlia che Piange* is typical of. Pound was comparing Provençal lyrics, which had specially influenced his own lyrical writing, with early Italian lyrics. Provençal is for singing; its metric is elaborate, but its sentences are short and abrupt, like Pound's sentences in many of his own poems. Early Italian verse, the verse of the *dolce stil nuovo*, is to be read, and to be read on the page; the sentences are longer, the words more weighted with thought, the connections of thought more carefully worked out. The type of poetry which I divined through *La Figlia che Piange* was, I think, that of the *dolce stil nuovo*. Similarly, what one feels about 'Sweetest love, I do not goe' is that Donne, if he had not had other work in hand, might have developed the conventional Elizabethan lyric towards a new deep and sober intimacy of tone. I am not a very original writer myself; I am lost, on the whole, without a convention of some sort, and so, I suppose, I may have been among the few to notice that, if Mr. Eliot had not had more important things to do, he could have become a poet of restrained and sad lyric grace in a quite conventional tradition. That possibility would naturally not be of much general interest. What must, however, have interested every young poet who read him was that immediacy of language to which I have already drawn attention: what has been called, too vaguely, his conversational tone.

What do we mean, in fact, by his conversational tone? As his work progresses, that description becomes less apt; the language of *Ash Wednesday*, of some of the Ariel Poems, of the *Four Quartets* is, indeed, 'a language by itself'. It can hardly influence anybody, for it has exhausted its own possibilities. For the ordinary reader, admiring Mr. Eliot's later poetry, the first impulse must be, not to go and do likewise, but to go and do something else; and such contemporary writing as has modelled itself on that later manner (some of Mr. Henry Reed's poems, for instance) strikes me as mere accomplished cold pastiche. *Prufrock*, on the other hand, the first poem of Mr. Eliot's that we all read—for we all open the book at the beginning, and we all find it impossible to dip or skip—is another cup of tea. As the first thing of Eliot's that we read, and are absorbed by, it has a great practical influence on our own work. And *Prufrock* is very largely an exercise in Mr. Eliot's peculiar conversational tone, and may help us to define that.

Eliot's conversational tone in *Prufrock* is not, for instance, that of Pope, even when Pope is most direct and least mannered:

> 'Nothing so true as what you once let fall:
> "Most women have no characters at all." '

It is not that of Byron in *Don Juan*, a garrulous, loquacious tone. It is not the buttonholing, breathing-down-your-neck tone that Browning has sometimes. It may, however, have something in common with all these three writers; like Pope, Mr. Eliot gives an effect of frequenting always the best company, who can quickly pick up a hint or an allusion; like Byron, he can be apparently inconsequent and flippant; like Browning he can conceive a poem most effectively as a sort of dramatic soliloquy. Yet it is more illuminating to go back, once more, to Donne. Compare

these two passages of verse in a conversational tone, one by
Donne, the other by Pope, rewriting him:

(*Donne*)

'Sir, though (I thank God for it) I do hate
Perfectly all this town; yet there's one state
In all things so excellently best,
That hate towards them breeds pity towards the rest.
Though poetry, indeed, be such a sin,
As I think, that brings dearth and Spaniards in:
Though, like the pestilence and old-fashioned love,
Riddingly it catch men, and doth remove
Never, till it be starved out; yet their state
Is poor, disarm'd, like Papists, not worth hate.'

(*Pope*)

'Yes, thank my stars! as early as I knew
This town, I had the sense to hate it too:
Yet here, as e'en in Hell, there must be still
One giant vice, so excellently ill,
That all beside, one pities, not abhors:
As who knows Sappho, smiles at other whores.
I grant that poetry's a crying sin:
It brought (no doubt) the Excise and Army in:
Catched like the plague, or love, the Lord knows how,
But that the cure is starving, all allow.
Yet like the Papist's is the poet's state,
Poor and disarm'd, and hardly worth your hate.'

Pope, in correcting Donne's 'rugged and most unmusical
versification', has missed his point. Donne's stretch and
contortion are deliberate, they have a rhetorical purpose, as
in the blank verse of another of Mr. Eliot's models, Cyril
Tourneur. What Pope has lost, rhetorically, by a metrical
regularity may be seen by comparing

'Is poor, disarm'd, like Papists, not worth hate.'

where the asyndeton accumulates the climax (and the

phrase 'like Papists', where the climax piles up, looks both back and forward in the line) with the flat amenity of

'Poor and disarm'd and hardly worth your hate.'

Donne adapts his language and his metrical framework to his thought: Pope adapts his thought to a conventional language (how weak, for instance, is the polite, pert 'Thank my stars!' compared to the fierce, 'I thank God for it!') and to a strict metre. His passage seems smart and vapid, at the most mildly facetious: Donne's, on the other hand, has sinister force. That comes out in things that Pope just leaves out—the adverb 'riddingly', and the phrase, 'old fashioned love'—which might mean normal love, as opposed to homosexual love, in which one ran less risk of the pox; or even love itself, the romantic and chivalrous love of the Petrarchan tradition, as opposed to fashionable lust. . . . Eliot has a perpetual elegance of language, a conscious refinement, which makes him in one sense more like Pope than Donne; but like Donne he dramatizes (and we should remember, in justice to Pope, that the background of Donne's passage is Elizabethan tragedy; the background of Pope's merely the Addisonian polite essay, gentlemanly chatter about literature); and like Donne he is always adapting his language to his thought, never his thought to a fixed convention of language.

What shall we say, then? The language of *Prufrock feels* like conversation, but it is rather a dramatic imitation of conversational language: heightened, condensed, contorted, with an uncanny precision which ordinary conversation could never have. *Prufrock*, for all its setting at a fashionable party, for all its air of being a Henry James short story, drastically boiled down (the 'story' left out, and the moral, the atmosphere left in) is really a tragi-comic soliloquy. It makes remarks which one doesn't, in fact, make at parties, though one may think afterwards that one has made them; but one is remembering odd thoughts and perceptions that flashed, unbidden, to one's mind,

'And I have known the arms already, known them all—
Arms that are braceleted and white and bare
(But in the lamplight, downed with light brown hair!)'

What it creates rather (and memories of a party create this
too, for if one arrives at a party late, sober, one finds that
very trite and disconnected things are being said) is the
illusion of conversation: the illusion that, in a quiet corner
near a noisy group, one is being talked to quietly, or is
quietly talking to oneself. That illusion creates a lull, a
soothingness: against the lull, the images flash out, like
lightning against a dark sky, with all the more startling
effect, the famous evening

'. . . spread out against the sky
Like a patient etherized upon a table;'

the paragraph in which the fog is stated to be a great
animal, the crustacean velleity,

'I should have been a pair of ragged claws
Scuttling across the floors of silent seas.'

and then at the end in a passage, after so much petulance,
wit, and triviality, after such a deliberate excess of the
'personal touch', suddenly purely formal, utterly impersonal,
drained of all these polite hesitations of the voice, the
mermaids:

'I have seen them riding seaward on the waves
Combing the white hair of the waves blown back
When the wind blows the water white and black.

We have lingered in the chambers of the sea
By sea-girls wreathed with seaweed red and brown
Till human voices wake us, and we drown.'

As the Russians all came out of Gogol's *Overcoat*, we
might say that we all came out of Prufrock's drawing-room.
Nearly every important innovation in the English verse of

the last thirty years is implicit in this poem. If some of the younger poets, at least, know when to be easy and when to be formal; if they know how to lead up quietly to a startling image; if they know that the point of highest concentrated feeling in a poem must be the most objectively, the most impersonally expressed—they could have learned these things, and to a large extent they *have* learned these things, from *Prufrock* and from Mr. Eliot's other early poems. Our gratitude for the later poems is, as I have already suggested, of another sort; it is a gratitude which we share with the general reading public, for these later poems mark out a path which only Mr. Eliot himself could have trodden— there is everything in them to admire, but, from the point of view of a young poet who is just beginning, there is nothing in them to imitate. It would be as fatal for him to imitate the language of *Samson Agonistes* or *The Tempest*. But *Prufrock* is a beginner's poem, and it has lessons for all of us in the art of how to begin. It refreshed, as I have already suggested, the whole language of poetry in our time. Thinking of Mr. Eliot's work, poets must share the general admiration of the public for enormous talent, for enormous learning, and for a steady, sad, and noble vision of the world; but they have also, as I have been trying to suggest, this special gratitude to him, as a craftsman who has provided them with new, sharp tools, and as a teacher from whom they have learned how to use these tools and how to keep them clean. Our time has been a terrible one, and for poets that terror has expressed itself as a struggle to say anything at all, to find any resource in language. Yet, like the 'girl of Tereus' in the *Pervigilium Veneris*, Eliot, by his example, has helped us to transform the grief of the time to art:

'iam loquaces ore rauco stagna cycni perstrepunt:
adsonat Terei puella subter umbram populi
ut putes amoris ore dici musicos,
et neges queri sororem de marito barbaro.

illa cantat, nos tacemus: quando ver venit meum?
quando fiam uti chelidon ut tacere desinam?
perdidi musam tacendo, nec me Apollo respicit:
sic Amyclas, cum tacerent, perdidit silentium.

Noisy, with harsh cries, swans now thrash the pools.
The girl of Tereus sings in the poplar shadow
So you would think a love song coming from her
And not a sister's complaint of a cruel spouse.

She is singing, we are silent: when will my spring come?
When may I be as the swallow that I may cease to be
                                                    silent?
I lost my Muse by silence, Apollo does not look at me:
So the Amyclae, they were silent, silence lost them all.'

Silence will not lose *us* all, though we may lose much: but
we too have heard (in Eliot's poems, as well as in other
places) the voices under the poplar shade of Philomela and
Procne:

'The change of Philomel, by the barbarous king
So rudely forced; yet there the nightingale
Filled all the desert with inviolable voice
And still she cried, and still the world pursues,
"Jug Jug" to dirty ears.'

Not all the ears have been dirty, and, in the desert of our
time, Eliot's voice has been inviolable; seeking, as I have
been seeking all through this essay, for some final adequate
compliment to pay to him, I am driven back, as I feared I
would be driven back, on that 'language by itself' that I was
seeking for—I pay him back, as we are all forced to pay
him back in the end, in his own coin: his own incomparable
words.

E. E. Cummings and Wallace Stevens: The Sensationalist and the Aesthete

❋

Here are two beautiful books,[1] to handle and look at, and books, for their contents, that anybody who cares about modern poetry will want to possess. The sight of them is also a little unnerving; what they demand of the reviewer is not a progress report but an attempt at a total judgment, a final placing. It is like a party, after the visitors have left: set it out of your world, in my shabby autumnal Chelsea. 'How very amusing Mr. Cummings was!' 'Yes, and so direct and touching, too.' 'I couldn't quite follow all the jokes—that peculiar dialect, is it *Bronx*?' 'And he does go on a bit about *sex*, doesn't he—about the machinery of it, I mean?' 'Oh, that's the 1920s, my dear. Rather charmingly old-world, in its way.' 'Yes, of course, but isn't he rather *sentimental* sometimes?' 'Oh, I would say mainly very innocent and sincere. What are his politics, do you think?' 'Oh, what we would call an old-fashioned Tory-anarchist. American politics are so very difficult; they do that in a kind of radical tone of voice.' 'Yes, but didn't you get the impression that he has mixed feelings about Jews—mixed feelings about Negroes, possibly—and then, of course, one must take it for granted most Americans don't like *us*.' 'Oh, I think you're quite wrong. There's a natural tendency

[1] *Poems, 1923–1954*, by E. E. Cummings (Harcourt, Brace, 1954); *The Collected Poems of Wallace Stevens* (Alfred A. Knopf, 1954).

toward emotional impatience and violence, but nothing Fascist. Fundamentally, he's an anarchist and a pacifist.' 'Is that why he seems to hate so many people?' 'Oh, yes, he believes in love. Don't you remember what a lot he had to say about love? That must make you hate a lot of people. And he's very much of an individual, a kind of metropolitan Thoreau, and so he dislikes ordinary, conventional people—you do remember your Tocqueville, and all that, about America, the extraordinary pressure of the urge to social conformity on the American with ideas?' '*I* thought he was lively, but to some extent he did seem to be saying the same thing over and over again.' 'I think poor Aunt Nelly was quite embarrassed by that anecdote, lively as it was, about the girls in the whorehouse. Though, of course, she's very broad-minded.' 'It was a little *anatomical*, I did think.' 'But what about Mr. Stevens?' 'Much more cultured, certainly. I must say when Americans go in for culture they go in for it regardless of time, trouble, and expense.' 'I found it hard sometimes to catch his drift. He's rather shut up in himself, would you say?' 'I don't know; we had a long conversation, over there in the corner, about the nature of poetry—I don't know if I could quite summarize the upshot for you, but it seemed very deep at the time.' 'Oh, deep, he is deep!' '*I* thought he talked wonderfully about painting and landscape and music and things, though, mind you, I found it hard to *pin him down*.' 'I thought sometimes of a remote Chinese hermit-sage in his mountain hut, and then I thought, it would be a very *natty* hut, wouldn't it? I think Mr. Cummings has been a bit more battered by life.' 'What a good thing they can't hear us. They are right, really, to dislike us on the whole. We *are* cats. . . .'

Mr. Cummings and Mr. Stevens have, in fact, for an English reader, an extra-poetic fascination—for the light they throw on the roots of American culture—that might easily, for us, deflect discussion of them into the kind of gossipy guesswork, in twittering birdlike voices, I have parodied above. Roughly, of course, we find ourselves fitting Mr. Cummings into a tough and native, Mr. Stevens into a cosmopolitan and sophisticated American tradition. Mr. Cummings has a crude and forceful directness which it would be hard to match in a contemporary English poet; Mr. Stevens a conscious refinement which it would be equally hard to match. It is, however, an Alexandrian rather than an Attic refinement. Mr. Robert Graves is an English poet (an early and late admirer of Cummings) who shares Cummings's cult of what, in a large and loose sense, can be called romantic love; but in his passionate propriety and fastidiousness of diction he is quite unlike Mr. Cummings, and yet equally, when one looks for counterbalancing resemblances, unlike Mr. Stevens. Mr. Graves is an Atticizing writer, he wants words and phrases to be apt, discreetly so, rather than showy; colour and showiness are indispensable instruments for Mr. Stevens, his language is opulent, *recherché*, queen of its own mode; every poem might have stepped long-legged and starry-eyed, with tempting shadows on its thighs, wearing this year's lightest and most expensive girdle, from a poetry fashion magazine, an aesthetic equivalent of *Vogue*. There *are* American poets —Mr. Robert Frost is one—of whom it can be claimed (as Bagehot claimed for Wordsworth, as against Tennyson and Browning) that they use language classically. Bagehot, who tagged the epithet 'grotesque' on to Browning and the epithet 'ornate' on to Tennyson might have used these respectively for Mr. Cummings and Mr. Stevens. It would be fairer to describe Mr. Cummings's use of language as *sensationalist* (and therefore occasionally sentimental, occasionally brutal); and Mr. Stevens's use of language as *aesthetic* (and therefore occasionally precious, occasionally vacuous). Thus, these are two very good and important poets, but judging them by the very highest standards (Chaucer, Shakespeare, Donne, Milton, Pope, Wordsworth, Blake, Yeats, say) one is forced to point out that some element of human experience or range within it traditionally thought of as central, is left out. Mr. Cummings and Mr. Stevens do not fulfil Matthew Arnold's function for the poet of strengthening and uplifting the heart; the very genuine stimulation they offer us is mixed with temptations to evasiveness and relaxation, to various kinds of self-flattery. And that comes out in the off-centre language.

What does Mr. Cummings leave out? For one thing (and this may appear a rash statement, for Mr. Cummings, in his more lyrical poems, might be thought to write about almost nothing else), the complex personal relationships of men and women. What Mr. Cummings seems to me to substitute for this fine traditional theme is, firstly, a celebration of the sexual appetites and achievements of the hearty male animal; and, secondly, the celebration of a kind of mystical attitude toward life in general that may indeed spring from a happy and stable relationship between a man and woman, but need not always do so, and is something quite different as a theme. Mr. Cummings's love poetry is, in a bad sense, *impersonal*; and I would connect this impersonality of the love poetry with a general characteristic of the poetry as a whole, its steadily sustained youthful strident energy, of which the dark shadow is its almost complete failure to mature. Mr. Cummings wrote in 1923 as well as he does now, and not very differently. The marks of permanent adolescence in his work are many. Let me list some: (1) an almost entirely uncritical devotion to parents, lovers, and a few chosen friends combined with an attitude of suspicion and dislike toward 'outsiders': (2) a general tendency to think of *all* political and economic activities as in the main a sinister conspiracy against the young: (3) a wholehearted universalistic pacifism, deeply emotional, not argued out, combined with a natural violent irascibility: (4) the instinctive generosity of youth (always side emotionally with the rioters against the police) combined with an equally deeply rooted provincial intolerance (unless I am obtuse in finding this intolerance in the dialect parodies and in some

of the references to people with Jewish or German names):
(5) the violent capacity of the young for disgust (recurrent
references to drunkenness, vomit, and so on) which can
itself, uncriticized, become disgusting: (6) a youthful, not
very well-balanced religiousness, a 'reverence for life' combined with a youthful refusal to accept death as a fact ('No
young man thinks that he will ever die. . . .'), leading, of
course, to a morbid preoccupation with death: (7) in-
decency, scatology, even here and there something that
strikes me as very like pornography—physical frustration
leading to emotional frustration, and making even physical
fulfilment finally emotionally frustrating, and final emotional fulfilment the object of a kind of private religion. To
sum all this up: Mr. Cummings's sense of life is the 'lyrical'
rather than the 'tragic' or 'comic' sense. The poet who has
not learned to accept 'society', 'others', the idea of the City
in some sense, will never become sufficiently mature for
tragedy or comedy. Mr. Cummings's satire is an aggres-
sive defensive manœuvre on behalf of his small private
corner in a, for him, still unsullied Garden of Eden;
salesmen, politicians, generals, the late President Harding
and the late S. S. Van Dine must keep out. Some such dras-
tic preliminary 'limiting judgment' is necessary if we are
to do justice to Mr. Cummings's achievement within his
limits.

Part of that achievement is readability. *Poems*, 1923–1954
is a volume of 468 pages and can be read straight through
like an American novel of the 1920s, or a volume of essays
by Mencken. It is, indeed, of Mencken, Scott Fitzgerald,
early Dos Passos that I think when I read Cummings and
not—except for turns and tricks, and moods, that sometimes remind me of Pound—of other poets. If Mr. Cummings were a less raw and vulnerable, a more balanced and
integrated person his poems would not be such a magnificent documentation of the stresses of the American scene.
Some of them have value, perhaps, *merely* as documentation:

'yoozwiddupoimnuntwaiv un duyyookusumpnruddur
givusuhtoonunduphugnting
(*anglice*: youse with the permanent wave and the yuke or
somethin' or other
give us a tune on the ****ing thing!)'

Others, like the deliciously funny epitaph on President
Harding (a footnote to Mencken's essays), call up in us a
tolerant nostalgia for the simpler stupidities of yesterday:

'. . . if he wouldn't have eaten them Yapanese Craps
somebody might hardly never not have been unsorry,
perhaps.'

As a clown, Cummings can make us laugh aloud. But he is
at his best (as in some of the war poems, the one about the
conscientious-objector conscript, the one about the Yale
boy marching off to war, and 'My sweet old etcetera') as an
angry and tender clown. Angry and tender clowning begins
to pivot over to lyricism in some of the poems about
whores: what begin as half-mockery,

'should i entirely ask of god why
on the alert neck of this brittle whore
delicately wobbles an improbably distinct face,'

end with intense sinister and pathetic dramatization,

'or why her tiniest whispered invitation
is like a clock striking in a dark house.'

The anger is never purged from even the most purely
lyrical poems: with their recurrent theme that love, love is
the only real thing and damn—damn and hate and torture
—any evidence to the contrary. The finest explicit statement
of this is the long, very beautiful poem beginning,

'my father moved through dooms of love,'

and ending magnificently, in a noble, almost 'metaphysical'
paradox:

'and nothing quite so least as truth
i—say though hate were why men breathe—
because my father lived his soul
love is the whole and more than all.'

The later lyricism is gentler, the 'real world'—so, crudely
and inadequately in both directions to call it—held more
safely at a distance.

'o by the by
has anybody seen
little you-i
who stood on a green
hill and threw
his wish at blue. . . .'

So what shall one say, on the whole? There is some of the
matter of life here; there is an extraordinary technical dex-
terity; there is an unurbane wit of a very savagely effective
sort; a disturbing gift for evoking sexual situations below
head-level; one of the most notable talents for direct and
simple lyrical utterance of this century: and, over and above
all these, there is something which, however narrow and
callow, has been held to obstinately enough to deserve the
honorary title of 'a philosophy of life'. It is the philosophy,
say, of the adolescent who wants the moon down out of the
sky, but wants it to stay up there and shine on him, too.
But far deeper even than this there is the fact that Mr.
Cummings's comparative undevelopment as a civilized
human being does not, any more than the wrong-headed,
peevish, or illogical remarks he makes, prevent one from
feeling that in some way he is in close direct touch—in a
way that the rest of us, the denizens of the 'unreal city' are
not—with a source and justification of being. His silliness in
a sense is locally traditional, it is in the line of Thoreau's
silliness or Emerson's, and carries with it its counterbalance
of raw insight. In an orthodox age, like the early seventeenth
century, the insight would have been chastened and civilized

by a social background; it has had to fight grimly to maintain its right to existence against a social background that seemed to make nonsense of it. That accounts for the stridencies. But a tough, temperamental consistency holds Mr. Cummings's book together; and lust, disgust, highjinks, and despair do not manage to crowd out the impression that love and joy, precariously defended, are what this poet understands most profoundly.

There are no stridencies in Mr. Stevens. And to the question about what is the central thing lacking the answer might be, in his case, just that 'matter of life' which is there, for all his faults, in the work of Mr. Cummings. And, indeed, again, the crude and obvious thing to say about Mr. Stevens—yet like many crude and obvious things, the centrally just one—is that, not having wanted to cope with that 'matter of life', he has tried to substitute for it a 'matter of mind'. His poems, to continue on this crude level, are about perception and reflection on perception. They are about what the mind can make of experience, not about experience as raw. They become more and more not only reflective but self-reflective, poems about what the poem is, poems in which the poet asks himself what he is doing, and in answering is still writing the same poem, and so indefinitely can or indeed has to extend his answer. Thus, many of Mr. Stevens's later poems are like commentaries on themselves that could be added to for ever, section by section, like expanding bookcases. Something of a similar sort is true of earlier and shorter poems; there are thirteen ways of looking at a blackbird, but there might be fifteen, or twenty, or any number. What the mind picks out from perceptual experience is always one of many possible aspects, and one of many possible ways of presenting that aspect, and about the choosing of the aspect, and the choosing of the mode, there must always be something arbitrary. The whole tone of polite irony, of urbane mystification that pervades Mr. Stevens's work stems, I think, from this central predicament of the reflective aesthete who, philosophically, is a kind of pragmatic solipsist. The world, for Mr. Stevens, that the poet lives in is the world that he chooses to shape by the arbitrary emphases of a detached attention not itself shaped by the compulsions, for instance, of hunger or love. We feel continually, in reading Mr. Stevens, that his actual *gifts* are comparable with those of the very greatest poets (we do not feel this, about Mr. Cummings, when reading him). Probably no modern poet has a more supple, rich, commanding, and evocative vocabulary; within certain limits— Mr. Stevens would be incapable of achieving the changes of pace, and the suddenings, slackenings and concentrations, of *The Waste Land* or *Ash Wednesday*—few modern poets are more notable masters of rhythm; very few contemporary poets, again, combine as Mr. Stevens does the three apparently disparate gifts of evoking impressions with imagistic vividness, shaping long poems with musical care, and pursuing through a long poem a single, very abstruse, metaphysical argument. Yet in one's heart one does not quite think he is a 'great' poet in the sense that, say, Yeats and Eliot are 'great' poets. What is it that one misses? Partly, or perhaps mainly, the whole area of life that lies between detached aesthetic perception and philosophical reflection on it; and, as a chief corollary to that, the urgency of ordinary human passion, the sense of commitment and the moment of final concentration. In one crude human sense, Mr. Stevens's enormous talents are being exploited a little frivolously; in all one's continuing pleasure and admiration, while reading him, there is the sense all the time of a lack of the highest tension. It would be impertinent to illustrate the merits of such a distinguished and famous writer by quotation; but here and there Mr. Stevens does seem to me to show an awareness of this lack, in his work, of human grasp, of human contact:

> 'I cannot bring a world quite round,
> Although I patch it as I can.

E. E. Cummings and Wallace Stevens

I sing a hero's head, large eye
And breaded bronze, but not a man,

Although I patch him as I can
And reach through him almost to man,

If to serenade almost to man
Is to miss, by that, things as they are,

Say that it is the serenade
Of a man that plays a blue guitar.'

A society gets the poets it deserves, and America has obviously deserved very well to get a poet of the painful, raw honesty of Mr. Cummings and such a first-rate artist in verse, and profoundly interesting reflective poet, as Mr. Stevens. The gaps that one finds in them are gaps also which (in England today, as much as in America) one finds in oneself. It is not enough to 'plunge into' life or enough, aesthetically and intellectually, to 'transcend' it. Saying that, is not saying that anybody else could, set in the perspective of these two poets, have done better. Only a more humane society than we have seen for a long time or are likely to see soon will prove a proper stamping ground for the fully humanist poet.

The Poetry of Robert Graves[1]

If we wanted to introduce Mr. Graves's poetry to some receptive and intelligent person who did not know much about it—and there are many such people, for Mr. Graves as a poet is merely a fine artist preoccupied with a rather strange personal theme, what he says has sometimes a good deal of philosophic interest, but he has neither a warning nor a consoling message for his age—where would we start? We would wish to illustrate the solid excellence of style in much of his poetry, its occasional intense lyricism, a certain defiant toughness of mood which it expresses; and we would also wish to hint at that strange personal theme. 'Ulysses' might be as good a poem to start with as another. It opens in a workmanlike way:

> 'To this much-tossed Ulysses, never done
>   With woman whether gowned as wife or whore,
> Penelope and Circe seemed as one:
> She like a whore made his lewd fancies run,
>   And wifely she a hero to him bore.'

A cultivated reader would appreciate at once the rotundity and neatness of that, and the fashion in which the 'she' and 'she', standing for *illa* and *haec*, reproduce in a neat inverted

[1] This essay was first published in 1947, before *The White Goddess* had appeared or Mr. Graves had become fashionable. I let it stand as it was first written. I think *The White Goddess* is likely to distract one from what the poems actually do and say. And I still think the dualistic theme, or the theme of agonizing tension between mind and body, is central to Mr. Graves's poetry.

135

antithesis (it is Penelope, though she is his wife, who makes
his lewd fancies run, and Circe, though she is his whore,
who bears a hero to him) the effect of an Ovidian elegiac
couplet. It is of Ovid, in fact, that we think at once, rather
than of later poets like Dante and Tennyson who have also
seen what they could do with Ulysses. Once the reader,
however, has settled down to expect a smooth Ovidian
treatment, he will be disturbed in the next stanza by two
lines of bitingly vivid romantic imagery: these women,

> 'Now they were storms frosting the sea with spray
> And now the lotus orchard's filthy ease.'

The first of these images is too romantically beautiful for
the Ovidian setting; the second, with the violent epithet,
'filthy', too full of sharp self-disgust. The next stanza is a
piece of angry moralizing:

> 'One, two, and many: flesh had made him blind,
> Flesh had one pleasure only in the act,
> Flesh set one purpose only in the mind—
> Triumph of flesh, and afterwards to find
> Still those same terrors wherewith flesh was racked.'

And the last stanza clinches the thought: the brave hero, the
great amorist, was really to himself a *worthless* person, in
all his successes he was fleeing from something he was
afraid of, yielding to a weakness that he despised.

> 'His wiles were witty and his fame far known,
> Every king's daughter sought him for her own,
> Yet he was nothing to be won or lost.
> All lands to him were Ithaca: love-tossed,
> He loathed the fraud yet would not bed alone.'

Mr. Graves sets out, like Ovid, to comment, from an un-
heroic point of view, on a well-known heroic story; but his
comments are more searching than Ovid's, and though this
poem can stand by itself, it also fits into the general body of
his work as a variation on his favourite theme, which is the

relationship particularly between love and sexuality, more generally between the spirit and the body, more generally still between the mind and nature. That relationship Mr. Graves sees as sometimes a comic, sometimes a tragic, but always essentially an *awkward* relationship; it is never happy and harmonious.

Mr. Graves is peculiar among poets in that (though unlike Leopardi, for instance, who had something of the same attitude, he is a man of robust physical energy) he has a sense of awkward and unwilling attachment to his own body; and that awkwardness and unwillingness are, again and again, the main *theme* of his poems. He can treat the topic in a thoroughly amusing fashion, as in the comic and rather indecent little poem which begins, 'Down, wanton, down!' Addressing an intractable part of himself, he says, with a sort of affectionate contempt,

> 'Poor bombard-captain, sworn to reach
> The ravelin and effect a breach—
> Indifferent what you storm or why
> So be that in the breach you die!'

But his more common attitude to the body, to its lusts, to its energies, to its mortality, to the clogging foreign weight that it hangs about him, is a far more sombre one. In 'The Furious Voyage' it is a ship, on a great uncharted sea, containing no land:

> 'And it has width enough for you,
> This vessel, dead from truck to keel,
> With its unmanageable wheel,
> Its blank chart and its surly crew,
>
> Its ballast only due to fetch
> The turning point of wretchedness
> On an uncoasted, featureless
> And barren ocean of blue stretch.'

In a perhaps less effective poem, 'The Castle', it is a sort of gothic bastille in which he is imprisoned:

'Planning to use—but by definition
There's no way out, no way out—
Rope-ladders, baulks of timber, pulleys,
A rocket whizzing over the walls and moat—
Machines easy to improvise—'

Baudelaire (but Baudelaire was a sick man, aware that his
body was breeding its own ruin) has similar images in some
rough notes of a dream: he explores a crumbling and gothic
interior, full of labyrinths and tottering statues, a fabric
which is at any moment going to fall and crush him, but
from which there is 'by definition no way out'. But Mr.
Graves is concerned not so much with the body's mortality
as with what he regards as the bearable, just bearable, nasti-
ness of ordinary physical life. Should we after all, he asks in
one poem, be grateful

'That the rusty water
In the unclean pitcher
Our thirst quenches?

That the rotten, detestable
Food is yet eatable
By us ravenous?

That the prison censor
Permits a weekly letter?
(We may write: "We are well.")

That with patience and deference
We do not experience
The punishment cell?

That each new indignity
Defeats only the body,
Pampering the spirit
With obscure, proud merit?'

Most of his emblems for the body, it should be noted, are *inorganic*: a ship, a castle, a prison cell. (In the little comic poem I have quoted, the male sexual organ, the 'poor bombard-captain' is a sort of obstreperous puppet-character like Mr. Punch.) As a love poet, Mr. Graves is essentially a romantic, along the same lines as (though probably not consciously influenced by) the troubadours and the poets of the *dolce stil nuovo*: a critic like Mr. Denis de Rougemont would connect his hatred of the body with their alleged Catharism, and it is true that Mr. Graves, in his latest novel, shows a great interest in the Gnostics, for whom the real fall was the creation of the world. But I think Mr. Graves's philosophy, in so far as he has one, springs from a fact about his personal nature: the fact does not spring from a philosophy. This sense of awkward and unwilling attachment to his body is, as it were, a *given* factor for him. A critic, too, must take it as a given factor.

Much of Mr. Graves's poetry, then, will be concerned with the dissatisfaction of the lover with sex, of the spirit with the body, of the mind with nature; and yet with facing the fact that love is bound to sex, spirit to body, and mind to nature. It is revealing to read, in this connection, some of his abundant and on the whole unsatisfactory early verses. Mr. Graves's early work does not show much promise of his present strikingly individual and distinguished style. He became known first as a war poet. After the war he relapsed for a little into very weak writing in the Georgian bucolic style, and in the preface to 'Whipperginny' (1923) he describes some of these rustic pieces as 'bankrupt stock', and this whole manner as the result of a mood of 1918, 'the desire to escape from a painful war neurosis into an Arcadia of amatory fancy'. These escapist pieces have most of the qualities that we dislike today in the Georgians, the bucolic-hearty strain,

'Contentions weary,
It giddies all to think;

> Then kiss, girl, kiss,
>   Or drink, fellow, drink.'

the manly beer-drinking note,

> ' "What do you think
> The bravest drink
> Under the sky?"
> "Strong beer," said I.'

and what Mr. Belloc, in 'Caliban's Guide to Letters', calls the prattling style,

> 'No! No!
> My rhymes must go
> Turn 'ee, twist 'ee,
> Will-o'-the-wisp like, misty;
> Rhymes I will make
> Like Keats and Blake
> And Christina Rossetti,
> With run and ripple and shake,
> How pretty. . . .'

How pretty, indeed, we feel inclined to murmur. And today when we come upon this self-conscious rusticity, these awkward assumptions of innocence in verse, we remember the advice of Patrice de la Tour du Pin: 'Do not play, like children, with the parts of yourself that are no longer childish.' But if these escapist pieces are mostly rather mawkish, the war neurosis did not itself produce very memorable poetry. Consider this postscript to an otherwise rather sentimental 'Familiar Letter, to Siegfried Sassoon':

> '. . . to-day I found in Mametz wood
> A certain cure for lust of blood,
> Where propped against a shattered trunk
>   In a great mess of things unclean
> Sat a dead Boche: he scowled and stunk
>   With clothes and face a sodden green;
> Big-bellied, spectacled, crop-haired,
> Dribbling black blood from nose to beard.'

In a passage like that there are the roots of the horror which is a recurring theme in Graves's later poetry; just as in the bucolic pieces he seeks in nature something which, in later, better poems he will know he has not found. But though the passage is obviously extremely sincere, it is poetically unconvincing. Compare the amount of control in it with that shown in some verses on a similar theme by the most mature battle poet of the war that recently ended. Keith Douglas. Douglas is writing about another dead soldier, this time in the Western Desert:

> 'Three weeks gone and the combatants gone,
> returning over the nightmare ground
> we found the place again and found
> the soldier sprawling in the sun.
>
> The frowning barrel of his gun
> overshadows him. As we came on
> that day, he hit my tank with one
> like the entry of a demon. . . .

Douglas's dead man has a picture of his girl in his pocket:

> 'But she would weep to see to-day
> how on his skin the swart flies move,
> the dust upon the paper eye
> and the burst stomach like a cave.
>
> For here the lover and killer are mingled
> who had one body and one heart;
> and Death, who had the soldier singled,
> had done the lover mortal hurt.'

This is a very much better passage than Graves's, partly because Graves expresses mere disgust (and mere disgust is itself disgusting); because the dead soldier in this passage is seen as a person, and the 'dead Boche' in the other as a mere object. There are also technical reasons why it is a better passage. Some of them have to do with the changing technique, not of poetry, but of war; mobile warfare, more than trench warfare, permits a certain control and detachment; Keith Douglas, not quite perpetually having his nose rubbed in the smell of death, is able to look on his dead man as an example of the fortunes of war and the large paradoxes of human life. The horrid foreground does not block all background. But also Douglas is beginning to write in a handier period, with neater tricks of rhetoric available to him. His lines move on the verb (the repetitions of 'gone' and 'found' in the first stanza), his visual images are conveyed by the antiseptically exact epithet and the isolated noun ('the *swart* flies', 'the *paper* eye', 'the *burst* stomach', 'the *frowning* barrel', and even, deliberately trite but appropriate, 'the *nightmare* ground'; and the two similes, 'like a *cave*', 'like the entry of a *demon*', at once natural and surprising). Moreover the deliberate formality of the language ('*nightmare* ground', '*swart* flies', '*weep*' instead of 'cry', particularly) and of the balanced syntax,

> 'and Death, who had the *soldier* singled,
> had done the *lover* mortal hurt,'

give an effect of aesthetic distance. With Graves that effect is not created, he merely presents unpleasant raw material, too close to him to be art. And neither verbs nor nouns are used in Graves's passage so as to activate the line. He has one terribly feeble inversion ('things unclean'), and he makes his main descriptive effect,

> 'Big-bellied, spectacled, crop-haired,
> Dribbling black blood. . . .'

in the weakest way, by piling up adjectives. Yet we may well suppose that the ardours and horrors of the 1914–18 war, and his retreat into 'an Arcadia of amatory fancy' afterwards, provided Mr. Graves with his main poetic material; in his later work he has, we may say, been largely concerned with refining, controlling and generalizing the practical attitudes that were forced upon him in these exacting years. He had a facile success as a war poet and a writer of bucolics; it is very much to his credit that he should have struggled through from that sort of success to one more lonely but very much more worth having.

Examples of his early style at its least satisfactory can be found in *Poems, 1914–1926*. Mr. Graves's second volume of collected poems, *Poems, 1926–1930*, has an epigraph from Miss Laura Riding:

> 'It is a conversation between angels now
> Or between who remain when all are gone,'

and his style in this volume has suffered the astonishing purgation that this epigraph suggests. The Arcadianism has gone. Nature and a self-conscious bucolic childishness are no longer considered as cures for a poetic, or a metaphysical unease that has become a far deeper and wider thing than any war-neurosis. In one of the rudest poems ever written about nature (a poem which, like much else in the volume, beautifully anticipates Mr. Auden's earliest manner), he says, with all the spite of a disillusioned lover (I quote the original version from that volume, not the revised version from 'No More Ghosts'):

> 'Nature is also so, you find,
> That brutal-comic mind,
> As wind,
> Retching among the empty spaces,
> Ruffling the idiot grasses,
> The sheep's fleeces.
>
> Whose pleasures are excreting, poking,
> Havocking and sucking,
> Sleepy licking.
>
> Whose griefs are melancholy,
> Whose flowers are oafish,
> Whose waters, silly,
> Whose birds, raffish,
> Whose fish, fish.'

143

The total effect of such a passage is probably indescribable in prose. The poem, in fact, like most of Mr. Graves's later pieces, is very much itself and not what a critic can say about it. But if you read these lines out to yourself aloud, you will find they have a slow, sad movement, a melancholy perched on the edge of a yawn, a humour on the edge of a sigh, that lulls and depresses, that seems at once to confirm and contradict what the poem says: for this oafish, idiotic and melancholy nature has its own perverse charm, too, conveyed much more intensely in these lines than in Mr. Graves's earlier straight poems about rustic life, in such volumes as *Country Sentiment*. There will also be, in very much of his later work, that knack of flat and final statement,

> 'Whose birds raffish,
> *Whose fish, fish,*'

as well as that ability to make a jocular manner go with a sad tone of voice, that ability to seem, whetever is being said, not entirely committed to it. Mr. Graves's reader had better be suspicious and alert; or else choose another poet.

Mr. Graves, in his volume of 1930, anticipates Mr. Auden's early manner so often and so startlingly—as in the beautiful poem that begins:

> 'O Love, be fed with apples while you may,
> And feel the sun and go in royal array,
> A smiling innocent in the heavenly causeway—'

that we may wonder why he did not enjoy a revival of prestige in the 1930s, on the tail, as it were, of Mr. Auden's sumptuous early renown. The chief reason was probably that, unlike Mr. Auden (who has had a succession of messages), Mr. Graves has no obvious message for the age. He is probably most moving and most beautiful as a poet in these love poems which are concerned entirely with themes from his personal life. As far as politics are concerned, he has expressed, in a poem called 'The Tower of Siloam', his objection to becoming a prophet, an announcer of calamities:

'It behoved us, indeed, as poets
To be silent in Siloam, to foretell
No visible calamity. Though kings
Were crowned with gold coin minted still and horses
Still munched at nose-bags in the public streets,
All such sad emblems were to be condoned:
An old wives' tale, not ours.'

About politics, as about war, as about life in general, his feeling seems to be that people are to do their duty and not to expect things to turn out well. His Belisarius hates the corrupt, cowardly Justinian, rather admires the straightforward virtues of the barbarians he is fighting against, but never thinks of ousting Justinian from his place, or going over to the other side; and Belisarius is a hero very much to Mr. Graves's taste. He has a poem about that period, 'The Cuirassiers of the Frontier': the soldiers who speak in it say

'We, not the city, are the Empire's soul:
A rotten tree lives only in its rind.'

Does Mr. Graves feel about the British Empire, or about western European civilization generally, more or less what he feels about Byzantium? He gives no hint about that. But whereas when he fought it was the horrors of war that came most closely home to him, in his later poetry he thinks more of the honour and nobility of a soldier's life, of the good fortune of an early death. As in the poem, 'Callow Captain', in which he may perhaps be thinking of the *persona* of himself, the young, gallant soldier, who stalks through *Good-bye to all that!*

'A wind ruffles the book, and he whose name
    Was mine vanishes: all is at an end.
Fortunate soldier: to be spared shame
    Of chapter-years unprofitable to spend,
To ride off into history, nor throw
    Before the story-sun a long shadow.'

Yet if he has managed, in retrospect, to purge war of its horror, horror of another kind has gathered in his later poetry around the love in which he sought an escape from war. His love poems are nearly all, though wonderfully touching, almost unbearably sad. That poem of which I have quoted three lines closes (I quote again the earlier version) sadly and sinisterly enough:

> 'Be warm, enjoy the season, lift your head,
> Exquisite in the pulse of tainted blood,
> That shivering glory not to be despised.
>
> Take your delight in momentariness,
> Walk between dark and dark, a shining space,
> With the grave's narrowness, but not its peace.'

'The tainted blood', 'the shivering glory' (the uncontrollable shivering of the body in a fit of lust), 'not to be despised'. Even in a love poem Mr. Graves cannot repress his faint grimace of disgust at the body; and in the saddest of all his love poems, 'A Love Story', he describes how love had dispersed the winter whose horror besieged him, transformed it, how his loved one, 'warped in the weather, turned beldamish', how the horror came back again, and how he realized that it had been a mistake 'to serenade Queen Famine'. His advice, in fact, about love, as about other things, seems to be to make the most of the good in the evil, of the good moment which heralds the bad change. But his final note is always sad:

> 'And now warm earth was Arctic sea,
>   Each breath came dagger-keen;
> Two bergs of glinting ice were we,
>   The broad moon sailed between;
> There swam the mermaids, tailed and finned,
> *And love went by upon the wind*
>   *As though it had not been.*'

Only the lucid wintry fantasy there, and the compelling

canorous voice, only the romantic trappings of which Mr. Graves had never entirely divested himself, console us for the cruel thing said.

It would be wrong to think of Mr. Graves as an entirely pessimistic poet. He is pessimistic about the world that exists. He has no message for the age, in that he does not think that things will turn out well (as, in their different ways, Mr. Auden and Mr. Eliot do). Some writers, like Mr. Orwell, who expect things to turn out badly, are at least very much concerned about this: and that also gives them, in a sense, a message; it is their part 'to foretell visible calamity'. Mr. Graves seems, on the whole, to think that it is in the nature of things to turn out badly, and only a fool would make a fuss about it. But there is some realm or other of subsisting value (in a recent poem, he calls it 'excellence') which the change, which is the badness, cannot touch: the ravaging worms

> 'were greedy-nosed
> To smell the taint and go scavenging,
> Yet over excellence held no domain.
> Excellence lives; they are already dead—
> The ages of a putrefying corpse.'

And in his last volume there is also a religious poem (largely translated from ancient Greek texts), 'Instructions to the Orphic Adept', in which it is suggested that complete self-recollection is a way of escape from change. The regenerate soul is admonished:

> 'Man, remember
> What you have suffered here in Samothrace,
> What you have suffered.
> Avoid this spring, which is Forgetfulness;
> Though all the common rout rush down to drink,
> Avoid this spring.'

In his poetry, Mr. Graves has obeyed these instructions; he has remembered what he has suffered, and, in remembering, has transformed pain into the excellence of art. He is a very fine poet, and a poet whose vision of some things, of love, of suffering, of pain, of honour, is much deeper, stronger and calmer than the vision that most of us can claim. His temperament may estrange intimacy; his chief preoccupations may be irrelevant to our most urgent contemporary problems. And when he deals with the theme of the body in a prison he may be dealing with a theme rather excessively private (in the sense that readers, like myself, who have not a parallel feeling about their own bodies, have to make a rather conscious effort of sympathy). Nevertheless, in his later work in verse—as, indeed, in his better work in prose—he is a model for young writers of a strong and pure style. His journeys may lie rather aside from what we think of as our main roads; but his is a very pure and individual talent, which, if we do care at all for good and honest writing, we ought not to ignore or decry.

Auden as the Young Prophet

———— ✸ ————

The Orators, an English Study came out in 1932, when its author, Mr. W. H. Auden, was in his twenty-sixth year. It was his second important book (the first was the *Poems* of 1930). He thinks it, now, a failure. Judging very stringently, he is right, but I wish there were a poet of twenty-five who was likely to give us in the late 1950s a failure equally exciting. The great and notable quality of the language, prose and verse, throughout *The Orators*, is punch, impact, vigour. The verse can be as striking as this: the speaker, one should explain, is a beggar, one of the dispossessed of the classical world, feeling that 'the barbarians may be some sort of solution': he is also one of the dispossessed of liberal, and growingly Fascist, Europe in the 1930s, looking wistfully towards a symbolic Russia:

   ' "Won't you speak louder?
  Have you heard of someone swifter than Syrian horses?
  Has he thrown the bully of Corinth in the sanded circle?
  Has he crossed the Isthmus already? Is he seeking brilliant
    Athens and us"?'

The prose can be as pungently concentrated as this, an image of the human spirit crucified by excessive self-love:
  'With odd dark eyes like windows, a lair for engines, they pass suffering more and more from cataract or deafness, leaving behind them diaries full of incomprehensible jottings, complaints less heard than the creaking of a wind pump on a moor.'
  The book, of course, contains other passages that have

149

worn less well. In the six odes at the end, in particular, there is too much of that scoutmasterish breeziness, the one aspect of Mr. Auden's complex poetic personality which I have never been able to stand:

> 'Queer to these birds; yes, very queer,
> But to the tryers such a dear,
> Only hard
> On smugging, smartness, and self regard. . . .'

Whether this is Dr. Arnold as God, or God as Dr. Arnold, it is equally hard to take. What may also annoy readers now, though it was very stimulating in 1932, is the insolently ostentatious privacy of many of the references:

> 'Of all the healers, granny in mittens, the Mop,
> the white surgeon,
> And loony Layard.'

Mr. Layard, I discovered recently, is a Jungian psychologist who may have been the first to introduce the young Auden to Groddeck. Who or what 'the Mop' was must remain a mystery till some thesis-manufacturer bothers to write to Mr. Auden and ask. But to a young reader in the early 1930s, these incidental obscurities did not seem to matter so much. The general drift seemed so clear.

Was it, though? If you had asked me what *The Orators* was 'about', twenty-four years ago, when I was an undergraduate, I should have said it was about the decay of English energy and the need to renew that energy through insight and action; and that the action was envisaged, in the book, mainly as that of small groups—discontented sons of the ruling classes—of dedicated young men. That would have been correct, up to a point. But the interesting thing is this. In the 1930s, I took it for granted, as everyone did (and as Auden, with his description of himself as a 'pink liberal' probably at a surface level also took for granted), that the implied politics were more or less Marxist. They seem to me now the politics of a romantic radical of the

Right. What the airman, in the prose section which is the moral core of the book, *Journal of an Airman*, dreams of is the renewed simplicity of a patriarchal order:

'The man shall love the work; the woman shall receive him as the divine representative; the child shall be born as the sign of the trust; the friend shall laugh at the joke apparently obscure.'

Or, in the verse, even more strikingly:

'All of the women and most of the men
Shall work with their hands and not think again. . . .'

These are not liberal or democratic sentiments. Manual therapy may be as good for a sick society as for a sick individual, but all the same these are the sentiments of idealistic Fascism. 'All of the women . . .', also, does take one aback. And the bias behind the phrase is a recurrent one: 'There is something peculiarly horrible about the idea of women pilots', and ' "What a wonderful woman she is!" Not so fast. Wait till you see her son.'

The airman of the *Journal* feels, in fact, that what is valuable in his heritage comes from men. The dead Uncle, who initiated him into the meaning of life, is spiritually more truly his 'ancestor' than his uncomprehending mother is. Auden works out this idea, with a diagram, in rather boring detail. But it is a key idea: one negative way of describing the atmosphere of his work throughout the 1930s is to say that the image of the Muse is absent except in the sinister transformed shape of the 'terrible Mother'. A mother-landscape image is sinisterly transformed in the prologue to *The Orators* itself. When the Hero returns from completing his task, the Muse who should welcome him has become (because he has subtly betrayed her) an ogress:

'And yet this prophet, homing the day is ended,
Receives odd welcome from the country he so defended:
The band roars "Coward, Coward," in his fever,
The giantess shuffles nearer, cries, "Deceiver".'

For the poets of the 1930s, in fact, the Hero has ceased to be the Muse's lover, he has become her competitor. Similarly it was not the female image of Nature ('By landscape reminded once of his mother's figure') that interested them so much as the male use of nature, the ruined power-houses, the hangars, the pylons.

So, if I were asked now what I thought *The Orators* is 'about', I should say something like this. It is about romantic male solidarity, about the idea of being initiated into the group of young braves of the tribe. Or, to take another image, it is about knightliness ('airman' equals 'cavalier'). In England, the ordinary working-class or lower-middle-class young man gets such an initiation into an all-male society only when there is a World War. The upper middle classes and the aristocracy get it all the time from the public-school tradition, from compulsory games, for instance, the prefect system, and the O.T.C. Baden-Powell tried to give it to everybody, or to a much wider section of the population, through the Boy Scouts. These are the reasons why the first book of *The Orators* is called 'The Initiates', why it begins with a parody of a school prize-giving speech, and why in the odes one is sometimes reminded (not so incongruously as might at first appear) of Kipling or Newbolt:

> 'Time to change guard:
> Boy, the quarrel was before your time, the aggressor
> No one you know.'

Moreover, *The Orators* is not only about romantic male solidarity in general; more particularly, it is about the fantasies of power and the daydreams of violent social change which this solidarity can evoke, in periods of decay, among gifted and discontented young men. Auden is certainly imaginatively attracted, in many passages of *The Orators*, to a mood that can engender Fascism; but the great moral distinction of the book is how he steps back on his tracks. In *Journal of an Airman* he in the end undermines, with ruthless insight, his own fantasies.

That ruthless insight lies behind such a passage as this:

'In hours of gentleness always to remember my Uncle,
the connection between the last desperate appeals of the lost
for help scribbled on the walls of public latrines and such a
letter as this.'

There is a less compressed, but very moving, passage in
which the 'I' of the *Journal* has a long conversation with an
imaginary critic who asks him what conceivable general
interest an accumulation of private fantasies and allusions,
a myth and an ethos derived from the shared experiences of
the 'small group', can have. Desperately trying to convey
'the interest', all the 'I' can do is to recall private jokes, give
lists of names of friends, sketch out obscurely a traumatic
experience. His interlocutor replies inexorably: 'Yes, but
the interest?' It is partly the same sort of 'interest' as that of
the 'Mortmere' world, the world of small-group folklore,
described by Isherwood in *Lions and Shadows*. To a wider
audience, much of 'the interest', in this sense, *must* remain
incommunicable; but is the very *existence* of this 'interest'—
a severe critic of Mr. Auden, like Dr. Leavis, would tend to
say so—merely a small group's self-flattering delusion?

The 'I' of *The Journal of an Airman* moves on from such
self-questionings to hysterical (though also hysterically
funny) fantasies about violent revolution. He has already
sketched out, with paranoiac wit, as the opposite of the
'airman' with his 'self-care', the many faces of the 'self-
regard' of the 'enemy':

'Three kinds of enemy face—the June bride—
the favourite puss—the stone in the rain.'

It is the enemy's 'self-regard' which introduces 'inert velo-
cities' into what would otherwise be a self-regulating system. But at the end the 'I' recognizes that these are 'thoughts
suitable to a sanatorium'. He recovers humility. He is suddenly able to relate his humiliating kleptomania, his compulsive pocketing of small objects, to the element of

grossness—of self-flattery, blindness, and brutality—in his fantasies. His hands 'stole to force a hearing'. He realizes also (to put it more simply and flatly than Auden does) that 'the enemy' is essentially a projection of his own unconscious inner aggressiveness, his will to dominate. He breaks off a relationship which he values, because he feels that God must disapprove of it. He faces calmly some ordeal he has to face (in view of the sinister 'Letter to a Wound' in an earlier section, and of the many scattered references to surgery throughout *The Orators*, it may be an operation). The last entry is: 'Hands in perfect order.'

It is disturbing, however, in the six odes which follow *Journal of an Airman*, that Auden still often seems to be functioning at the level of the airman's fantasies rather than his insights. There is a strange effect of double focus, insight mounted on fantasy. Nothing could be more effective than some of the hard-hitting satire, rather Skeltonic in tone, on well-known iniquities of the early Thirties; but all this is set in a framework of a world that is to be made over by Rex, Christopher, Stephen, loony Layard, and the rest of 'the boys'—in the framework of an inanely complacent vision of a revolution working from the top down, engineered by an *élite*. There is not really that sentimentalization of the working classes of which the poets of the 1930s are sometimes accused:

> 'Dyers and bakers
> And boiler-tube makers,
> Poofs and ponces,
> All of them dunces.
> Those over thirty,
> Ugly and dirty. . . .'

One would say that Auden didn't trust or respect the common people enough. And to make two sharp observations: it was the 'Dyers and bakers/And boiler-tube makers', not Rex or Wystan, who at El Alamein in 1942 did in fact 'throw the bully of Corinth in the sanded circle'; it was the people who ought to 'work on the land and not think again', not Christopher or Stephen, who brought about the profoundly important peaceful social revolution of 1945. Yet if Auden's solutions were often fantastic, his eye for the problem was unerring: 'What do you think about England, this country of ours where nobody is well?' And he was right to seek the roots of that illness in misdirected and inadequate love, in the wrong use of the spirit. He was right, also, to harangue and clamour. In the sort of detailed social remedies it suggests, *The Orators* may be as far off the mark as Carlyle's *Past and Present*. But like that book it stirred the consciences of intelligent young men in a bad time. That, in modern times, is what we expect a prophet to do.

Auden in Midstream

'With his unattractive stock-in-trade, and his clap-trap,' says Kathleen Raine, 'Auden, nevertheless, as none of the rest do, touches the human heart.' The unattractive stock-in-trade is, I suspect, for Miss Raine the facile use of generalizations—the taking of a leading idea from Freud, from Marx, and now from Kierkegaard, and seeing how it works out in a different context. It is the adoption, by a powerful but not a very scrupulous intellect, of any convenient 'working scheme'. (The first section of *The Orators*, with its startling application of Dante's ideas about love, as the only human motive, to the problems of public-school life, is an admirable example of Auden's pragmatism at its most fruitful and illuminating level.) God, like the libido, or like the dialectic, is for Auden chiefly a useful generalization; assuming the existence of God, he finds it possible to solve certain problems. The clap-trap is the unction, the over-persuasiveness, the mixture of blarney and bullying that goes with this sort of pragmatism. Hugh Sykes Davies, an excellent critic, who writes too little, has hinted at the morally repellent side of Auden's attitudes . . . the element that has something in common even with Buchmanism. 'It is not possible', Sykes Davies says, 'to adopt a new theory or a new loyalty overnight for valid reasons, and the reasons for such overnight changes are always invalid. The crisis in the patient's ideas and feelings does not arise from observation and speculation, but from internal psychological problems, of course unperceived; and the solution is determined not by observation and speculation, but by the needs of the psychological condition. . . . Every convert is psycho-

logically ill. . . . Morally, he disgusts because the act of conversion solidifies personal neuroses into social form. *In time,
converts band together in such numbers that they, the diseased, can
interfere with the healthy unconverted—and they are always
anxious to do this.*' It must be admitted that it is almost too
easy to apply this generalization to Auden. He has, since he
began, been threatening his readers with a variety of calamities—disease, madness, death in war or revolution, and now
eternal damnation. He has, as he admits himself,

> 'adopted what I should disown
> The preacher's loose, immodest tone.'

Yet, when all this is said, Auden does remain the most
considerable poet of his generation. He does, as Miss Raine
says, touch the human heart. He cannot be dismissed just by
saying that one doesn't believe what he says, and doubts
(because he is too emphatic about it) whether he really believes it himself. Auden's attitudes, reduced to average
prose, would result in a writer as unpleasant as, say, Mr.
Middleton Murry. But they are not reduced to average
prose. They are *used* for rather extraordinary poetry.

Let us take an example of the clap-trap—the gift for
sinisterly effective Kiplingesque slogans. 'We must love one
another or die.' Has anybody thought of a more nasty and
horrid motive for our loving one another? (Just what
would a love vamped up on such prudential considerations
be really worth?) But it has its effectiveness as a slogan, as
telling clap-trap, just because it leaves to the reader the
choice of the level at which he wishes to interpret it. There
is the level of mere platitude: 'Isolated people wither away.'
There is a level of frightful cynicism: 'Though all my im-
pulses are selfish, I need other people as a source of new
energy.' 'I am so lonely, that I must love you, though there
is nothing in you to love.' There is the level of fear: 'I had
better love you, for otherwise you may kill me.' There is
even an honest level, as in Christ's answer to the rich young
man who asked what should he do to inherit eternal life.

'I admit that to try to love everybody, in a quite undis-
criminating way, is a terrible strain and a sacrifice. But you
are not forced to. You can always die . . . the more usual,
and perhaps the more dignified choice.' But the total effect
of such slogans is *mainly* frightening, revealing a ghastly
hollowness, but putting up a sort of façade in front of it, or
suggesting a cheap way out. . . .

What touches the human heart is certainly not Auden's
solutions (which are other people's solutions, ready-made
solutions, taken over) but the situation in which Auden, and
most of us, more often than we care to admit, find ourselves: that of complete isolation. Isolation is the disease, and
Love, however much he cheapens the word, can still
remain the word that suggests a remedy:

> 'Released by Love from isolating wrong
> Let us for Love unite our various song,
> Each with his gift according to his kind
> Bringing this child his body and his mind.'

That is from *For the Time Being* and, according to the
Christian framework of this oratorio, Love in the first line
would mean charity, in the wide sense, and Love in the
second God, or more precisely the Christ-child; but the
effectiveness of the passage is partly due to the fact that,
owing to the vague echo of the Counter-Reformation—the
note of Dryden and Purcell—in the style, we *also* think of
sexual love in the first line and of Cupid in the second. Thus
to 'bring this child my body', while it *ostensibly* means to
bring the Christ-child a body dedicated to chastity, *also*
suggests bringing Cupid a body dedicated to pleasure; this
faint and trembling ambiguity creates more effective poetry
than a merely Christian, or a merely pagan statement possibly could. We are aware of the death from which Auden's
Love ('Winter and Love', says a more subtle poet, 'are
desperate medicines') is an escape; we forgive him a great
deal because we, too, are aware of the 'isolating wrong'.
Admittedly, Auden's escape has never been into personal

love in the ordinary sense; rather into something larger and vaguer and more full of energy than the ordinary human situation—the dialectic (loss of oneself in history), the libido (loss of oneself in sexual ecstasy), and now God (surrender of one's will to another much more powerful one). He has been seeking situations less painful and complicated, with less of a prosaic drag about them, than this. His success as a poet, perhaps, is his failure to remain satisfied with his escapes. The pathos, what touches the human heart, is that after all these efforts the great waves move away, and the poet is as much alone as ever, lying awake in bed and regarding the other body

> 'mortal, guilty, but to me
> The entirely beautiful.'

Something like this perhaps is true—whether wholly intended by Auden or not—about Auden's Prospero, a Gerald Heard type, in 'The Sea and the Mirror'. That he quite fails (as Antonio maliciously suggests) to break his wand. There is an obvious comparison. Shakespeare was not intensely or especially a religious writer, yet in that conventional little epilogue to *The Tempest* with, as Walter de la Mare says, 'its curiously apt overtones'.

> 'now I want
> Spirits to enforce, art to enchant,
> And my ending is despair
> Unless I be relieved by prayer,
> Which pierces so, that it assaults
> Mercy itself, and frees all faults . . .'

in that, we feel a consciousness of the 'last things', so habitual that it does not need, so to say, to write itself up.

Auden's Prospero, on the other hand, in what might be an expansion of this passage, writes himself up to some tune.

> 'When the servants settle me into a chair
> In some well arranged corner of the garden
> And arrange my mufflers and rugs, shall I ever be able

To stop myself from telling them what I am doing—
Sailing alone, out over seventy thousand fathoms?
Yet if I speak, I shall sink without a sound
Into unmeaning abysses. *Can I learn to suffer*
Without saying something ironic or funny
About suffering?'

I would say, no; the old gentleman will be talking. . . .
(In passing, these three lines I have italicized show one
weakness in the style of this volume—an excessive bookish-
ness. They are like bad Aldous Huxley. They irritate because Auden's Prospero has given no evidence, sententious,
loquacious, and sometimes eloquent as he is, that he is at all
capable of thinking of anything very effectively ironic or
funny to say; and people may be irritated, too, at the notion
of suffering as a rather expensive and special luxury for the
truly high-minded.)
But one sees the differences. Shakespeare is a dramatist
but his people are not, in quite this sense, incessantly
dramatizing themselves. For Auden the dramatic gesture
(not the dramatic incident) is all important. Everything he
would do would be this special sort of thing, with its sharp
rhetorical edge to it—'Leave for Cape Wrath to-night!'
or, 'Seeing our last of Captain Ferguson.' Yet ordinary
common little people pray and repent, and feel the
emptiness of their small successes, just as they work for a
political party, or go to bed with their wives: it was not,
after all, Auden who invented religion or sex or politics.
Like Miranda, Auden finds novelty everywhere and everywhere assimilates it; as with her brave new world, ' 'tis new
to *him*'. This is part of what Miss Riding and Mr. Graves
meant by calling him a synthetic, not a traditional, writer.
Everything has to be questioned, everything explained.
This partly explains the queer and rather unfeeling detachment Mr. Spender has noted: for Auden's Prospero,

'A stranger's quiet collapse in a noisy street
Is the beginning of much lively speculation,'

not the beginning of doing anything practical for the
stranger.

That everything is seen from the outside, and as new, and
as having to be explained (that is, as having to be set against
a wider background, which is assumed, so that there may be
explanations) is one reason, perhaps for certain faults of
taste and feeling which are rather noticeable in *For the Time
Being*. He ignores the fact that lives of ordinary routine,
which look dull and simple from the outside, from the inside, broken down into their day-to-day detail, may seem
interesting and complicated enough. And this causes him
occasionally to indulge in a peculiarly unpleasant mixture of
spiritual and social snobbery:

> 'The solitude familiar to the poor
> Is feeling that the family next door
> The way it talks, eats, dresses, loves, and hates
> Is indistinguishable from one's own.'

Both the facts, and the values implied here, seem to me
wrong. It is the upper classes in all ages, who have tended to
conventionalize their behaviour; Goldsmith somewhere has
an acute remark about the manners of the gentry being the
same all over eighteenth-century Europe—one must look
both for national characteristics, and individual eccentrici-
ties, among the peasantry. I am sure, I am much more *like*
any other middle-class intellectual of my age, than a
plumber in Bradford is like a plumber in London. Secondly,
I do not see what is wrong with the family next door being
like my family. Real conversation, real intimacy, is, in fact,
only possible when two people share a general background
of behaviour, and indeed of reading, and of taste, which is
so much taken for granted that it need not be talked about.
The individualism which Auden *seems* to be advocating here
is rather like that which, along so many English streets,
jostles together the fake-Tudor or neo-lavatorial pub, the
commercial Renaissance bank, and the jazz-modernistic
cinema. I prefer the amenity of the Georgian crescent. An

even more snobbish (and very badly written) passage is this

> 'Redeem for the dull the
> Average Way
> That common ungifted
> Natures may
> Believe that their normal
> Vision can
> Walk to perfection.'

It is not really such a colossal and crushing tragedy not to be Mr. Auden; and the best of us are very common and ungifted, in very many directions, and the most limited of us is capable of sacrifice and love.

This stuffiness is all the more depressing when one re-members Auden's former gift, in a poem like 'August for people and their favourite islands', of summing up, quite easily and lazily, the whole atmosphere of a place and the people there; and he seems to have lost that, and to have lost the unaffected pleasure he once felt in the sight of people being easily and lazily themselves; America could have offered him Coney Island, instead of these depressing and unconvincing generalizations, but the American scene, the American atmosphere, the speech habits of America, appear not to exist for him. I think there is a reason, a sociological one. The façade of English life is a very composed one, the flaws in the surface are difficult to detect, and one of the things that made Auden before the war a poet of such ex-treme social significance was his ability to put a finger on points of extreme, but hidden, stress. But America does not present a composed façade; it makes a cult, almost, of the incongruous; it is almost blind to the incongruous; and American writers tend, like Henry Adams, or the Southern Regionalists, either to invent a manner adapted to a com-posed society which doesn't exist, but ought to, or like Sin-clair Lewis, in his earlier and less regrettable days, to shout at the top of their voices to draw attention to incongruities which, even for the least sensitive English observer, would

be glaring enough. A writer like Auden for instance, or like
Rex Warner, might do a fruitful parody of a leader in *The
Times*, the *Economist*, or the *Spectator*; but a leader in the
Saturday Evening Post parodies itself. There is a degree of
rusticity which exhausts the resources of language. In
America, I suppose, there are only three alternatives: one
surrenders, one becomes hysterical and hoarse like Mark
Twain or Sinclair Lewis, or one withdraws. Auden seems
to have withdrawn, and America, for all it exists for him,
might be a desert island. There is only one outbreak of the
old beautiful malice and mischief, a poem which I first read
in a scribbled copy over a bar in Cairo:

'In the Retreat from Reason he deserted on his rocking
    horse
And lived on a fairy's kindness till he tired of kicking her,
He smashed her spectacles and stole her cheque-book and
    mackintosh
Then cruised his way back to the Army.
George, you old numero,
How did you get in the Army?'

That is nicely done. But, on the whole, and at least for
the time being, Auden seems to have lost that promise he
had once of being our best poet in a conversational style
(that is, our best poet with an adult social sense) since the
Byron of 'Don Juan' or perhaps even since Pope.

On the other hand, Auden is steadily increasing his mastery over the actual craft of verse. There is almost no form,
no metre at which he is not capable of having a pretty com-
petent try. His most interesting metrical innovation in 'The
Sea and the Mirror' is the borrowing of syllabic metre from
Miss Marianne Moore. He uses this in what is perhaps his
most perfect single poem to date, 'Alonso to Ferdinand'.
Each line has exactly nine syllables, the stanzas have an
elaborate and difficult rhyme scheme, but since stressed can
rhyme with unstressed syllables the number of possible full
rhymes in English is greatly extended; the general effect of

the metre, in Auden's use of it, is to give an effect of careful but successful concentration, like a military slow march with the soldiers counting their steps, or like counting your steps when you are dancing a slow waltz. His use of the metre is quite unlike Miss Moore's who always has the air of balancing, say, a pile of plates which are always about to topple over but never quite do; the air of doing something surprising, difficult, acrobatic, sometimes almost (elegantly) clownish . . . indulging, as she does, in lines of varying length and slyly concealed rhyme patterns. Auden's use of the metre is more straightforward, his effect smooth, grave, and majestic. I think syllabic metre is a very important and useful innovation in English verse . . . much more so, for instance, than Hopkins' type of metre, which tends to distort the natural syntax and cadence of the English language, and can only be used effectively, indeed, in Hopkins's own peculiar type of rhetoric. It would be a mistake, of course, to attempt to read 'Alonso to Ferdinand' without any stresses at all; what the reader will find himself stressing is what the French call the 'mobile accent' . . . or those words on which, from the sense pattern (of the individual line, not of the sentence or paragraph) there is a natural rhetorical stress. That stress, however, will be a modulated one, so as not to rack the slow and grave syllabic pattern.

With this advance in metrical accomplishment there goes, however, that tendency towards an impressive vagueness, even towards a triteness or woolliness, of metaphor and simile first noticed by Julian Symons. The contrast with the tightness of Auden's earliest poems is striking and from some points of view depressing. 'My dear one is mine as mirrors are lonely.' That, as reviewer after reviewer has pointed out, is a very lovely line. But just how does my dear one being mine resemble mirrors being lonely? (To anybody with some knowledge of how poems are composed, it must seem possible that Auden may have written first, 'My dear one is mine *though* mirrors are lonely,' and then, by the alteration of a syllable, created at once a more euphonious and a more mysterious line.) It might be a mere comparison of degree: mirrors are so lonely that they reflect everything which is in front of them, and my dear one just as completely reflects me (or I may be, indeed, comparing myself to the mirror; I am so lonely for my dear one as a mirror is for everything, and for me there is nothing else, my dear one is everything). That is enough to satisfy the syntax, but the sadness and the beauty of the line come partly, I think, from the fact that mirrors are so obvious a symbol both of understanding and separation; I am reflected completely in the mirror, but I also, my real self, remain completely outside the mirror; or, in love with you, I reflect you completely, but you are free, as a person, to move away, while I still possess—for a little time—your image. And if *both* you and I are like mirrors, we only know each other as reflected in each other, and being in love is important as a way of possessing oneself. But this possession is illusory, for the surface never melts away, never quite dissolves even in love, and we can never, like Alice, enter the looking-glass kingdom, and wander together there, hand in hand. All these ideas are more or less relevant, and there are probably others I have missed. The point is that one can't, of course, stop to work them all out while actually reading the poem. One has the impression, merely, of something moving, intricate, and perhaps true, and passes on. This intricate vagueness has its own fascination and I cannot agree with Mr. Symons in regarding it as mere laziness on Auden's part. He knows very well, I should think, its peculiar effectiveness.

I have been delaying coming to grips with Auden's thought. William Empson has a striking little poem, 'Reflection from Rochester', in which he says that the mind

> 'now less easily decides
> On a good root confusion to amass
> Much safety from irrelevant despair.
> Mere change in numbers made the process crass.'

Auden is not a thinker in the sense that Empson is; but what he has really been doing all along is seeking, in politics, or psychology, or religion, for a good root-confusion which would make the despair (which is, I think, his centrally important experience) irrelevant. Partly for that reason his politics, his psychology, and now his religion are always off-centre. And they are, in fact, confusing. They are ways both of explaining and of attempting to get rid of—but also to infect others with a personal sense of guilt. He does seek in that sense, in Sykes Davies's phrase, to solidify personal neuroses. The particular type of religious thinking to be found in *For the Time Being* is not new in his work. It is to be found in the famous poem that begins,

> 'Sir, no man's enemy, forgiving all
> But will, his negative inversion, be prodigal . . .'

and that ends with the rather undergraduate line,

> 'New styles of architecture, a change of heart.'

It is a religion of emotional conversion, and, among historical forms of Christianity, it resembles Lutheranism more than either Roman Catholicism or High Calvinism. It makes much more of God's will and less of His reason, much more of the individual's direct response to God and less of the idea of fellowship in a Church, than Roman Catholicism, but it does allow some scope for man's emotions (if not for his reasonable will) to co-operate with God, and it does not go all the way with that type of extreme Protestantism which makes man's salvation or damnation *entirely* dependent upon God's particular election. The general effect of such a religion would be to make men feel that, whether or not necessarily wicked, they are certainly weak, and that perhaps it is better to sin strongly and to repent strongly than to be puffed up with a sense of one's strength and virtue. (Herod, the good administrator, in Auden's oratorio, is the man who tries to rely on his own will and reasoned moral standards; he is rather venomously treated. Caesar, in another poem, stands for all man's attempts to stand on his own feet—in science, in culture, in philosophy, as well as in politics—and it is made clear that from Auden's standpoint all these are equally wicked and disastrous.) The dangers of this particular type of religion, with its emphasis on some sort of emotional surrender, are seen more clearly in 'The Sea and the Mirror'. Antonio's great crime is that he has not surrendered to Prospero,

> 'Your all is partial, Prospero;
>   My will is all my own;
> Your need to love shall never know
>   Me; I am I, Antonio:
>   My choice myself alone.'

But if Prospero can be a symbol for God, he might also be a symbol for Hitler. No man has the right to compel another man's love, unless he can prove himself worthy of it; no God either, for that matter, unless he can prove that, as well as being powerful, he is good. 'God is not without sin. He created the World,' says an old proverb from the East, and it is not very noble to worship a God just because he is powerful and can harm us. Auden, indeed, does show that he is aware of this dilemma:

> 'Alone, alone, about a dreadful wood
> Of conscious evil runs a lost mankind,
> Dreading to find its Father lest it find
> The Goodness it has dreaded is not good . . .'

but his solution is Kierkegaard's, that of the emotional leap in the dark, not Milton's, that of justifying the ways of God to man. We have seen some of the results of the emotional leap in the dark in politics (and German politics have suffered greatly from the tradition of passive obedience that goes with Lutheran pietism) and German politics, when Hitler played Prospero, suffered greatly from the lack of a few Antonios. Auden has perhaps found a temporary solution for a number of his own personal difficulties, but I do not think that he has lighted on a very useful root-confusion for the rest of us. He seems to me, on the whole, to be *less* illuminating than in the days of his psychological and political probings.

He is not, I think, fundamentally a religious poet, any more than, for example, Milton was.[1] A person with the genuine piety, the sense of mystery and awe, of, say, Dr. Johnson could never have made out of the truths of the Christian religion the purely mythological pattern—the argumentative deity and the cannonading angels of *Paradise Lost*. The artist and the dialectician were strong enough in Milton to make use of this dangerous material and the artist and the dialectician are strong enough in Auden. But I find no evidence anywhere in this book of Auden's, any more than anywhere in Milton, of any profound *personal* spiritual experience; such as one finds, for instance, in Mr. David Gascoyne's *Noctambules* or in some short poems of Miss Kathleen Raine's. He is not a religious poet in that sense, and though *For the Time Being* has some affinities with *The Rock*, I do not see Auden going on to write something like *Four Quartets*. His gifts are of another sort, and his strength is of another sort. Antonio's mockery is true,

---

[1] I hope this doesn't sound too paradoxical. The distinction is between grasping a theology as a coherent parable, or a coherent system of ideas, which is what Milton and Auden do, and having a certain kind of personal experience, a sharp and immediate sense of goodness or of evil. Or perhaps it might be described as the difference between generalized and personal experience, between accepting a set of ideas because on the whole they seem to fit, and being absolutely gripped and held by a certain sort of experience. Neither Auden nor Milton seem to be gripped and held. They choose, rather, to grip and hold. They could let go.

Because they could let go, poets like Auden and Milton are more anxious to persuade than poets, like Herbert, or Vaughan, or Crashaw, of actual religious experience. One does not need to argue about actual experience. One has had it, and can merely attempt to record it.

'Antonio, sweet brother, has to laugh.
How easy you have made it to refuse
Peace to your greatness! Break your wand in half,
The fragments will join; burn your books or lose
Them in the sea, they will soon reappear
Not even damaged: as long as I choose
To wear my fashion, whatever you wear
Is a magic robe. . . .'

We can allow no peace to Auden's greatness. He will not be satisfied until he has written something which is utterly moving, persuading, convincing to *everybody*, and, of course, he will never do this. There will always be the schoolboy who doesn't attend, the scout who skips the parade, the man who chooses dying instead of loving, the heckler with the awkward question, the fellow conjuror chiefly interested in how he does the trick—there will always be Antonio. Prospero, again and again, will have to postpone the breaking of his wand. But, after all, is it to be regretted? There are so many professional mystagogues; so many dull preachers; so many cheapjacks with their bottled spiritual cure-alls; but of all poets writing today, there is only Auden with just that range and scope. His strength is not in what he accepts, but in what he discards. It lies just as much in a certain fundamental ruthlessness as in the love about which he talks so vaguely and so much. He is a much greater man than his ideas; as a poet, a major voice, as a thinker, about on the level of Mr. Middleton Murry. Because he has a major voice, what he says will always be relevant, without having to be, in a sense, true. (In one sense, it always will be true; it will always be a possible synthesis of an unusually wide reading and experience—it will always be pragmatically true, a possible 'working scheme'.) 'All I have is a voice. . . .'

Auden's Later Manner

Of all the poets whom I have dealt with in this volume, I feel that I have treated Mr. Auden least fairly. Irritation not so much with his ideas as with his manner of entertaining ideas has, through the years, when I have had occasion to deal with him, betrayed me into a carping, petulant, suspicious tone; and I am now beginning to see that to argue whether his ideas were right or wrong had as little to do with the strict function of a critic of poetry as treating, for instance, Dryden's *Religio Laici* or Tennyson's *In Memoriam* as pamphlets about natural religion, to be supported or refuted by logical arguments. I tended, in all my earlier writing about Mr. Auden, to take elements in a composition for statements in a pulpit, or a witness-box. I nagged at a social attitude which irritated me, where I should have taken the social attitude as 'given', and reverted to it only when I thought some inadequacy in it helped to explain some inadequacy in what was poetically made of it. Let me try, now, to make some belated slight amends.

He does remain, of course, the most considerable Anglo-American poet of his generation. As Mr. Richard Hoggart says, in an admirable recent British Council Pamphlet about him, one still hesitates to accord him major status—to put him 'up there', as it were, with Yeats, with his own early master, Hardy, with Mr. Eliot—but he does remain, at fifty or so, the most exciting and promising 'younger poet' of our generation. Nobody else of around the same age—except in his narrower but perhaps sometimes deeper mode, Mr. Empson—rivals him in speculative agility or technical adroitness. And Mr. Empson has written only three or four new poems since 1940. Nobody at all, of all poets who are active now, rivals Mr. Auden in fertility of invention. And yet, I suppose, over the last ten years or so few of us have been wholly happy about the way his poetry has been going. I shall say nothing about *The Age of Anxiety*. A learned Italian critic, Signor Melchiori, in his book *The Tightrope Walkers*, thinks of it as a triumph in a new baroque manner, square and solid in construction, but with lavish extravagant ornamentation; it uses a very primitive metrics, that of Anglo-Saxon poetry, for a very sophisticated theme: and I remember a fine scholar saying to me, when it first came out, 'If one is seeking to be "mannerist", to play on one's sense of the jarring inappropriateness of subject to handling, of content to form, why not instead try out the metre of *Hiawatha*?' But two volumes of shorter poems, largely of 'light' poems, *Nones* and *The Shield of Achilles*, deserve both a warmer welcome and a more respectful consideration.

Let me take the second of these volumes first, *The Shield of Achilles*. And let me relate it to the two aspects of Mr. Auden's work which have most worried recent critics. One of these is a growing lack of personal immediacy; the other is an over-piling of verbal ornament. That lack of immediacy is very noticeable, for instance, in the first seven poems in *The Shield of Achilles*, the set called 'Bucolics'. These are like the notes of a very intelligent lecturer in human ecology done into verse. Thus, when we turn to the poem (among the poems on plains, mountains, and so forth) on islands, we do not get a vivid image like Mr. Pound's

> 'Tawn foreshores
> Washed in the cobalt of oblivions.'

We get instead reflections, pungent, intelligent, but faintly chilling, on penal colonies and dying Pacific races:

> 'Once, where detected worldlings now
> Do penitential jobs,

Exterminated species played
Who had not read their Hobbes.'

Nothing could be neater but (as in the fine 'Ode to Gaea' in another section) it is our world seen from an aeroplane. The poet, on the whole, brackets his personal life off from his poetry. We find ourselves longing for some concentration of direct experience, out of which the generalizations could grow.

Mr. Auden, of course, has always been a generalizer. He has never been interested either in his own experience, or the experience of other people, for its own sake; he has been interested in it as an instance of a general case, of the sort of thing that happens. He has a classifying mind; he is at the very, very extreme opposite pole from a poet like Hopkins with his passionate concentration on *haecceitas*, thisness, 'sakes', 'selving' and 'unselving', 'inscape'. The worry that critics may have had about his attitude to language in his recent books is not about this 'given' element in him; it is about a painstaking frivolity, a preoccupation with ornament. He does manfully defend the baroque mode:

'Be subtle, various, ornamental, clever,
And do not listen to those critics ever
Whose crude provincial gullets crave in books
Plain cooking made still plainer by plain cooks. . . .'

Walter Bagehot was one of 'those critics' and I agree with Bagehot that the way to make a basket of fish poetical is *not* by calling it, as Tennyson did in *Enoch Arden*,

'. . . Enoch's ocean-spoil
In ocean-smelling osier. . . .'

Or that way of handling it *does*, of course, make it 'poetical': but in a soppily vulnerable way, a way for the tough and wry who hate poetry to kick at.

Let us consider, with this suspicion of 'the poetical' in mind, such a passage as this of Mr. Auden's, from his recent work:

172

'The horn gate and the ivory gate
Swing to, swing shut, instantaneously
Quell the nocturnal rummage
Of its rebellious fronde, ill-favoured,
Ill-natured and second-rate,
Disenfranchised, widowed and orphaned
By an historical mistake. . . .'

But for the Fall, the basic sense of that passage is, our
dreams would not be Freudian dreams—would not be so
shabby, guilty, and incoherent as they are (the shabbiness
expressed by 'nocturnal rummage', 'rebellious fronde', and
so on: the Fall, ironically, by 'an historical mistake'). The
rhetoric, the mechanism of persuasion, in such a passage is
one of expansion; the plain, underlying prose sense is 'like
gold to ayery thinness beat'; the lines *look* as if they were
making a much more portentous and complex statement
than they are making.

The title poem of *The Shield of Achilles*, a grim meditation on power politics, perhaps on the *Iliad* itself as what
Simone Weil called 'the Poem of Force', had a bleak impressiveness: three victims being (not exactly) crucified:

'The mass and majesty of this world, all
   That carries weight and always weighs the same
Lay in the hands of others; they were small
   And could not hope for help and no help came:
   What their foes liked to do was done, their shame
Was all the worst could wish; they lost their pride
And died as men before their bodies died.'

That impresses me poetically, impresses me morally, and
yet there is something about the attitude implied in it that
very frighteningly raises the whole question, in the context
of which in the 1930s one always, perhaps obtusely, would
discuss Mr. Auden's poetry of the power of poetic perception to influence events. An hour or so before I copied out
these lines I read, in *The Manchester Guardian*, a translation

of passages from M. Alleg's book, *La Question*. M. Alleg is the editor of a Communist newspaper, who was tortured by parachutists in Algeria. His torturers told him that they were modelling themselves on the Gestapo, that they hoped to torture Frenchmen, including liberal or radical political leaders, in France, too, and be done with the Republic. I reflected that if there is any country in Europe which men of other countries have turned to as a centre of civilization, have loved second to their own countries, it is France. I reflected also that as at least a sympathizer with Communism M. Alleg must have in his time turned a Nelson eye to the possibility that men were being tortured behind the Iron Curtain; and yet, standing up to torture himself, he seemed to speak not as a partisan but for all men. In a sense, Auden speaks also in these lines for all men—but hopelessly? In the 1930s, he seemed often ahead of events, warning us of what we might still do to dodge our fates. In a poem like *The Shield of Achilles*, he is like the chorus in a Greek tragedy, which makes all the appropriate moral comments, but knows it cannot prevent the awful thing happening. By classical standards, this should make him a more universal poet; and by revealing starkly what is worst in us, he may in fact, in such a poem, be nerving us to pursue what is better. And yet, in a cruder way, did he not move us more when he took sides more, when he seemed to speak with even crude power, like an orator? Was 'the preacher's loose, immodest tone', which he once often protested against, not part of his early power over one?

In fact, the vein which I often find most attractive in Mr. Auden's later poems is not this harsh, bleak vein but one of playfulness. There was much of this in the volume which preceded *The Shield of Achilles*, the volume called *Nones*, the most variously pleasurable for me of all Mr. Auden's more recent volumes. Nones is the daily office of the Church originally said at the ninth hour, or three o'clock in the afternoon; it was between the sixth and the ninth hour, while Christ hung on the Cross, that there was a darkness

over the earth, the sun was darkened, and the veil of the
Temple was rent. So far, certainly, the title does not suggest
a mood of cheerfulness. But there is another meaning of the
word more directly relevant to the mood of at least the
lighter pieces in the book. 'Nones' is the old spelling of
'nonce'. Many of the poems in *Nones* are nonce-poems
(poems inspired by unrecurring occasions or written, in
some cases, for public declaration at American graduation
ceremonies): many of these are also full of nonce-words:

> 'On the mountain, the baltering torrent
>   Sunk to a soodling thread,'

for instance; the once battering but now faltering torrent
sunk, I suppose, to a soothing and dawdling thread. One is
half tempted on reading such lines to wonder whether Mr.
Auden's inspiration has itself begun to soodle, but, if there
was little or nothing in *Nones* in Mr. Auden's old, urgent,
hortatory vein, that was because of a feeling that all 'sane
affirmative speech' has been so 'pawed-at' and 'profaned'
by newspapers and politicians that the only civilized tone
of voice for a poet today is

> 'the wry, the sotto voce,
> Ironic and monochrome.'

And in fact Mr. Auden has rarely written with more confident ease than in the lighter pieces in *Nones*. He hits just
the note he wants to, even when he is seeking to hold the
restless attention of an audience of undergraduates:

> 'Between the chances, choose the odd;
> Read *The New Yorker*, trust in God;
>   And take short views.'

Whether under the ease of the surface of such poems
there is a slackness of will is another question; also, how far
irony and humour at this level can unconsciously betray an
undue complacency of spirit. There is a *New Yorker* side to
Mr. Auden, and the recipe for the *New Yorker* type of

humour is to step far enough back from the routines we are all immersed in to feel sophisticated about them; but not far enough back to cease to be one of the boys. But Auden can be one of the boys at several levels and there is a quite different snob highbrow pleasure, for instance, in recognizing the tessellations of Horatian syntax in these lines addressed to Mr. Brian Howard:

> '. . . what bees

> From the blossoming chestnut
> Or short but shapely dark-haired men
> From the aragonian grape distil, your amber wine,
> Your coffee-coloured honey. . . .'

To read a volume like *Nones* is, in fact, to recognize once again that Mr. Auden is more adroit—almost unscrupulously adroit, perhaps—than anyone else now writing verse; he can be back-slapping, ominous, port-winy, or abstruse, as the occasion demands. Yet even where he does not aim at major statements, there are major themes, above all the Christian theme, in the background; the frivolity is in a sense permissible because the last things, death, judgment, hell, heaven, are always in Mr. Auden's mind, and the worldly hopes men set their hearts upon have been rejected. In the interim, there is nothing against a little harmless enjoyment. Mr. Auden's type of Christianity strikes me, as I have said in an earlier essay, as being a sophisticated Lutheranism. He does not exactly say to us, *Pecca fortiter*, but to avoid despair he has put most of his money on Grace since he knows he is going to fall down on Works. One trouble about such a type of Christianity is that to the outsider it might not seem to make much practical difference:

> 'But that Miss Number in the corner
> Playing hard to get . . .
> I am sorry I'm not sorry . . .
> Make me chaste, Lord, but not yet.'

Humility consists of recognizing one's impurity, but also

provides an excuse for going on being impure:

> 'The Love that rules the sun and stars
> Permits what he forbids.'

I saw the poem from which these lines come first in type-script. Auden had sent it to a Roman Catholic lady, a friend of mine, who was editing a literary magazine and she was embarrassed, much admiring Auden's work generally, but feeling that the allusions to St. Augustine and Dante in that jazzy context were in desperately bad taste; I agreed with her then, but now feel that I was silly and squeamish. It is one of the strengths of Auden's handling of the theme of Grace and Original Sin that he doesn't worry about shocking *les bien pensants*. And when he expresses, as he sometimes does, his more intimate and personal convictions, he can be very moving, as in these lines from one of the most beautiful of all his recent poems, the loveliest poem in *Nones*, 'In Praise of Limestone':

> 'Dear, I know nothing of
> Either, but when I try to imagine a faultless love
> Or the life to come, what I hear is the murmur
> Of underground streams, what I see is a limestone
> landscape.'

Nones was a disconcerting book, but I would say it more often embodied positive values (it is certainly a value that somebody can go on unashamedly enjoying himself today, as Mr. Auden seems to) than *The Age of Anxiety*, where the theme of our awkward *malaise* was all too faithfully mir-rored—Professor Yvor Winter's 'fallacy of imitative form' —in the elaborately maladroit handling. From all sorts of official and respectable points of view, *Nones* was a quietly outrageous little book, and one liked it all the more for that. Deliberately slackening down a little when everybody else is keyed up, taking a humorous view of guilt and anxiety as part of the set-up—'throwing it away', as the actors say of a strong line—is, after all, a defensible human attitude when everybody else is getting shrill, frightened, and nasty. But one's admiration for Auden, from first to last, remains mingled with doubts. From his beginnings, he could be spotted as a potentially major talent: will the moment come, or has it come already, or is it too late for it to come now, when we shall look back on all that he has done and salute a major achievement? Or will he always remain for critics the problem prodigy, the boy who 'might have gone anywhere', but who always, when the obvious goals were pointed out to him, chose to go somewhere else?

Evasive Honesty:
The Poetry of Louis MacNeice

It is probably an error, at least of tact, to bring into an appraisal of a living poet one's impression of his personality as a man. But there is a real sense, as Roy Campbell once remarked about Dylan Thomas and about William Empson, in which good poets are, when you meet them, like their works; they talk and behave in a way you expect them to. And it follows, conversely, that one's impression of the personality of a notable poet may throw some light on his work.

In any case, this personal impression will be a superficial one; I have talked or listened to Mr. MacNeice, at B.B.C. pubs, at his friend William Empson's, at the Institute of Contemporary Arts when I have taken the chair for him, I suppose half a dozen times in the last ten years; and I have seen him often in pubs or at parties without talking to him. He gives a paradoxical impression of at once extreme and genial sociability, and remoteness. His talk flows easily and wittily, and his remarks on people, on ideas, on works of literature come out with an unpremeditated spontaneity. At the same time, one has often the impression that he is thinking at the back of his mind about something else; that the alertness and the sparkle are very much on the surface of his mind, that his *ripostes*, however apt, are almost absent-minded, that a whole elaborate apparatus of thinking and feeling is behind a fire curtain.

Something like this I feel also about his poetry. Nothing

could be more vivid, more frank, more candid, even in a sense more indiscreet than some of his best poetry. All the cards seem to be, even casually, on the table. At the same time, reading his poems one has the feeling sometimes that one has been subjected to an intelligence test; or that his hands, as he deals the cards on the table, move with disquieting speed. To use another metaphor, he is both in life and in poetry a man whose manner, at once sardonic and gay, suggests that he is going, perhaps, to let one in on a disquieting secret about something; one finds that he hasn't. The quality that one is left remembering, the poetic as well as the personal quality, is a kind of evasive honesty. Both the strength and the weakness of his best poems, like the strength and the weakness of the personal impression he makes, rest on the sense that a good deal is held in reserve. What it is, I have only a faint idea; but I have a feeling that he would be a more important poet, if it were less fully held in reserve, yet that the strength even of his slighter poems depends on one's intuition that there is so much of it.

He is a poet, I think, whom it is sensible to discuss in terms of his conscious attitude to life, his moral tastes and preferences, what he feels about the problematical world we are living in, since that mainly, and only occasionally deep personal feelings, seems to be what his poems are about. When his *Collected Poems* came out in 1948, he was the one poet of the 1930s in whose work the years of the Second World War did not seem to have brought about a sharp break. Mr. C. Day Lewis, for instance, in the 1930s was often writing, to my mind rather unsuccessfully, either in a manner diluted from Hopkins or in a manner taken over from Mr. Auden's coarser scoutmaster vein. He was writing about the 'state of the world', rebelling against it. At some period in the 1940s, one noticed that he was writing, much more successfully, in a manner that owed something to Hardy, something to Browning and Clough, and that he was writing about the personal life. As for Mr. Auden himself, he has run through styles almost as Picasso has, he has reminded one of Laura Riding, Byron, Rilke, Yeats, he has perversely forced interesting matter into what seems a strangely inappropriate mould, like the Anglo-Saxon alliterative metre of *The Age of Anxiety*; the very beautiful purely personal manner with its long lines and its florid vocabulary which he has forged for himself in recent poems like 'In Praise of Limestone' is composite, not simple; through the kaleidoscope of successive styles, we now see that he has had a more consistent attitude all along than we thought. Mr. MacNeice's attitude has always been a firmly fixed one, and his style has changed only from a young man's concentration on images to an older man's care for structure. His short poems have been much more often successful than his poems of a certain length (the only two of his longer poems that I admire quite whole-heartedly are two from the middle of the 1930s, *Eclogue for Christmas* and *Death and Two Shepherds*). In this again, he is not exceptional; the number of poems of more than three or four pages which are completely successful in their way is, I suppose, a very small fraction indeed of the number of poems of three or four stanzas which are completely successful in theirs. There is a case, in fact, for thinking of Mr. MacNeice as a poet who has sacrificed an unusual gift for concentration to a misguided ambition to deploy himself at length. But, failures or successes, Mr. MacNeice's poems express from his beginnings to now an attitude to life which is admirably coherent: that of the left-of-centre Liberal, and, morally, that of the man who is out at once to enjoy life and to shoulder his social responsibilities. The typical attitude is one of a sane and humorous, and sturdily self-confident, social concern.

What may put some readers off is that this is so much (polished, learned, alarmingly witty though Mr. MacNeice is) the decent plain man's attitude. Decency, measure, courage, a lack of pretence, a making of the best of good things while they last, and a facing up to bad things when they have to be faced, these are the good insider's virtues. Mr.

Evasive Honesty: the Poetry of Louis MacNeice

MacNeice's standpoint is the standpoint of common sense. He is subtle enough, however, to realize that the standpoint of common sense can be defended only through dialectic and paradox; he does not try to fight the plain man's battles with the plain man's weapons. It is on an acceptance of paradox that his own consistency is based (he was very interested in his youth in the paradoxes of the modern Italian idealists, not only Croce, but Gentile):

> 'Let all these so ephemeral things
> Be somehow permanent like the swallow's tangent wings.'

Thus one of Mr. MacNeice's favourite figures (as he has noted in a lively and perceptive essay on his own work) is oxymoron: the noun and epithet that appear to contradict each other. He might himself be described in that figure as an intolerant liberal or a large-hearted nagger. He wants a world in which all sorts and conditions of men can have their say; but when their say, as so often, proves slack, or insincere, the say of

> 'The self-deceiving realist, the self-seeking
> Altruist, the self-indulgent penitent,'

he loses his patience. It takes all sorts to make a world, certainly, but making is an activity, and the sorts he approves of must really put their shoulders to the wheel, must really creatively work to *make* it. More broadly, to underline yet again this paradoxical consistency, one might that it is Mr. MacNeice's taste for variety, contrast, obstinate individuality—combined with his feeling that all these things, all 'the drunkenness of things being various', must somehow join in the 'general dance'—that unifies his vision of the world. (The problem of the One and the Many, like the problem of Essence and Existence, crops up again and again in Mr. MacNeice's poetry. The swallows are ephemeral existents but the pattern their tangent wings make seems to claim to be an eternal essence. Perhaps the submerged nine-

tenths, both of his poetry and his personality, is a speculative
metaphysician, of an unfashionably ambitious sort).

The danger of Mr. MacNeice's liberal, humanistic attitude, so admirable in so many ways in itself, is that it is too
often, especially in his longer poems, liable to slacken down
into mere moralizing. Take such a passage as this:

> '. . . it is our privilege—
> Our paradox—to recognize the insoluble
> And going up with an outstretched hand salute it.'

One agrees, of course, at some though not at all levels, with
what is being said (one does not agree, but this is certainly
not an application Mr. MacNeice will have had in mind,
that one should greet the apparently insoluble political
divisions of our time, as Browning greeted the Unseen,
with a cheer). One is unhappy about the way of saying. Is
not the tone of voice, too flat in one sense, and too stretched
in another, the orator's tone rather than the poet's? When,
in a long, ambitious poem, full of such moralistic passages,
I come for instance on this,

> 'The paradox of the sentimentalist
> Insisting on clinging to what he insists is gone,'

I do feel, I confess, a sense of relief. The tone is right, there,
these two lines are tight, witty, hit straight home. The
moral *fact* is presented, the moral judgment is left (as I think
it should be) to the reader.

Readers of that collected volume of 1948 often found
themselves, I imagine, like myself, lingering a little wistfully over the dash, vividness, and gaiety of the earlier
poems. But the later poems also deserved careful reading.
Mr. MacNeice was tired, as he explained in a prose piece
written about that time, of 'journalism', and tired of
'tourism', tired of the poem as a mere footnote to experience; he aimed now at making all the parts of a poem fit
coherently together, even if that involved the sacrifice of
the brilliant inorganic image and the witty irrelevant sally.

'Thus the lines', he wrote, 'that I am especially proud of in my last book are such lines as these (of the aftermath of war in England):

> "The joker that could have been at any moment death
> Has been withdrawn, the cards are what they say
> And none is wild . . ."

or (of a tart):

> "Mascara scrawls a gloss on a torn leaf"

(a line which it took me a long time to find).' Both passages are essentially exploitations of the poetic pun. A card in a gambling game that can become any other card is called 'wild'; the joker, which is not really a proper member of the pack, is often used in this way as a 'wild' card. But the wider connotations of death as a cruel practical joker, or as a wild beast in the jungle waiting to spring on one, emotionally reinforce what might have been a mere piece of knowingness. The second pun, I think, is even subtler. Mascara scrawls either a sheen on a torn piece of foliage (the tart's sad eyelid shaped like a leaf) or a commentary on a torn page (from a diary say, a record of illicit self-indulgence to be destroyed). And the tart herself is like a leaf torn from the living tree of life, and the false gloss of the mascara on her eyelid is a commentary on her fate. Such Empsonian economies certainly demanded harder work from Mr. MacNeice's readers than his old pieces of 'tourism',

> '. . . impending thunder
> With an indigo sky and the garden hushed except for
> The treetops moving,'

or his old pieces of 'journalism', his shrewd remarks in passing,

> '. . . that a monologue
> Is the death of language and that a single lion
> Is less himself, or alive, than a dog and another dog.'

Evasive Honesty: the Poetry of Louis MacNeice

The danger, however, that Mr. MacNeice at the end of the 1940s seemed to be facing was that of sometimes relapsing —as a relaxation from the strain of much close writing and as a sop to his sense of moral urgency—into the very 'monologue' which in these lines he deplores. How far, in the last ten years, has he surmounted that danger?

Perhaps he did not wholly surmount it. In 1952, he brought out *Ten Burnt Offerings*, a set of fairly longish poems which had been originally conceived for radio (they took about fifteen minutes each to broadcast). In that book, one had a sense of an inner flagging battling with an obstinate ambition. The relevance of the themes of these ten poems, both to common problems of our day and to what one took to be Mr. MacNeice's personal predicaments, seemed real but oddly oblique. The themes of the poems were themes that might have suited a prose essay: the paradox of Elizabethan culture, the dung and the flower: the harsh roots of modern ethics in Greek and Hebrew guilt and sacrifice: Ulysses and Jacob as twin competing symbols of searching and driven man: Byron as the romantic for whom the conscious pursuit of liberty becomes the subconscious pursuit of death. Such a range of topics was impressive; but it had a touch about it, also, of the Third Programme Producer with his fatigued fertility in 'new approaches'. The language showed, sometimes, that fatigue. When Mr. MacNeice wrote about the Elizabethans,

> 'Courtier with the knife behind the smile, ecclesiastic
> With faggots in his eyes,'

it was impossible to forget how much more freshly they said the same sort of thing about themselves:

> 'Say to the Court it glows
>   And shines like rotten wood;
> Say to the Church it shows
>   What's good and doth no good.'

A wider reach can imply a shallower local penetration.

As if aware of the dangers of a stretched thinness, Mr.
MacNeice was fecund in metaphor:

> 'because your laugh
> Is Catherine wheels and dolphins, because Rejoice
> Is etched upon your eyes, because the chaff
> Of dead wit flies before you, and the froth
> Of false convention with it. . . .'

Nothing could be gayer than the 'Catherine wheels and
dolphins'. But were the more painful connotations of
'etched' (a needle on the iris?) intended or relevant. Are
'chaff' and 'froth', themselves examples of conventional
dead metaphor, appropriate because 'dead wit' and 'false
convention' are what they refer to—but, even if so, is there
not still an unpleasant though faint clash between the 'froth
of false convention' and the real and beautiful sea-froth
churned up, three lines back, by 'dolphins'? The ornamentation, in fact, in this book had often the air not of emerging
spontaneously from the theme, but of being trailed over it,
like roses over a trellis. A trellis, to be sure, would be
nothing without roses, but the gaunter outlines of Mr.
MacNeice's thought, often half-hidden here, were interesting in themselves. His language was best where it was
barest: as in the section on Byron in Lowland Scots,

> 'I maun gang my lane to wed my hurt,
> I maun gang my lane to Hades,

or the aside about history,

> '. . . the port so loved
> By Themistocles, great patriot and statesman,
> Great traitor five years on,'

or the statement of the poet's own predicament:

> 'This middle stretch
> Of life is bad for poets; a sombre view
> Where neither works nor days look innocent
> And both seem now too many, now too few.'

Even in these fine lines, there was something to question about the texture. 'A sombre view of the situation' is a worn politician's phrase; was it being accepted with a sort of fatigue, or alluded to with a sort of irony? Bareness, at least, seemed in the early 1950s to be Mr. MacNeice's growing-point: his danger, that facility of the practised writer which is so very different from spontaneity—the temptation to write because one can, not because one must.

In *Autumn Sequel*, which came out in 1954, it seems to me that he yielded almost fully to that temptation. Certainly in calling these twenty-six Cantos of that very intractable metre in English, *terza rima*, 'a rhetorical poem', Mr. Mac-Neice rather cunningly anticipated one's own verdict, that the poem was a triumph not only of skill but of determination. Of course, for Mr. MacNeice 'rhetoric' is not, as for Sir Herbert Read, the natural enemy of poetry, but, in the traditional sense of the word, the art of eloquent and persuasive writing, or, as for Hopkins, 'the common teachable element in poetry'. *Autumn Sequel* was partly an exercise, a deliberate display of skill. And it was an exercise written with a particular medium in view (though it had not, in fact, been commissioned in advance by that medium). The bulk of the poem was, in fact, broadcast on the Third Programme before it was published, and a passage from the fourth Canto, about the dangers and rewards of radio for the creative writer, is both an example of the tone of the poem at its most effective and partly a definition of that tone:

> '. . . as Harrap said
> Suggesting I might make an air-borne bard
> (Who spoke in parentheses and now is dead),
> "On the one hand—as a matter of fact I should
> Say on the first hand—there is daily bread,
> At least I assume there is, to be made good
> If good is the right expression; on the other
> Or one of the other hands there is much dead wood

187

On the air in a manner of speaking which tends to
  smother
What spark you start with; nevertheless, although
Frustration is endemic (take my brother,
He simply thinks me mad to bother so
With people by the million) nevertheless
Our work is aimed at one at a time, you know. . . ." '

Throughout the poem Mr. MacNeice was at his best in the
recording, as there, of conversation, Harrap's mannerisms of
hesitation and deviousness, partly *mere* mannerisms, partly a
technique for checking 'stock responses' in himself, are
caught more fully than either a novelist or a realistic prose
dramatist could afford to catch them. Mr. MacNeice makes
us listen for the sake of listening, listen for the essential
quality of something, instead of listening to see what comes
next.

Harrap's remarks also suggest why *Autumn Sequel* makes
a paradoxical, and in the end rather disturbing and unsatis-
fying, combined impression of impersonality and intimacy.
A poem written for the ear—and though the poem was not
commissioned in advance, it cannot have come as a very
great surprise to Mr. MacNeice that the Third Programme
should decide to broadcast it—must take every trick as it
comes and some tricks, the less obvious ones, two or three
times over. It must be painted in poster-colours. Its visual
images should have the punch and the concentrated exaggeration of good descriptive journalism. Its shifts from one
topic to another must be as smooth as a change of gears. Its
moral reflections must be made explicit, must be hammered
in, even at the cost of stridency. Its human characters must
establish themselves at once in clear outline even at the cost
of over-simplification and flattening out. All the goods
must be in the shop-window; for the listener, with no text
in front of him to go back over and puzzle about has not,
even ideally, access to the rest of the shop. Technically,
Autumn Sequel is exactly what a long poem conceived

primarily in terms of radio ought to be. Criticisms of it, therefore, must fundamentally be criticisms of the limitations of radio as a primary medium for poetry. The paradoxical 'limiting judgment' about *Autumn Sequel* is that the more Mr. MacNeice apparently succeeds in taking us into his confidence, the more we admire his public skill in 'putting himself over'. The poet throughout, even and perhaps especially at his moments of most extreme genial informality, has been on parade. *Autumn Sequel* was not only, as Mr. MacNeice himself rightly commented, less 'occasional' than its predecessor of the late 1930s, *Autumn Journal*; it was also much less the poetic equivalent of a journal, like Amiel's, written primarily for the writer's own eyes.

The poem's nearest traditional equivalents, perhaps, were those poems of the late eighteenth and early nineteenth centuries which mingled moral reflections, natural descriptions, and sketches of human character in a blank verse subdued to the tone of polite conversation, like *The Task* or *The Excursion*. *Autumn Sequel* is, in a slightly brittle way, much *brighter* reading than such poems. The easy amble of pedestrian blank verse does not keep many modern readers alert; and the very difficulty of *terza rima*, and its apparent unsuitability for a sustained conversational use enable Mr. MacNeice to keep us waiting restlessly for the next rhyme, the next glide at a tangent to a new topic. Yet perhaps readers will not return to *Autumn Sequel* as they find themselves returning even to the flatter patches of Cowper or Wordsworth. Everything, here, is on the surface. No nail is not hit on the head; and what we miss—in spite of what I have said earlier about my feeling that there is a great bulk of Mr. MacNeice that is permanently submerged, that never surfaces in poetry—is the sense of an area of unused resource outside the poem. (Of unused *conscious* resource: that may explain my apparent contradiction of myself, for it is the unconscious sources, probably, that Mr. MacNeice is always scary of tapping.) This, for all its abundant and sometimes too facile archetypal imagery, the sinister Parrot

189

gabbling the cult of flux, the Garden, the Quest, the mountain which must be climbed 'because it is there', is above
all a poetry of consciousness, as also of an admirable social
conscientiousness. It lacks the beauty of necessity.

A few short quotations may illustrate, in a more particularized fashion, some of the poem's flaws and felicities.
Mr. MacNeice is at his best a witty writer, but his wit can
lapse into a pointless allusive facetiousness:

'Oxford in October
Seems all dead stone (which here hath many a Fellow. . . .'

'Stone dead hath no fellow': our memories are jogged
flatteringly, but then we reflect that 'stone dead' does not
mean 'dead stone' and that the impeachment of the Earl of
Strafford has nothing really, at all, to do with what Mr.
MacNeice is talking about. A similar fault is a recurrent
facile smartness. Visiting Bath, Mr. MacNeice tells us at
length that he does not like the eighteenth century:

'Accomplishments were in, enthusiasm out,
Although to our mind perhaps it seems a pity,
That prose and reason ran to fat and gout. . . .'

A deeper and today a more usual observation would be that
in its greatest writers, in Swift, in Pope, in Gray, in Cowper,
in Johnson, the prose and reason ran to spleen, melancholia,
or actual madness; Mr. MacNeice is attacking an Austin
Dobson view of the eighteenth century which nobody now
holds.

Here and there also in the descriptive passages of *Autumn
Sequel* one feels that Mr. MacNeice is very much the Third
Programme feature-writer, mugging up the background in
advance, and determined to discover something quaint.
But more usually Mr. MacNeice is at his best in the
descriptive passages, as here, on Oxford stone:

'. . . I roll on
Past walls of broken biscuit, golden gloss,

> Porridge or crumbling shortbread or burnt scone,
> Puma, mouldy elephant, Persian lamb. . . .'

I have noted already his excellence in the recording of conversation. Some passages expressing personal feeling, notably those on the character, death and funeral of the poet
Gwylim (an archetypal joyous maker, modelled, with the
warts rather carefully left out, on Dylan Thomas) are
genuinely moving, though, because Mr. MacNeice is shy
about the direct expression of feeling, when he does express
it directly he often seems just on the verge of becoming
sentimental. One respects also the passages of moral exhor-
tation, on the importance of being and making, of struggling and giving and loving, of not yielding to drift. The
whole poem is extremely readable, but it is in these personal and moral passages that one gets farthest way from the
sense of something extremely skilful, but also too consciously and too wilfully 'contrived'.

Both *Ten Burnt Offerings* and *Autumn Sequel* gave me,
then, the sense that a fine talent was forcing itself. I read
with far more genuine pleasure Mr. MacNeice's most recent
volume, *Visitations*, in which he seemed to have got back
for the first time in ten years or so the bite that he had in
the 1930s; and in which he got away also from the snare of
the blown-up, big poem, of a length suitable for broadcasting. In these new short poems or sequences of short
poems he had freed himself from the twin temptations of
moralizing at the drop of a hat, and of ad-libbing. His mood,
from the beginning of the book, was agreeably cantanker-
ous (it is very difficult to discuss him, except in oxymorons!):

> 'Why hold that poets are so sensitive?
> A thickskinned grasping lot who filch and eavesdrop. . . .'

He attacked snooty reviewers (or the snooty reviewer in
himself):

> 'Yet the cold voice chops and sniggers,
> Prosing on, maintains the thread

Is broken and the phoenix fled,
Youth and poetry departed.

Acid and ignorant voice, desist.
Against your lies the skies bear witness. . . .'

It is time, perhaps, that I did stop prosing on about him, that my own acid and perhaps ignorant voice did desist. I have said already, I think, all the general things I want to say. I should say finally that one would not have registered so sharply the degree of one's dissatisfaction with some of Mr. MacNeice's recent poetry unless one had a very high respect for, and therefore made very exacting demands on, the range and flexibility of his art and the integrity and scope of his mind. He has tried, with a strain of conscious effort, to make himself into the wrong sort of major poet. I think that if he had only waited a little more patiently for the pressure to gather, for the poem to force itself upon him, he might have been a major poet of the right sort. He has brought intelligence and poetry together; but the intelligence has too often seemed something superadded to the poem, rather than something used up in its proper shaping.

'Not Wrongly Moved...'
(William Empson)

———————————✵———————————

Towards the end of Mr. William Empson's long expected, and long delayed, *Collected Poems* there is a short and moving poem called 'Let it Go'. It is one of the only three poems he wrote during the Second World War, when he was very busy at the Far Eastern Section of the B.B.C.

'It is this deep blankness is the real thing strange.
    The more things happen to you the more you can't
    Tell or remember even what they were.
The contradictions cover such a range.
The talk would talk and go so far aslant.
    You don't want madhouse and the whole thing there.'

From these six lines, a critic, new to Mr. Empson's work, and starting this collection of poems—like dishonest readers of detective stories—at the end instead of the beginning, might deduce a great deal about the poet's art and temperament and moral attitudes.

In Mr. Empson's tone and diction, such a critic might first notice an apparent casualness. The six lines at first sound like a few touching but slightly disjointed remarks flung out by a very tired man in conversation. Yet, having had that impression, he may then notice that they are a formal whole; the metre is regular, the rhyme-scheme strict, the rhymes themselves exact. And he will notice also that Mr. Empson, though here imitating the effect of conversation, is by no means slavishly bound by a conversa-

N   193

tional word-order. He inverts that here twice, and in both cases for rhetorical emphasis:

'It is this deep blankness is the real thing *strange*. . . .'

'Tell or remember *even* what they were. . . .'

The prose order would be 'the real strange thing' and 'even remember'; though, in fact, the first of these two lines is, like many of Mr. Empson's lines, covertly elliptical—it opens out as, 'It is this deep blankness (that) is the real thing (that is) strange.'

The next thing our critic with a fresh eye might notice is that the throw-away mannerism, the artifice of the off-hand statement, of the lucky stray shot, conceals—or rather holds down, and reveals with polite indirectness—an enormous pressure of inner disturbance. The phrase 'deep blankness' points to the state which psychologists call protective emotional fatigue; but points to it, unexpectedly, with gratitude. And the phrase 'madhouse and the whole thing there' is similarly an eloquently reticent paraphrase for what psychologists call 'total recall'. The poem is about deciding not to go mad, or about being grateful to Nature for her odd, her sometimes rather flat and depressing ways of stopping us from going mad. The use of the word 'madhouse' instead of 'madness', which would have been the more obvious choice, contributes to the peculiar tone of pragmatic irony. Poets can talk about their 'madness' rather smugly, remembering Plato's theory of inspiration or Dryden's:

'Great Wits are sure to Madness near alli'd
And thin Partitions do their Bounds divide. . . .'

Even if these associations are not present, the word 'madness' has a ring of awe and pity. But 'madhouse' is a brutal word (it has not even the remoteness of 'asylum' or the gentility of 'mental hospital'). Mr. Empson's use of 'madhouse' reminds us that it is weak and inept to go mad if you

'Not wrongly moved. . .' (William Empson)

do not have to; you get shut up and your friends, however kind they are, tend to feel superior. 'The whole thing there,' if we compare it with 'total recall', has the same flavour of tart common sense. A 'total recall' suggests an experience which might be terrific but would also be awe-inspiring: 'the whole thing there' sharply reminds us that emotional problems, like all problems, should be tackled piecemeal. Though it deals with a mood of apathy, the poem does not express such a mood. It expresses a firmness of moral decision. And in an odd way the poet's fatigue bears witness to his energy, and his deliberate façade of blankness to the range of his experience and the power of his passions. There are clues, here, that will help us with much more complex poems. When Mr. Empson writes in 'Ignorance of Death',

> 'Otherwise I feel very blank upon this topic,
> And think that though important, and proper
> for anyone to bring up,
> It is one that most people should be prepared
> to be blank upon,'

only a fool would take this as an expression of complacency, obtuseness, or indifference. And when, discussing the poetic schools of the 1930s, he writes jauntily in 'Autumn on Nan-Yueh':

> 'Verse has been lectured to a treat
> Against Escape and being blah.
> It struck me trying not to fly
> Let them escape a bit too far,'

he might be having a dig at some of his young poetic disciples of our own decade.

Many young poets have in the past five years or so, in this country, been profoundly influenced, and rightly so, by an admiration for what could, most broadly, be called Mr. Empson's 'tone of voice': its assurance, its moderation, its sanity. But some of the verse produced by this discipleship has been, to say the least, prosy. Mr. Empson is a master of

195

the line that makes its point by not making it, by a sort of terse reticence, the line like,

'The contradictions cover such a range . . .'

'It seemed the best thing to be up and go . . .'

'There is not much else that we dare to praise . . .'

but, when he wants to, of something that Matthew Arnold himself would recognize as 'the grand style';

'Matter includes what must matter enclose,
Its consequent space, the glass firmament's air-holes.
Heaven's but an attribute of her seven rainbows.
It is Styx coerces and not Hell controls.'

His flat manner has been easier to learn than his grand manner; and in a conversation with some young poets about Matthew Arnold's 'touchstones', Mr. Empson, indeed, once himself suggested that 'the grand style' was a thing most good poets could lay on for a line or two when it was wanted, and by itself no sure test of a poet's rank. Yet his own flatness,

'Blame it upon the beer
I have mislaid the torment and the fear,'

gains its authority from the possibility of the grand style always in the background. His love of sanity springs not from phlegm but from a passion, obstinately sustained in 'a mad world'. His advice to us to be sensible and pragmatic springs from a deep awareness of the attraction of various kinds of emotional excess. When his young disciples have endured as sturdily as he has the ravages of time and the contradictory tugs of temperament they may begin at last to speak to us, in his tones, with something of his authority.

Mr. Empson is proverbially a 'difficult' poet. He has written elaborate notes to many of his own poems; and his best poems do deserve to be considered individually, and in detail. In a short, general survey of his poetic achievement, like this, however, the detailed examination of individual poems would be out of place. What may be more humbly useful, and what is perhaps new, is to sketch the kind of moral framework within which, in the broadest meaning of the phrase, Mr. Empson's poems 'make sense'; to consider them as the expression of a coherent attitude to life. Mr. Empson is a poet who has a religious temperament, a scientific world view, the attitude to politics of a traditional English liberal of the best kind, a constitutional melancholy and a robust good-humour, a sardonic wit, a gift for expressing the diffidence and passion of romantic personal attachments, a belief in pleasure, a scepticism about abstract systems, and a sharply practical impatience with anything he considers cant. The total complex of his attitudes has more in common with that of the attitudes of an essayist like, say, Montaigne than with that of most other poets. Many subjects have 'poetic' interest for him that to other writers would appear matters for prose disquisitions. He resembles the metaphysical poets (the greatest single ancestral influence on his work has been the poetry of Donne) in his power to fuse the activities of 'thinking' and 'feeling', in his power of finding or making connexions between apparently disparate objects and themes, and also in not being (in the broader sense of the word, as it is used by philosophers rather than literary historians) in the least 'metaphysical'. It has often been pointed out, recently, that a poet like Spenser, who is not metaphysical in the literary historian's sense, has something like a coherent metaphysics (or a coherent traditional philosophy), whereas a poet like Donne has not. Mr. Empson's attitude towards philosophy in the strict sense of the word is one of scepticism, sometimes good-humoured and sometimes impatient:

'Two mirrors with Infinity to dine
Drink him below the table when they please.
Adam and Eve still breed their dotted line,
Repeated incest, a plain series.
Their trick is all philosophers' disease.'

197

'Not wrongly moved. . .' (William Empson)

Mr. Empson's note to this is: 'Two mirrors have any number of reflections (the self-conscious mind): a dotted line is used for "and so on". The mind makes a system by inbreeding from a few fixed ideas.' Like one of his intellectual masters, Dr. Richards, Mr. Empson has a profound distrust both of 'systems' and of 'fixed ideas'.

The philosophical attitude has its place, in the scale of human interests, somewhere between the religious attitude and the practical attitude; and both men of religious genius and men of practical genius have often shown an impatience, something like Mr. Empson's, with philosophy. What is profoundest in Mr. Empson's religious attitude is expressed, more compactly than anywhere in his poems, in the quotation at the beginning of them from the Buddhistic 'Fire Sermon':

'When he is weary of these things, he becomes empty of desire. When he is empty of desire, he becomes free. When he is free he knows that he is free, that rebirth is at an end, that virtue is accomplished, that duty is done, and that there is no more returning to the world; thus he knows.'

Mr. Empson's practical attitude, on the other hand, is perhaps expressed more compactly than elsewhere in the masque 'The Birth of Steel' (with additions by other hands) which he wrote for performance before the Queen when she visited Sheffield University. The final choruses, with their gaily plebian rhymes, glorify that industrial revolution which is the hard gritty core round which British greatness, art, culture, manners and all the rest of it must now be built:

> 'MEN: Puddling iron, casting iron,
>   Is the work of this environ;
>   And it suits the British lion
>   Puddling iron.
> WOMEN: Blending steel, rolling steel,
>   That's the way to get a meal,
>   And we're right ahead of the field,
>   Blending steel. . . .'

'Not wrongly moved. . .' (William Empson)

The reader who finds it hard to reconcile the moods which these two quotations evoke should note perhaps in the extract from 'The Fire Sermon' the remarks about duty— 'that virtue is accomplished, that duty is done'. He might remember also Santayana's phrase about 'the long way round to Nirvana'. There certainly does seem to be a sense in which, for Mr. Empson as for the Buddhists, all existence not only involves suffering but *is* suffering. But, like the Buddhists, also, he refuses to believe that there is any short cut away from suffering. We must see that 'duty is done'. And, apart from its constitutional melancholy, there is perhaps in Mr. Empson's temperament something 'mere English', unaffected by Eastern profundities; a Yorkshire doggedness, a plain man's common sense, a cheerfulness that keeps breaking in.

The aristocratic tradition and the Christian tradition have both, at times, attracted him:

'We could once carry anarchy, when we ran
Christ and the magnificent milord
As rival pets; the thing is, if we still can
Lacking either.'

There are times also when he seems to feel that any religious attitude is at best a piece of gallant make-belief in a universe neither hostile nor friendly but neutral, in which man is an isolated creature. In a fine early poem, 'The Last Pain', he solemnly and eloquently recommends such make-belief, the postulating and sustaining, as objective, of values that one knows in one's heart not to be objective:

'Feign then what's by a decent tact believed
And act that state is only so conceived,
  And build an edifice of form
  For house where phantoms may keep warm.

Imagine, then, by miracle, with me,
(Ambiguous gifts, as what gods give must be)

'Not wrongly moved. . .' (William Empson)

What could not possibly be there,
And learn a style from a despair.'

Mr. Empson's later statement of this position in 'Your Teeth are Ivory Castles' is more complex. There is a hint that something, after all, might 'possibly be there'; and a far greater liberality about the range of attitudes which, if consistently adhered to, might make possible some sort of 'good life':

'though you
Look through the very corners of your eyes
Still you will find no star behind the blue;

This gives no scope for trickwork. He who tries
Talk must always plot and then sustain,
Talk to himself until the star replies,

Or in despair that it could speak again
Assume what answers any wits have found
In evening dress on rafts upon the main,

Not therefore uneventful, or soon drowned.'

Among a number of younger critics there is a doctrine current that Mr. Empson's best poems are half a dozen of his early ones, those in which he makes a magnificent Donne-like use of metaphors and images from mathematical physics and from natural history; it seems to me that he is a consistently good poet, though, of course, not always at the top of his form; and that what his later poems lose through a greater relaxation or expansiveness (some of them, like 'Autumn on Nan-Yueh', are positively chatty), they gain through a wider range of reference, a deeper warmth, a more direct and contemporary human appeal. It is unfashionable to deal with a contemporary poet, as Mr. Empson has been dealt with here, in terms of his 'ideas', even in terms of his 'message'; yet it seemed justifiable in the case of a poet whose mind is so original and distinguished, whose preoccupations are, basically, those of so many thoughtful and sensitive men of our time. The passages already quoted have illustrated the assurance but perhaps not the range of his verbal art. He can write like Pope, and as well as Pope:

> 'Still stand uncalled-on her soul's appanage;
> Much social detail whose successor fades,
> Wit used to run a house and to play Bridge,
> And tragic fervour to dismiss her maids.'

He can write with an intense lyrical pathos,

> 'But oh
> The lovely balcony is lost
> Just as the mountains take the snow.'

His talent is, as he himself once said in a broadcast, perhaps a 'narrow' one; it is also deep.

A Poetry of Search
(Stephen Spender)

———————————— ❄ ————————————

'A poet may be divinely gifted with a lucid and intense
and purposive intellect; he may be clumsy and slow; that
does not matter, what matters is integrity of purpose and
the ability to maintain the purpose without losing oneself.
Myself, I am scarcely capable of immediate concentration
in poetry. My mind is not clear, my will is weak, I suffer
from an excess of ideas and a weak sense of form. For every
poem that I begin to write, I think of at least ten which I
do not write down at all. . . .'

A poet, if he can strike the right balance between modesty
and candour, between due humility and proper pride, is
sometimes his own profoundest critic. Mr. Stephen
Spender's *Collected Poems* should be read not only along with
the poet's concise and charming introduction, but along
with his more elaborate essay, from which the above quotation is taken. 'The Making of a Poem', published in *Partisan
Review* in 1946. Mr. Spender there describes the patient
compositional tactics of an intuitive poet of the slow intro-
vert type. He describes how he is always given something
to start with (is given more than he can use, endless sketches
and ideas in notebooks) and how, having chosen among
many possible beginnings, he works forward from the
given element in a poem, not so much by a logical process
as by a series of patient gropings, exploring and retreating
from blind alleys, towards the completed poem, 'the final
idea'. This groping forward, for Mr. Spender, is partly a
matter of reviving, around two or three given lines, or dis-

connected sets of lines which he feels to be potentially parts of the same poem, or perhaps sometimes round a single phrase, past experiences with all their emotional associations. Thus, for Mr. Spender, the Muses are the daughters of Memory, Imagination is a function of Memory, and he would not agree with Landor that 'Memory is not a Muse'.

'It is perhaps true [he writes] to say that memory is the faculty of poetry, because the imagination is itself an exercise of memory. And our ability to imagine is our ability to remember what we have already once experienced and to apply it to some different situation. . . . Here I can detect my own greatest weakness. My memory is defective and self-centred.'

Poets, Mr. Spender goes on to say, are men not saintly (they have not renounced ambition) but men 'ambitious to be accepted for what they ultimately are as revealed . . . in their poetry. . . .' Since there can be no cheating, the poet, like the saint, stands in all his works before the bar of a perpetual day of judgment. But the poet is like the saint at least in that he has renounced 'the life of "action" which . . . is in fact a selective, even a negative kind of life.'

It is easy to see in the light of such statements why, when Mr. Spender's poems first appeared, they were hailed with such enthusiasm by critics like Sir Herbert Read who look on the Romantic movement as the last great unifying force in European literature. Like the great romantics, Mr. Spender sees the poet as a man dedicated, set apart. We are reminded, not indeed of Coleridge's transcendantalism, but of Keats on 'negative capability', and of Wordsworth on 'emotion recollected in tranquillity', on the life-enhancing quality of certain remembered 'spots of time' and on the association of ideas. When Mr. Spender says, 'There is nothing we imagine which we do not already know,' we could, indeed, give the remark a Coleridgian or Platonic turn, but we may be pretty sure he himself does not intend to give it such a turn. He is not what he himself calls a 'visionary' poet, like Blake or Coleridge, or like Rimbaud, or Rilke, or Yeats. His feet are on the ground. No myth, or hunger for myth, obsesses him. He is a sensitive agnostic, whose soul indeed might be described as naturally religious or even *naturaliter Christiana*—few living poets have such a spontaneous and patient sympathy even with uncomely weakness and even with deserved suffering—but who feels it would be intellectually dishonest to accept the consolations of faith. Even on a secular level Mr. Spender is not a man to be contained by rigidities. If his poems of the Spanish civil war annoyed Mr. Roy Campbell, they also annoyed Communists, because of their tenderness towards cowards and deserters, their refusal to strike heroic attitudes, or to regard war, even for a cause assumed to be just, as anything but the most horrible necessity. Mr. Spender's deep sympathy in these poems is with the individual who wishes, however self-centredly, to escape.

It is, in fact, this 'self-centredness' which Mr. Spender rightly regards as in some ways a weakness of his that also gives him his peculiar uncomfortable honesty; and it is his deepest link with those masters of lyrical or symbolic autobiography, the great romantic poets. Mr. Auden, in one of the introductions to the admirable anthology, *Poets of the English Language*, which he edited along with Professor Norman Holmes Pearson, has the following acute remarks on the ethos of the romantic poet:

'The divine element in man is now held to be neither power nor free-will nor reason, but self-consciousness. Like God and unlike the rest of nature, man can say "I": his ego stands over against his self, which to the ego is a part of nature. In this self he can see possibilities; he can imagine it and all things being other than they are; he runs ahead of himself; he foresees his death.'

This passage might almost be a comentary on one of the most penetrating of Mr. Spender's early poems:

'An "I" can never be a great man.
This known great one has weakness

A Poetry of Search (Stephen Spender)

To friends is most remarkable for weakness:
His ill-temper at meals, of being contradicted,
His only real pleasure fishing in ponds,
His only real wish—forgetting.

To advance from friends to the composite self,
Central "I" is surrounded by "I eating",
"I loving", "I angry", "I excreting",
And the great "I" planted in him
Has nothing to do with all these,

Can never claim its true place
Resting in the forehead, and calm in his gaze.
The great "I" is an unfortunate intruder
Quarrelling with "I tiring" and "I sleeping",
And all those other "I's" who long for "We dying".

No poet is totally unaffected by the climate of his age, and the tone of this poem, its irony and the flatness of its pessimism, would have puzzled the great romantics. There is a deep inherited wish in Mr. Spender to yield to the romantic afflatus; there is also a strong contemporary impulse to question it and check it. He knows that, for the taste of the age, his emotions can be triggered off too easily. 'The Pylons' and 'The Funeral', two poems which he reprints with reluctance in this collection, 'for the record', are instances of how dangerously in Mr. Spender's work the platform speaker, shy and hesitant and at a certain level very 'sincere', but fatally responsive to the mood of his audience, can take over from the poet. Aware of this danger, Mr. Spender lets his finger hover very delicately indeed round the trigger. The typical quality of his style, arising from this paradoxical combination of a desire to 'let himself go' and a fear of 'letting himself go' is a stumbling eloquence or a sweeping gesture suddenly arrested; or sometimes, starting off in a mood of careful constriction, he works rather flatly or awkwardly towards a sudden concentration

—a concentration the more striking because of the painful effort with which it has been arrived at. It might be said that, unlike the great romantics, Mr. Spender is 'self-conscious', in the colloquial sense, *about* his self-consciousness. It remains true that his poetry, like theirs, is an exploration of the possibilities of the self and a search for the 'unfortunate intruder', 'the great "I" ' that transcends these.

It is this centring of the poetic process on the quest for the transcendental ego—or for the inner perspective, a vanishing one, from which everything can be understood and forgiven—that explains aspects of Mr. Spender's work that have exasperated more robust or perhaps more simple-minded critics. He often shows deep sympathy towards characters, actions, or feelings not in themselves admirable; towards, in the Spanish civil war poems, the shirker rather than the fighter; towards, in the poems grouped in this volume under the theme of 'love and separation', the traditionally ridiculous figure of the cuckold rather than the traditionally attractive figure of the Don Juan; towards jealous, neurotic, and inadequate rather than towards simply happy lovers; towards that kind of liberalism commonly described as muddled or as wanting to have its cake and eat it too rather than towards coherent and consistent attitudes like those of the Communist, the Conservative, or the Pacifist; towards moods of hysteria rather than towards states of balance; towards people who become symbolically significant after they are dead rather than towards people who fulfil themselves while living; towards self-pity rather than stoicism, weakness rather than strength, failure rather than success. Yet critics, like Mr. Roy Campbell or Mr. Peter Russell, who have been infuriated by what they consider the unvirility of such attitudes, ought to ask themselves whether they are not in fact traditionally Christian attitudes—of humility about one's own weakness and charity for the weaknesses of others; and whether 'tougher', more 'manly' attitudes, of a Nietzschean sort, may not have in them something of vulgar kowtowing to strength, crude male self-gratulation, worship of success, 'the bitch goddess'.

Let us admit, however, that the greatest poetry is heroic, and that there was sense in what Yeats said about passive suffering not being a theme for poetry. The answer, on Mr. Spender's behalf, would be that suffering is an inescapable feature of our time and that in a persistent active sympathy with suffering, a refusal to withdraw from imaginative participation in it, there *is* something heroic. It would be easy, of course, in Mr. Spender's case as in Byron's, to jeer at 'the pageant of his bleeding heart'; but it is a gentle heart, and the age has given it something to bleed for. It may at times, to be sure, bleed a little too easily, and we may wonder whether the bleeding really hurts. Mr. Spender's feelings are near the surface, and he is often a little ashamed that they are so near the surface. He might, perhaps, have integrated his feelings more fully if he had not been born in the land of the straight bat, the jolly good show, and the stiff upper-lip; if he had belonged to some country like Spain or Italy or Germany where the direct expression of emotion is not thought slightly shameful, and where it is not obligatory for poets to have 'a sense of humour'. Yet, as has been hinted above, the real answer to those who object to the emphasis in Mr. Spender's poems on weakness —on 'I eating', 'I tiring', 'I sleeping'—is that these, our vulnerabilities, belong for him to the self of possibilities, they are not ultimately real, they are transcended by the 'central ""'. And the search for that, the playing of the cards through weakness up to strength, is his own special and distinctive courage as a poet. On a more technical level, of course, a similar remark might be made about Mr. Spender's verse craftsmanship. It is his consciousness of his 'weak sense of form'—and uncertain taste for language— that makes him work so hard on his poems, that makes him doubt whether even anthology pieces are quite 'finished'.

Mr. Louis MacNeice once described Mr. Spender as a poet patiently pressing *clichés* into poetic shape with steady and powerful hands. His syntax does, indeed, often seem either flat or awkward, his diction threadbare; and side by side with this drabness or clumsiness there goes a basic element of *cliché* of another sort, an eloquence that is real, but too like the eloquence of an orator. Yet, out of fumblings, out of over-emphatic gestures, the great white bird of poetry suddenly takes wing:

> 'Not palaces, an era's crown,
> Where the mind dwells, intrigues, rests;
> Architectural gold-leaved flower
> From people ordered like a single mind,
> I sing. This only what I tell:
> It is too late for rare accumulation,
> For family pride, for beauty's filtered dusts;
> I say, stamping the words with emphasis,
> Drink from here energy and only energy,
> As from the electric charge of a battery,
> To will this Time's change.
> *Eye, gazelle, delicate wanderer,*
> *Drinker of horizon's fluid line. . . .'*

With the two lines italicized, an extraordinary change of quality or dimension seems to come over the early poem of which this is the onset. The first eleven lines are, indeed, skilful, vigorous, and persuasive rhetoric; the line,

> 'Drink from here energy and only energy,'

is a particularly memorable one. Yet there is in the choice of words, in the order of words, in these first eleven lines something not exactly vulgar but a little strident, a little stale: 'an era's crown', 'dwells', 'rare accumulation', 'family pride', 'beauty's filtered dusts'—there is something in such phrases which suggests either a leading article or a conventional old-fashioned 'literariness'. 'This only what I tell' may irritate, for it is an ellipsis that may not (at a first try) fill out to make good sense. 'This is only what I tell' is not the required meaning, but 'This only is what I tell'. It would be a captious criticism, perhaps, to say that 'the electric charge of a battery' strikes us today as too much of a period image, like pylons, or arterial roads. It is sounder to say that throughout these first eleven lines we have a certain uncomfortable feeling of being 'got at'. But then, by its lyrical concentration,

> 'Eye, gazelle, delicate wanderer . . .'

utterly transforms these partly hostile impressions. The first eleven lines become 'right' again, for what they lead up to, for what they set off.

In quite a number of the earlier poems of this volume there are such moments of magical transformation. Many of the later poems, however, more lucidly organized round more coherent sets of feelings, have no need of such moments. In Mr. Spender's earlier work we can spot the moment when the poem, which has been roaring along the runway, suddenly soars. In beautiful late poems like 'Seascape' or 'Missing My Daughter' what holds us, frail and almost vanishing in its detail, yet delicately strong in its total composition, like a David Jones water-colour drawing of flowers in a glass bowl against a window, is the shining transparency of the single vision:

> 'The shore, heaped up with roses, horses, spires,
> Wanders on water, walking above ribbed sand. . . .'

Or the reflection of a child in a mirror already reflecting roses and the child's imagined image, the sense of her absence:

> 'The door, in a green mirage,
> Opened. In my daughter came.
> Her eyes were wide as those she has,
> The round gaze of her childhood was
> White as the distance in the glass
> Or on a white page, a white poem.
> The roses raced around her name.'

A Poetry of Search (Stephen Spender)

In such late poems we feel that the essential purity of Mr. Spender's vision has become purged at last of a youthful turbidness, of an awkward and contorting shyness, and of an encumbering, too facile, rhetoric.

Dylan Thomas

❋

I

When Dylan Thomas died in New York in his thirty-ninth year at the end of 1953, he had been a poet of considerable reputation for twenty years and, with the recent publication of his *Collected Poems*, was at the height of his fame. The collected volume was known to have sold, even before his death, more than ten thousand copies, an enormous figure by contemporary English or American standards. He was one of the two or three poets of his time whose name, like that of Mr. Eliot or Mr. Auden, was familiar to the man in the street. Shortly after his death, the success over the air and on the stage of his dramatic prose fantasy for radio, *Under Milk Wood*, introduced his work to an even wider audience than that which appreciated his poetry. It was not only, however, as a writer that Thomas was known to a wide public. He had a remarkable gift as an entertainer, and was a first-rate broadcaster, particularly of his own short stories based on his childhood in Wales. He was an extremely gregarious man, and had a very warm and lovable personality. His death produced a spate of tributes in prose and verse from scores of friends and acquaintances. And even for those who did not know him personally, Thomas had become, as few poets of our age have become, a kind of legend. He corresponded, as most poets do not, to some popular ideal, vision, or fiction of what a poet, in real life, should be. He was the pattern of the poet as a bohemian, and this was in many ways a misfortune for him. Had he been a more aloof, a less gregarious, a more prudent man; had he been less ready to expend himself in casual sociability; had he had less of a knack, in his later years, for earning money quickly and spending it even more quickly: in any of these cases, he might have lived longer and produced more; but he would not have been, in any of these cases, the writer that he is.

Thomas achieved, and has retained, a popular fame as a poet in spite of the fact that many of his poems are, at least on an intellectual level, extremely hard to comprehend. The design of at least many of his earlier poems is notably obscure; many of his later poems are much clearer in out-line than his earlier work, but they are still full of puzzling details. Yet he is one of the few modern poets who can be read aloud to a large, mixed audience, with a confidence in his 'going down'. There is a massive emotional directness in his poems that at once comes across. And the more critical reader, who may be suspicious of what seems a direct attack on his feelings below the level of the intellect, soon becomes aware that Thomas's obscurity is not that of a loose and vague but of an extremely packed writer. In one of the best short studies that has been written of Thomas since his death, Dr. David Daiches quotes what is certainly, at a first glance, an almost totally opaque passage.

> 'Altarwise by owl-light in the halfway house
> The gentleman lay graveward with his furies;
> Abaddon in the hangnail cracked from Adam,
> And, from his fork, a dog among the fairies,
> Bit out the mandrake with tomorrow's scream. . . .'

Dr. Daiches comments:

'The careful explicator will be able to produce informa-tive glosses on each of these phrases, but the fact remains that the poem is congested with its metaphors, and the reader is left with a feeling of oppression. . . . But it must be emphasized that this is not the fault of a bad romantic poetry, too loose and exclamatory, but comes from what can perhaps be called the classical vice of attempting to press too much into too little space.'

In spite of this excessive congestion of much of his poetry, Thomas obviously did succeed in communicating in verse, to a very large public by modern standards, something which that public felt to be important. What was that something, and how did Thomas get it across? It was certainly something very different from the public personality, the personality of an entertainer, which Thomas conveyed in a prose book, *Portrait of the Artist as a Young Dog*. Thomas was not, like Byron or Yeats, for instance, the poet as actor; he did not dramatize his personal life in his poetry, or build himself up as a 'character'. He did these things in conversation, and in the sketches and short stories, brilliant improvisations, which were fundamentally an extension of his genius for conversation. His poems are exceedingly individual, but they are also impersonal; when he writes about his childhood he is not so much recalling particular experiences as transforming them into a vision of innocence before the Fall. Yet at the same time, he is a concrete rather than a generalizing poet; he does not, like Mr. Auden, take a more or less abstract theme and proceed to relate it, in a detached way, to particularized observations about man and society. Both the appeal and the difficulty of his poetry come from the fact that it is a poetry of unitary response. Many of the best modern writers have been concerned with a kind of split in the consciousness of our time between what men think and what they feel or would like to feel, between what men suppose to be true and what they would like to believe, between what men feel is a proper course of action and what they feel is an attractive one. These urgent contemporary themes of stress, doubt, division in the self, tragic irony and tragic choice, do not enter into Dylan Thomas's poetic world. It is a world quite at one with itself. At the heart of his poetic response to experience there is a baffling simplicity.

II

It is Thomas's poetry that makes him important and, because of this baffling simplicity at the heart of it, his personal history, outside the history of his poems, can perhaps throw very little direct light on his achievement as a poet. His prose works, with the exception of *Under Milk Wood*, also throw little light on his poetry. They are second-level achievements, representing Thomas as the brilliant entertainer rather than the dedicated poet; they stand also, as so much of Thomas's personal life did, for that search for distraction which the concentrated nature of his dedication to poetry made necessary. Thomas's poetry is the main theme of this essay, but I shall precede my consideration of it by a few brief remarks on Thomas's life, his personality, and his achievements in prose.

Thomas was the son of a Swansea schoolmaster, a teacher of English in a grammar school, who had himself poetic ambitions; Thomas's father must have had remarkable gifts as a teacher, for many of the leading figures today in Welsh literary life were, at one time or another, his pupils. The Welsh, like the Scots, have a very strong family sense, and in his later years memories of holidays with farmer uncles meant a great deal to Thomas. He was not a particularly brilliant schoolboy, but he did very well at English, took an enthusiastic part in amateur dramatics, and wrote neat and very conventional poems for his school magazine. His father would have liked him to work hard to gain a scholarship to a university, but he did not do so. On leaving school, he became for a short time a reporter on a Swansea newspaper, a job which must have combined for him the appeal of bohemianism with that of the outer verges of literature.

Thomas's Welshness is an important part of his make-up. He never spoke or understood the Welsh language, and he very early taught himself to speak English not with the slight Welsh sing-song but with what he himself described mockingly as a 'cut-glass accent'. He disliked Welsh nationalism, and, indeed, all types of nationalism, but Wales remained to him home. His knowledge of the Bible, and his fundamentally religious—emotionally rather than intellectually religious—attitude to life were typically Welsh; his bohemianism was partly a reaction against the severe puritanism of much of middle-class Welsh life. His sense of verbal music, his feeling for the intricate interplay of vowel and consonant, and also, in prose and conversation, his love of the extravagant phrase and the witty exaggeration were Welsh. He was un-English also in his universal gregariousness, his unwillingness to make social discriminations, his complete lack of class-consciousness.

He first became known as a poet through contributing poems to, and winning prizes from, the poetry page of *The Sunday Referee*, edited by Victor Neuberg. *The Sunday Referee* finally financed the publication of his first volume, *Eighteen Poems*. Thomas was thus flung on the London literary world, particularly its bohemian side, as a boy of twenty, and in his early years in London he depended a great deal on the generosity and hospitality of friends. In his later years, however, his wide range of secondary gifts, as a broadcaster, a writer of sketches and short stories and film scripts, even as a comic journalist, were bringing him in a considerable yearly income; this tended, however, to be spent as soon as it was earned, and his payment of income tax was perpetually overdue. He lost, in later years, his taste for London life, and spent as much time as he could with his wife and children at Laugharne. It was monetary need that drove him to undertake the American poetry reading tours, which both he and those who organized them found a considerable strain as well as a stimulus, and on the last of which he died. Mr. John Malcolm Brinnin's book about these tours is obviously almost agonizingly accurate in its descriptions of many embarrassing episodes, but it is a portrait of a sick man under the strain of financial and moral worry, and of being perpetually on public show, and it should not be taken as giving a fair idea of the character or personality of Dylan Thomas as his English friends knew him. In particular it conveys a vivid impression of the element of stress, but no impression at all of the element of fulfilment, in Thomas's married life; Mr. Brinnin's remarks about this should be corrected by Roy Campbell's that Thomas and his wife were 'always in love, even years after marriage to the day of his death. They would quarrel like newly-weds on the slightest pretext with never a dull moment and make it up in two minutes.'

In America, Thomas tended to drink whisky rather than beer, though he knew spirits were bad for him. In England and Wales, he stuck on the whole to beer, not for its own sake, but as what his friend Mr. Vernon Watkins calls 'a necessary adjunct to conversation'. The tempo of his English life was slower, more genial, and less harassed than that of his tours in America. The charm of his rambling, vivid, extravagantly anecdotal conversation comes out in *Portrait of the Artist as a Young Dog* and in many of his broadcast sketches. The warmth of his personality, his zest in every kind of human oddity, his love for his fellow men, come out in his last completed work, *Under Milk Wood*. Here, more than in any other prose work of his, he managed to combine his prose gift for humorous fantasy based on realistic observation with his poetic gift for a piled-up richness of evocative language. *Under Milk Wood* is also, purely formally, notable as an invention. It derives not from any literary model, but from the radio form of the 'feature', in narrative and dialogue, evoking the spirit of a place; it turns that form into literature. It also makes more broadly and obviously apprehensible than, perhaps, any of Thomas's poems do that 'love of Man and . . . praise of God' which, in the introduction to the *Collected Poems*, Thomas wrote of as underlying all his work. *Under Milk Wood* is not, in the ordinary sense, dramatic. The characters are not confronted with choices; they behave according to their natures, mean, thriftless, or generous, and are to be accepted, like natural objects, for being what they are; and the movement is not dramatic, but cyclical, from early morning through day to night.

There are perhaps two moral centres in *Under Milk Wood*: the Reverend Eli Jenkins, with his touching 'good-bad' poems and his gentle appeals to a gentle God to look kindly on human failings; and the old blind sea-captain, the fire of whose lust and love—it is typical of Thomas's unitary response to refuse to distinguish between these—is not quenched even by the waters of death and of utter forget-fulness. Thomas was as a man, like the Reverend Eli Jenkins, utterly without malice. Reading *Under Milk Wood* it is possible to understand what a famous newspaper, in an remarkable obituary notice of Thomas, meant by asserting that he had the courage to lead the Christian life in public. 'The harlots and the publicans shall go into heaven before you.'

III

In an early statement about his poems, published in Mr. Geoffrey Grigson's poetry periodical of the 1930s, *New Verse*, Thomas spoke of the process of writing a poem as one of stripping away darkness, of struggling up to light; and also of that struggle as taking place through a dialectic of images. In his preface to his *Collected Poems*, on the other hand, he spoke, as we have seen, of his poems being written 'for the love of Man and in praise of God'. These two state-ments help us to measure a certain progress, or develop-ment, in a poetic achievement which is too often thought of as having been one of more or less stationary self-repetition. In many of his early poems, Thomas does, in fact, seem immersed, in a way that is bewildering to the reader and may have been bewildering to himself, in an attempt to grasp the whole of life, human and natural, as an apparently confused but ultimately single process. In his later poems, he more often seems to be, quite consciously and much less bewilderingly, *celebrating* that process—celebrating it, as Dr. Daiches says, religiously, and with sacramental imagery.

Perhaps also it is wrong to speak of him as celebrating some particular process; an American critic has suggested that what Thomas can be thought of as celebrating is the fact, or notion, of process in general, Mr. Eliot's 'three things', 'birth, and copulation, and death', seeing them as cyclical, seeing every birth as involving death, every death as involving birth, seeing also human life and natural process as exactly equated.

Such a set of clues certainly helps us a good deal with Thomas's earlier poems:

> 'The force that through the green fuse drives the flower
> Drives my green age; that blasts the roots of trees
> Is my destroyer.
> And I am dumb to tell the crooked rose
> My youth is bent by the same wintry fever. . . .'

Thomas, there, is massively identifying the body of man with the body of the world. The forces, he is saying, that control the growth and decay, the beauty and terror of human life are not merely similar to, but are the very same forces as, we see at work in outer nature. But how is Thomas able to hold and move us by saying this? In a way, it is a platitude: it is a statement, at least, which most of us would accept without too much excitement or perturbation up to a point, or with qualifications. Man, as an animal, is part of nature; is that a new or startling idea? My own answer, when many years ago I first considered the puzzle of the extremely powerful impact of this passage, was this. The man-nature equation here gains strength from an inter-transference of qualities between—or, more strictly, of our emotional attitudes towards—man and nature. We feel a human pity for Thomas's 'crooked rose', and, on the other hand, the 'wintry fever' of an adolescent's unsatisfied sexual desires acquires something of the impersonal dignity of a natural process.

Dylan Thomas

It is still, I think, the best clue that we have at least to Thomas's earliest volume, *Eighteen Poems*, to think of him as engaged in this way in bestowing on something humanly undignified, adolescent frustration, natural dignity:

'I see you boys of summer in your ruin.
Man in his maggot's barren.
And boys are full and foreign in the pouch.
I am the man your father was.
We are the sons of flint and pitch.
O see the poles are kissing as they cross.'

The American critic, Mr. Elder Olson, interprets the whole poem from which this stanza comes—the first poem in Dylan Thomas's first book—as a dialogue between perverse youth and crabbed age, with the poet occasionally intervening as an impersonal commentator. Mr. Olson's ingenuity leaves out, however, the most obvious thing. The poem is not only *about* the boys of summer in their ruin, but *by* one of them. It seeks to give oratorical emphasis and nobility of gesture to a subject which literature can usually touch on only furtively or with condescending pity—the subject of the sexual frustrations suffered by, and also the agonizingly intense erotic imaginings that obsess, in an advanced and therefore in many ways repressive civilization like our own, the middle-class adolescent male. Thomas began to write his poems in his late 'teens. It is in his late 'teens that the sexual desires of the male are at their most urgent, and that his sexual potency is at its greatest; it is in his late 'teens also, in our society, that he has least chance of satisfying or exercising one or the other in a normal fashion. What Thomas is doing in many of his earliest poems is finding poetic symbols adequate to this experience, which is centrally important in most masculine life-histories, but which it is difficult to treat not only with literary, but even with ordinary, decency. He also expresses the wider sense of traumatic shock, a shock at once of awe and horror, which is likely to accompany, for any young male in our civilization, the full imaginative realization of 'the facts of life'. He went on to do things more broadly significant than this; but this, in itself, was a significant achievement.

IV

Thomas's second volume, *Twenty-five Poems*, brought him on the whole more praise and more fame than his first. Dame Edith Sitwell, in particular, saluted it with enthusiasm in a memorable short review in *The Observer*. Yet like many second volumes of verse—and like all second novels!—*Twenty-five Poems* is in many ways unsatisfactory. It shows Thomas experimenting with new themes, new images, new styles. Two poems in the book have, indeed, been much praised, but to me it seems undeservedly. One is 'And Death Shall Have No Dominion', which strikes me as a set of large but rather empty rhetorical gestures, a poem in which the poet faced by the harsh fact of death is not properly confronting it but 'cheering himself up'. The other is Thomas's one political poem, 'The Hand That Signed the Paper'. That ends with this stanza:

> 'The five kings count the dead but do not soften
> The crusted wound nor stroke the brow;
> A hand rules pity as a hand rules heaven;
> Hands have no tears to flow.'

That stanza has been praised as an example of a poet splendidly and successfully mixing metaphors; may not some, with all respect, find it rather an example of bathos?

There are other poems in *Twenty-five Poems* like 'Should Lanterns Shine', which show us that Thomas had been reading both Rilke, probably in translation, and Yeats:

> 'And from her lips the faded pigments fall,
> The mummy cloths expose an ancient breast . . .
>
> I have heard many years of telling,
> And many years should see some change.

The ball I threw while playing in the park
Has not yet reached the ground.'

Such lines show a minor good taste in a composite manner which is essentially *not* Thomas's. He had become, in his second volume, much more uncertain about the way he was going than in his first, and there is one poem which expresses his doubts admirably. Was, perhaps, his poetic method a method of self-deception?

'I have longed to move away
From the hissing of the spent lie
And the old terrors' continual cry
Growing more terrible as the day
Goes over the hill into the deep sea;
I have longed to move away
From the repetition of salutes,
For there are ghosts in the air
And ghostly echoes on paper,
And the thunder of calls and notes.

I have longed to move away but am afraid;
Some life, yet unspent, might explode
Out of the old lie burning on the ground,
And, crackling into the air, leave me half-blind.
Neither by night's ancient fear,
The parting of hat from hair,
Pursed lips at the receiver,
Shall I fall to death's feather.
By these I would not care to die,
Half convention and half lie.'

Thomas very rarely uses in his poetry the wit and humour of his personal conversation and his narrative prose. But here he manages to evade deep fears by mocking at shallow fears: '. . . night's ancient fear,/The parting of hat from hair' is simply a grotesque image of a man's being so frightened that his hair stands on end and pushes his hat off: as in a comic drawing by such a cartoonist as H. M. Bateman. The 'receiver' is simply a telephone receiver, and the poet's lips are 'pursed', as in a melodrama, because he is receiving a horrifying message. 'Death's feather' has no deep, obscure symbolic meaning but is simply an allusion to the humorous Cockney phrase: 'You could 'ave knocked me down with a feather!' (That, I think, is its use here; but it is quite a favourite phrase of Thomas's, and what he has often in mind is the custom of holding a feather to a dead man's lips to make sure he is no longer breathing.) These thrillerish fears, or self-induced, half-pleasant shudders, are 'half convention and half lie'. Neither the poetic imagination, nor sane, practical common sense, can afford to pay much attention to them. But the spent lie from which some life, yet unspent, might explode as it lay burning on the ground, is another matter; so are the ghosts, the ghostly echoes on paper, the repetition of salutes.

This, in fact, is the one poem of Thomas's whose subject-matter is poetical self-criticism. The poet is pondering whether he ought to make a bonfire—accompanied by small fireworks, perhaps dangerous ones—of childish fears, obsessions, and superstitions; a bonfire, also, in his writing of poetry of 'given' phrases, lines, and images—'ghostly echoes on paper'—about whose source and meaning he is not clear. He is wondering whether he ought to become, like so many of his contemporaries of the 1930s, an 'adult' and 'socially conscious' poet. He decides that he cannot afford to make this bonfire for the reason that the poetic lie, the undue fearsomeness and rhetoric—the 'ghosts' and the 'repetition of salutes'—are somehow bound up with the possibility of the full, life-giving poetic vision. The old lie, exploding, might leave him half-blind; the terrors from which he wants to move away are somehow inextricably linked with an image full of peace, dignity and beauty:

> '. . . as the day
> Goes over the hill into the deep sea.'

I have been trying here to follow Mr. Robert Graves's ideal

technique of making a poem's drift clear by expounding it, at greater length, mainly in its own words. If the reader agrees with me about the poem's drift, he will admire the insight into his own poetic scope which Thomas shows in this poem. He was right to take the risk of regressiveness, rather than cut the tangle of links that bound him with his childhood; the obsession with childhood, even with its fictions and fantasies, was to lead him in the end to a rediscovery of innocence.

The most important and most obscure poems in *Twenty-five Poems* are, however, the ten sonnets beginning 'Altarwise by owl-light'. Mr. Elder Olson has argued very persuasively that these sonnets evoke in succession pagan despair, the new hope consequent upon the birth of Christ, the Christian despair consequent upon the Crucifixion, and the renewed Christian hope consequent upon the Resurrection; very ingeniously, but perhaps a little less persuasively, he has suggested that these ideas are expressed through an almost pedantically exact symbolism drawn from the movements of the constellation Hercules, standing both for man, and for the manhood of Christ. For other readers, the sonnets had always seemed the most baffling of Dylan Thomas's works, though to a sympathetic reader the Christian overtones and the occasional presence of 'the grand style' were obvious from the start. There are fragments in these sonnets —which as wholes remain, in Dr. Daiches's phrases, oppressive and congested even after one has grasped and accepted the main lines of Mr. Olson's exposition—more nobly eloquent than anything else Dylan Thomas ever wrote:

'This was the crucifixion on the mountain,
Time's nerve in vinegar, the gallow grave
As tarred with blood as the bright thorns I wept . . .

Green as beginning, let the garden diving
Soar, with its two black towers, to that Day
When the worm builds with the gold straws of venom
My nest of mercies in the rude, red tree.'

The sonnets, a failure as a whole, splendid in such parts as these, are important because they announce the current of orthodox Christian feeling—feeling rather than thought—which was henceforth increasingly to dominate Thomas's work in poetry.

V

Thomas's third volume, *The Map of Love*, which contained prose pieces as well as poems, appeared in 1939, on the verge of the Second World War. It had a great and in many ways unfortunate influence on some of the younger English writers of that time, in particular on the movement called at first the New Apocalypse, and later, when it became a wider and even more shapeless stream of tendency, the New Romanticism. The prose pieces in *The Map of Love* were not at all like the straightforwardly descriptive and narrative, funny and pathetic pieces of *Portrait of the Artist as a Young Dog*, which came out in the following year, 1940. They were much influenced by the belated English interest in the French Surrealist and Dadaist movements. Mr. David Gascoyne's excellent short book on Surrealism had appeared two or three years before *The Map of Love*, and more recently there had been Herbert Read's anthology of Surrealist texts and paintings published by Faber. The prose pieces in *The Map of Love* are not strictly Surrealist—they are too carefully worked over, as to their prose rhythms, and so on—but they have a semi-Surrealist flavour in their superficial incoherence, their reliance on shock tactics, and the cruelty or obscenity, or both, of much of their imagery. They are failures on the whole, artistically, but they have a real interest in relation to the total pattern of Thomas's work. They are his *pièces noires*, the pieces in which he accepts evil: they are one side of a medal of which the other side is Thomas's later celebration of innocence, and the benignity of the Reverend Eli Jenkins. In writing these pieces, Thomas was grappling with, and apparently succeeded in absorbing and overcoming, what Jungians call the Shadow.

Perhaps because of the comparative failure of these prose pieces, *The Map of Love* was the least popular of Thomas's volumes. It cannot have been printed in large numbers, or have gone into many impressions, for it is almost impossible —where with the other volumes it is fairly easy—to procure a second-hand copy of it. Yet it contains some of Thomas's most memorable poems, chief among them the elegy 'After the Funeral' for his elderly cousin, Ann Jones. This is a piece of baroque eloquence: in the poet's own words,

> '. . . this for her is a monstrous image blindly
> Magnified out of praise. . . .'

There are, however, three or four lines towards the end which transcend the baroque manner and which rank with the passages already quoted from the sonnets as among Thomas's finest isolated fragments.

Their appeal is simple, human and direct:

> 'I know her scrubbed and sour humble hands
> Lie with religion in their cramp, her threadbare
> Whisper in a damp word, her wits drilled hollow,
> Her fist of a face died clenched on a round pain;
> And sculptured Ann is seventy years of stone.'

Other, slighter poems in *The Map of Love* have interest as explorations of new aptitudes. A slight but charming poem, 'Once it was the colour of saying' gives a foretaste of one of Thomas's main later themes, the reminiscent celebration, through the evoking of a landscape that the perspective of time has made legendary, of childish innocence:

> 'Once it was the colour of saying
> Soaked my table the uglier side of a hill
> With a capsized field where a school sat still
> And a black and white patch of girls grew playing . . .

The gentle seasides of saying I must undo
That all the charmingly drowned arise to cockcrow and
    kill.
When I whistled with mitching boys through a reservoir
    park
Where at night we stoned the cold and cuckoo
Lovers in the dirt of their leafy beds,
The shade of their trees was a word of many shades
And a lamp of lightning for the poor in the dark;
Now my saying shall be my undoing,
And every stone I wind off like a reel.'

The 'capsized field' there—looking as if it had been upset or
overturned on the hillside, and also, from the distance, just
the size of a schoolboy's cap—is a delightful example of the
subdued punning which a careful reader of Thomas soon
learns to look for everywhere. Yet even as late as 1939,
Thomas's voice was still not always quite his own. Or
rather, he had his own voice, but he would still from time
to time try on other people's to see how they fitted. Asked,
for instance, who was the author of the following stanza
from *The Map of Love* an intelligent reader might well name
Mr. C. Day Lewis or Mr. W. H. Auden. The turn and the
mood of the last two lines, in particular, suggests that preoccupation of most of the poets of the 1930s with harsh
historical necessity, which Dylan Thomas on the whole did
not share:

'Bound by a sovereign strip, we lie,
Watch yellow, wish for wind to blow away
The strata of the shore and drown red rock;
But wishes breed not, neither
Can we fend off rock arrival. . . .'

It was biological necessity, rather, that preoccupied Thomas.
That comes out in the last poem in this volume, flatly
melancholy in its tone, but displaying a gift, new and unexpected in Thomas, for the forceful gnomic statement:

'Twenty-four years remind the tears of my eyes.
(Bury the dead for fear that they walk to the grave in
    labour.)
In the groin of the natural doorway I crouched like a tailor
Sewing a shroud for a journey
By the light of the meat-eating sun.
Dressed to die, the sensual strut begun,
With my red veins full of money,
In the final direction of the elementary town
I advance for as long as forever is.'

VI

Among many critics of Thomas, there has been a tendency to attempt to enclose him within a formula; that of
the man-nature equation used here to throw light on
Eighteen Poems: that of adolescent sexual excitement used
here for the same purpose; that of the religious celebrator
of natural process, that of the disorderly breeder of images,
struggling from sleep to wakefulness, and so on. There has
been no general agreement about which formula is right,
but there has been a general agreement that some formula
would be, and also that there is a remarkable similarity
about all Thomas's poems. I have been trying, in this sketch,
to deal with each volume of Thomas's in turn, almost as if I
had been reviewing it when it first came out. I hope I have
conveyed my impression—an impression which, when it
first came solidly home, very much surprised me—that in
tone, in style, in subject-matter Thomas is a much more
various, a much less narrowly consistent poet, and that in
attitude to life he is much more a developing poet, than
people make him out to be. In *Eighteen Poems*, for instance,
there is, in the ordinary senses of these words, no human or
religious interest; the sonnets, at least, in *Twenty-five Poems*
have a remarkable religious interest; and 'After the Funeral'
and some other poems in *The Map of Love* have a human
interest that is new.

Thomas was found unfit for military service and spent most of the years of the Second World War in Wales, coming up to London from time to time to see friends, do broadcasting work, or meet publishers. He never tackled the war directly as a subject, but at least two of his poems, the obscure but powerful title poem of *Deaths and Entrances* and the famous 'A Refusal to Mourn' have, for background, the bombing raids on London. I have been told that some work he did on a documentary film on the bombing raids, which in the end was found too grim for public release, had a profound effect on his imagination; an effect that may partly explain the retreat, in many of his later poems, to the themes of childhood innocence and country peace. Certainly, in these years, Thomas did more and more tend to turn, for the central themes of his poetry, to his Welsh childhood. The same episodes which, in *Portrait of the Artist as a Young Dog*, had provided material for comedy, now, more deeply explored, brought forth a transformation of memory into vision; a vision of a lost paradise regained.

Thomas's last English volume of new poems, *Deaths and Entrances*, came out in 1946. It increases the impression of variety, and of steady development, which the earlier volumes, read in the order of their appearance, give. It contains a remarkable number of successful poems of notably different kinds. One kind, in particular, at once caught the fancy of a wide public. It is a kind which, very roughly, throwing out words at a venture, one might call the recaptured-childish-landscape, semi-fairy-tale, semi-ode kind: more concisely, the long poem of formal celebration. Such, for instance, are seven late poems by Thomas: 'Poem in October', 'A Winter's Tale', 'Fern Hill', 'In Country Sleep', 'Over Sir John's Hill', 'Poem on His Birthday', 'In the White Giant's Thigh'.[1] All these poems have a larger and looser, a more immediately apprehensible rhythmical movement than most of Thomas's earlier work. They do not aim

[1] The last three of these are not in *Deaths and Entrances* but in *Collected Poems*.

at dark, packed, and concentrated, but at bright, expansive
effects. Their landscapes are always partly magical landscapes.
Their common flavour can, however, perhaps be better
conveyed by a series of quotations than by such remarks:

'Bird, he was brought low,
Burning in the bride bed of love, in the whirl-
Pool at the wanting centre, in the folds
Of paradise, in the spun bud of the world.
And she rose with him flowering in her melting snow . . .'
('A Winter's Tale')

'It was my thirtieth year to heaven
Woke to my hearing from harbour and neighbour wood
And the mussel pooled and heron
Priested shore
The morning beckon
With water praying and call of seagull and rook
And the knock of sailing boats on the net webbed wall
Myself to set foot
That second
In the still sleeping town and set forth. . . .'
('Poem in October')

'I hear the bouncing hills
Grow larked and greener at berry brown
Fall and the dew larks sing
Taller this thunderclap spring, and how
More spanned with angels rise
The mansouled fiery islands! Oh,
Holier then their eyes,
And my shining men no more alone
As I sail out to die. . . .'
('Poem on His Birthday')

'Now as I was young and easy under the apple boughs
About the lilting house and happy as the grass was green,
The night above the dingle starry,
Time let me hail and climb
Golden in the heydays of his eyes,

And honoured among wagons I was prince of the apple towns
And once below a time I lordly had the trees and leaves
    Trail with daisies and barley
  Down the rivers of the windfall light.'

('Fern Hill')

'The dust of their kettles and clocks swings to and fro
Where the hay rides now or the bracken kitchens rust
As the arc of the billhooks that flashed the hedges low
And cut the birds' boughs that the minstrel sap ran red.
They from the houses where the harvest kneels, hold me
    hard,
Who heard from the tall bell sail down the Sundays of the
    dead
And the rain wring out its tongues on the faded years,
Teach me the love that is evergreen after the fall leaved
Grave, after the Belovéd on the grass gulfed cross is scrubbed
Off by the sun and Daughters no longer grieved
Save by their long desires in the fox cubbed
Streets or hungering in the crumbled wood: to these
Hale dead and deathless do the women of the hill
Love for ever meridian through the courters' trees

And the daughters of darkness flame like Fawkes fires still.'

('In the White Giant's Thigh')

Neither the style nor the mood of these passages would
have been easily predictable even by an exceptionally acute
critic of Dylan Thomas's earlier verse. The mood is close
to some of the verse of Vaughan and some of the prose of
Traherne, or to take a closer and more contemporary comparison from another art, there is something in this glowing
transformation of everyday things—a boy in an apple tree,
a young man going out for an early walk in a seaside town
on his birthday—that recalls some drawings by David Jones
or some paintings by Stanley Spencer. One would not, with
the same confidence, mention Wordsworth or Blake; there
is a kind of massiveness and sobriety in Wordsworth's

explorations of childish memory, there is a naked directness in Blake's *Songs of Innocence*, that we do not find here. Thomas, like Vaughan, Traherne, Spencer, or Jones, could be described affectionately as 'quaint', his vision of paradise as a 'touching' one; such epithets would be out of place if one were discussing Blake or Wordsworth.

The style, also, has changed. Its main mark is no longer an obscure concision, a dense packing of images, but a rapid and muscular fluency that puts one in mind sometimes of a more relaxed Hopkins, sometimes of a more concentrated Swinburne. The tone of voice is a deliberately exalted one. The seven poems I have mentioned, and some of which I have quoted, are likely to remain Thomas's most popular pieces. But for the special effect he is aiming at in them he has eliminated that quality of cloudy pregnancy which, rightly or wrongly, was for many readers one of the main fascinations of his earlier poems. It is not that these eloquent, sincere, and moving long poems are in any sense shallow; they make us gloriously free of a visionary world; yet there does remain a sense, if the Irishism is permissible, in which the depths are all on the surface. The poems give what they have to give, grandly, at once. One does not go back to them to probe and question. A passion for probing and questioning can, of course, vitiate taste. Yet there will always remain critics (by his own confession, Professor William Empson is one) to whom these lucid late successes are less 'interesting' than other late poems, more dense and obscure, much less certainly successful but carrying the suggestion that, if they *were* successful, their success might be something higher still.

The quality that Thomas jettisoned in these late, long poems, rightly for his purposes, was a quality of dramatic compression. The title poem of *Deaths and Entrances* is, for instance, almost certainly on the whole a failure: if only for the reason that Thomas does not provide us with clues enough to find out what exactly is happening in the poem, and yet does provide us with clues enough to make us bother about what is happening. The setting is certainly the bombing raids on London:

> 'On almost the incendiary eve
>   Of several near deaths,
> When one at the great least of your best loved
>   And always known must leave
> Lions and fires of his flying breath,
>   Of your immortal friends
> Who'd raise the organs of the counted dust
>   To shoot and sing your praise,
> One who called deepest down shall hold his peace
>   That cannot sink or cease
>   Endlessly to his wound
> In many married London's estranging grief.'

To read that stanza is like seeing a man making a set of noble gestures on a tragic stage and not quite catching, because of some failure of acoustics, what he is saying. Yet the gestures *are* noble, and I would claim that the last line in particular,

> 'In many married London's estranging grief,'

is a fragmentary achievement of a kind of poetry higher in itself than the dingles and the apple boughs and the vale mist riding through the haygold stalls and even than the very lovely heron-priested shore; a kind of poetry which grasps and drastically unifies an unimaginably complex set of interrelated pains. Such a line suggests the immanence in Thomas, in his last years, of a poetry of mature human awareness.

There are some shorter poems in *Deaths and Entrances* that seem similarly to reach out for, and sometimes to grasp, a mature human awareness. Among them are the beautifully constructed 'The Conversation of Prayer', 'A Refusal to Mourn the Death, by Fire, of a Child in London' (of which Mr. William Empson has given a masterly exposition); the two very short, which are also among Thomas's few very personal, poems, 'To Others than You' and 'In My Craft and Sullen Art'; the plangent *villanelle*, with its Yeatsian overtones, addressed by Thomas to his dying father, 'Do Not Go Gentle into That Good Night', of which the intended sequel, recently reassembled by Mr. Vernon Watkins from Thomas's working notes, would have been an even more striking poem: and with less certainty 'There Was a Saviour'.

One of these poems, 'The Conversation of Prayer' is worth looking at on the page as an example of Thomas's extraordinary virtuosity as a creator of textures. I have marked, in italics, the hidden rhymes:

'The conversation of *prayers* about to be *said*
By the child going to *bed* and the man on the *stairs*
Who climbs to his dying *love* in her high *room*,
The one not caring to *whom* in his sleep he will *move*,
And the other full of *tears* that she will be *dead*,

Turns in the dark on the *sound* they know will *arise*
Into the answering *skies* from the green *ground*,
From the man on the *stairs* and the child by his *bed*.
The sound about to be *said* in the two *prayers*
For sleep in a safe *land* and the love who *dies*

Will be the same grief *flying*. Whom shall they *calm*?
Shall the child sleep un*harmed* or the man be *crying*?
The conversation of *prayers* about to be *said*
Turns on the quick and the *dead*, and the man on the *stairs*
Tonight shall find no *dying* but alive and *warm*

In the fire of his *care* his love in the high *room*.
And the child not caring to *whom* he climbs his *prayer*
Shall drown in a grief as *deep* as his true *grave*,
And mark the dark eyed *wave*, through the eyes of *sleep*,
Dragging him up the *stairs* to one who lies *dead*.'

Apart from the extraordinary complexity of this rhyme

scheme, the reader should notice that the vast majority of the words in the poem, most of the exceptions being participles, are monosyllables. The only word that is more than a disyllable is 'conversation' and it is also the most abstract word in the poem and the word that, as it were, states the poet's theme. No doubt any skilful craftsman might invent and carry through a form like this as a metrical exercise. But Thomas's poem does not read at all like an exercise; most readers, in fact, do not notice the rhyme-scheme till it is pointed out to them. Again, most poets would find it hard to construct a series of stanzas mainly in monosyllables without giving an effect of monotony. Thomas's line is so subtly varied as to defy an attempt at rule-of-thumb scansion. It is a four-stress line, with feet very freely substituted, and in one case the four feet are four anapaests but with a dragging effect, because of their setting, that anapaests do not usually have:

'For the *man*/on the *stairs*/and the *child*/by his *bed*.'

Usually, however, the effect is far more subtle:

'Who *climbs*/to his *dy*/ing *love*/in her/*high room*.'

There we have an iambus, an anapaest, an iambus and an unstressed two-syllable foot followed, according to English custom, by a two-stress foot. And that, to be sure, seems to make *five* stresses; but because 'high' chimes loudly with the first syllable of 'dying', earlier in the line, the word 'room' has actually only a secondary stress. Such minutiae are dry reading except for the teacher of metrics, but since Thomas has been accused by some critics, such as Mr. Geoffrey Grigson, of careless and slapdash writing it is worth providing an almost mechanical demonstration of his mastery of his craft.

Yet the crafts exists only for the sake of the art. 'The Conversation of Prayer', perhaps one of the most perfect of Thomas's short poems, may have been neglected because the idea around which it moves is, at least in Protestant countries, becoming marginal to our culture. It is the idea of the reversibility of grace; the idea that all prayers and all good acts co-operate for the benefit of all men, and that God, in His inscrutable mercy, can give the innocent the privilege of suffering some of the tribulations which have been incurred by redeemable sinners. The man in this poem might be the father of the boy, or he might have no connection with him; or the man and the boy might be the same person at different stages of their life histories. Both pray, and there is a sense in which prayer is eternally heard. The boy prays for 'sleep unharmed', for a night undisturbed by bad dreams, and the man whose wife or lover is dying prays that she may be better. The prayers, as it were, cross in the air, the man is granted his wish, for one night at least the sick woman is happy and well again, but the sleeping boy has to endure all the man's nightmare of climbing up the stairs to discover the loved one dead. Only this idea makes sense of the poem. How, it may be asked, could Thomas, bred a Bible Protestant, and never interested in abstruse notions, have come across it, or worked it out for himself? Perhaps it is an idea that all men who really struggle with prayer do, at least implicitly, work out for themselves. For, though Thomas's attitude to life was, as he grew older, an increasingly religious, and in a broad sense an increasingly Christian one, he was certainly not a poet, like Mr. Eliot for instance, to whom dry theological and metaphysical speculations were, in themselves, poetically exciting. His world was not a conceptual world and his coherency is not a conceptual coherency. Across the page in the *Collected Poems* from 'The Conversation of Prayer' there is the famous 'A Refusal to Mourn', whose drift Professor Empson has summed up as 'a pantheistic pessimism'. Thomas's longest personal religious poem, 'Vision and Prayer' offers us a naked confrontation of the desire for utter extinction with the hope of personal salvation. The last line of 'A Refusal to Mourn',

'After the first death, there is no other,'

has a resonance and authority both for unbelievers and believers. At one level, the meaning may be, as Professor Empson suggests, that life is a cruel thing and that the utter finality of physical death is welcome; but the logically contradictory Christian overtones—'Do not let us fear death, since, once the body is dead, the soul lives for ever'—cannot possibly be excluded. We must respect the baffling simplicity of Thomas's unitary response and not impose abstract categories on him.

One poem in *Deaths and Entrances*, 'The Hunchback in the Park', a more descriptive and 'realistic' poem than Thomas was in the habit of writing, may help us, perhaps, to grasp this simplicity by watching it operate at a less profound level. This begins with a long but not obscure two-stanza sentence:

> 'The hunchback in the park
> A solitary mister
> Propped between trees and water
> From the opening of the garden lock
> That lets the trees and water enter
> Until the Sunday sombre bell at dark
>
> Eating bread from a newspaper
> Drinking water from the chained cup
> That the children filled with gravel
> In the fountain basin where I sailed my ship
> Slept at night in a dog kennel
> But nobody chained him up. . . .'

The boys in the park, of whom Thomas is one, mock and torment the solitary hunchback who, ignoring them, seeks happiness in a dream in which the park stands for all the richness of life from which he is locked out; and the boys are locked out from the poetic understanding of that richness which the hunchback has attained to through deprivation and pain. They are part of the richness, and how should they understand it (that may be part of the implication of the phrase, 'the wild boys innocent as strawberries', which several critics have found sentimental)? Hunter and hunted; mocked and mocker; boys and hunchback; growth and decay, life and death, dream and reality: all sets of polar opposites are, for Thomas, at some level equally holy and necessary, holy is the hawk, holy is the dove. . . . This theme, the coincidence of opposites, runs through all Thomas's work and the end of this poem states it clearly: how the hunchback, the 'old dog sleeper'

> 'Made all day until bell time
> A woman figure without fault
> Straight as a young elm
> Straight and tall from his crooked bones
> That she might stand in the night
> After the lock and chains
>
> All night in the unmade park
> After the railings and shrubberies
> The birds the grass the trees the lake
> And the wild boys innocent as strawberries
> Had followed the hunchback
> To his kennel in the dark.'

Other poems in *Deaths and Entrances* show Thomas experimenting along still other lines. 'Ballad of the Long-Legged Bait' is his only poem, with the partial exception of 'A Winter's Tale', of which the movement is primarily a narrative one. It is a phantasmagoric narrative like Rimbaud's *Bateau Ivre*. Its immediate impact is extremely confusing. Mr. Elder Olson has worked out a logical structure for it. The poet goes fishing in a magic boat, using a naked woman for a bait, and all the sea creatures eat her up, and then as in the Book of Revelation, 'there is no more sea'. She is a woman, and she is also his heart, and he has been sacrificing the desires of his heart to restore a lost Eden. In the end, Eden is restored, and so is the woman, and the heart in its lost innocence; the poet steps out of the boat, now on dry land and

> 'stands alone at the door of his home
> With his long-legged heart in his hand.'

The poem, thus, for Mr. Olson is a kind of small allegory about the struggle inside Thomas, a typically Welsh struggle, between natural sensuality and puritan mysticism. Thomas himself, more modestly, over a bar in New York, said that the poem is about how a young man goes out fishing for fun and games, for all the excitements of the wild free life, and finds in the end that he has caught a wife, some children, and a little house. The poem, even with the help of these clues, remains unsatisfactory—it leaves one feeling a little sea-sick—but it is yet another example of Thomas's eagerness, throughout his poetic career, to go on extending his range. And as a whole *Deaths and Entrances* does remain one of the two or three most impressive single volumes of poetry published in English over the last ten years.

VII

Let us now try to sum up. In the few years since his death, Dylan Thomas's reputation as a poet has undoubtedly suffered at least a mild slump. He was always far too directly and massively an emotional poet, and in the detail of his language often too confusing and sometimes apparently confused a poet, to be acceptable to the analytical critics of the *Scrutiny* school who today exercise a far wider influence on general English taste than they did four or five years ago. Quite apart from that, there is quite generally in literary history a time lag, sometimes of as long as twenty or thirty years, between a notable writer's death and the attempt to reach a balanced judgment on him. The difficulty, also, at least at the level of attempting to explain in prose what the poet is doing, of Dylan Thomas's work has meant that the three short books so far published about him, by Mr. Henry Treece in his life-time (a revised edition has been published since Thomas's death), and since his death by Mr. Elder Olson and Mr. Derek Stanford, have been much more concerned with exposition of his sense than with attempts to 'place' him or even to illustrate in detail his strictly poetic art. Mr. Stanford thinks he may rank in English literary history rather as Gray ranks; this may be too high an estimate, for where is Thomas's long poem of mature moral interest, where is his 'Elegy Written in a Country Churchyard'? But he might well rank as Collins ranks; he has written some perfect poems, his poetic personality is a completely individual one, he brings in a new note. One might call Gray a minor major poet; one might call Collins a major minor poet. That, possibly, is also Thomas's rank, but at the same time we should be profoundly suspicious of this class-room, or examination-school, attitude to poets. There is a very real and profound sense in which poets do not compete with each other. No true poet offers us something for which anything else, by any other true poet, is really a substitute. It is enough, for the purposes here, to insist that Thomas was a good poet and worth our attention; and to attempt to define, and make vivid, his specific quality.

The reaction against Thomas, since his death, has, in fact, really been concerned to deny that Thomas was a good poet; or to assert that he might have been a good poet, but cheated poetically, in a way that disqualifies him. Thus, Mr. John Wain has remarked that a meaning, or a set of meanings, can nearly always be got out of Thomas's poems but that the critic's worry is whether Thomas ever cared much what the meanings were so long as the thing sounded all right. Even more sharply, in his witty and provocative Clark Lectures, *The Crowning Privilege*, Mr. Robert Graves condemns Thomas as a poet who takes care of the sound and lets the sense take care of itself: Mr. Graves compares Thomas to a soldier firing off a rifle at random while a confederate in the butts—the confederate being the gullible reviewer of contemporary poetry—keeps on signalling bulls and inners, whether or not the bullet has come anywhere near the target.

How much justice is there in such strictures? There are certainly poems by Dylan Thomas of which many readers must find even the main drift, as sense, hard to grasp; there is hardly any poem of Thomas's of which some details, at least, are not likely to puzzle most readers. But I hope I have shown two things: that in Thomas's best poems there is a coherent meaning, and that it is not always mechanically the same meaning. It is simply not true that he went on writing, with variations of form and imagery, the same archetypal poem over and over again; he grew and changed and at his death was still developing, in the direction of a wider and more genial human scope. The importance of *Under Milk Wood* is that it shows him, at the very end of his life, transforming into a kind of poetry that humorous apprehension of life which, in *Portrait of the Artist as a Young Dog*, is still something quite separate from poetry. Had he lived, he might have worked into his poetry the shrewdness and the gaiety that make him a first-rate entertainer. His feeling for life, at the end, was growing, not shrinking; and the separated elements of it, the outer and the inner being, the legendary sweet funny man and the fine solemn poet, were growing together.

Let me end this sketch by quoting a short, a very personal poem of Thomas's, which warns us wholesomely against the kind of undue familiarity to which his public legend, the memory of his personality, the critic's dangerous passion for summary judgements, might all invite us:

TO OTHERS THAN YOU

Friend by enemy I call you out.

You with a bad coin in your socket,
You my friend there with a winning air
Who palmed the lie on me when you looked

Dylan Thomas

Brassily at my shyest secret,
Enticed with twinkling bits of the eye
Till the sweet tooth of my love bit dry,
Rasped at last, and I stumbled and sucked,
Whom I now conjure to stand as a thief
In the memory worked by mirrors,
With unforgettably smiling act,
Quickness of hand in the velvet glove
And my whole heart under your hammer,
Were once such a creature, so gay and frank
A desireless familiar
I never thought to utter and think
While you displaced a truth in the air,

That though I loved them for their faults
As much as for their good,
My friends were enemies on stilts,
With their heads in a cunning cloud.

I hope that the truths displaced in the air in these pages have
been displaced towards their proper locations; I hope that
in all I have been saying my head, too, has not been in a
cunning cloud. I remember Dylan Thomas's own head,
benignly calm, as it looked in a photograph of his death-
mask which a close friend of his, the poet Ruthven Todd,
brought to show to Thomas's friends in London: it should
have made me think of two lines of Thomas's, not well
known:

'And when blind sleep drops on the spying senses,
The heart is sensual, though five eyes break.'

Experiment In Verse

———————❈———————

In 1956, the International P.E.N. Congress was being held in London. The Poetry Book Society did me the honour of asking me to edit a special number of their quarterly bulletin, to contain a small anthology of new English poems. This was presented to the delegates, to give them a notion of the current state of English poetry. John Wain, one of the poets I included, remarked to me that, nice as it was in its way, my little selection might almost have come out in 1916. There was nothing in it to suggest that over the past forty years English poetry had undergone something like a revolution. The poems were all lucid, carefully constructed, quiet, subdued. Such echoes as there were seemed to be from the great early and late Victorians. Here, for instance, Mr. C. Day Lewis seemed to be speaking in the voice of Hardy:

> 'Lot 96: a brass-rimmed ironwork fender.
> It had stood guard for years, where it used to belong,
> Over the hearth of a couple who had loved it tenderly,
> Now it will go for a song.'

The gathering of poetic associations around what seems an intractably prosaic object, there, the balancing of a conversational run of speech, and choice of words, against the artifice of rhyme and metre, are very Hardyesque. Mr. Michael Hamburger similarly echoed Browning's blank verse,

'Remarking this chair was new, that picture gone,
The room more crowded and the carpet thinner;
Yet wine and wit flowed freely as before,'

and some lines of Mr. Vernon Watkins's had the note of
Landor:

'No lesser vision gives me consolation.
Wealth is a barren waste, that spring forgot.
Art is the principle of all creation,
And there the desert is, where art is not.'

There was no poem, in fact, in this small selection, that
thirty or forty years ago would have alarmed or upset Sir
Edward Marsh. What, the reader of the selection might
wonder, had become of the influence of the 'modern movement' in poetry, what had become of the taste for the
vividly elliptical and the pregnantly obscure? What had
become of the influence of innovators like Hopkins, and the
later Yeats, and Mr. Pound and Mr. Eliot, and Mr. Auden
in his early work, and Dylan Thomas? Had the whole
'modern movement'—so far as its practical effect on contemporary poetry went—been sunk without a trace? Were
practising poets today, even the youngest of them, after the
interlude of two world wars and the disturbing years between them, simply taking up the threads where a sensitive
and intelligent Georgian poet like, say, Edward Thomas had
dropped them? Was the whole 'modern movement' beginning to seem, for the practising poet today with his feet on
the ground, a splendid irrelevance?

A good critic and a fine poet, Dr. Edwin Muir, has in fact
recently suggested that this, or something like this, may be
the case. In the 1920s, in a poem like *The Waste Land*, a poet
like Mr. Eliot was making a desperate effort to renew the
language and the imagery of poetry; in the 1930s, poets like
Mr. Auden, Mr. MacNeice, Mr. Spender and Mr. Day
Lewis were making an equally strong effort to relate poetry

to the poet's secular 'beliefs', to his immediate social and political hopes and fears. But there is, Dr. Muir thinks, a permanent substance of poetry, a traditional poetic method, to which such revolutionary attitudes, whether technical or ideological, may be largely irrelevant. There is, as it were, a tradition, or there are a set of inherited poetic habits, which, even after the most violent disturbances, tend to re-establish themselves. And it has, of course, become a commonplace of criticism to assert that the best contemporary English writing (the best English writing since, say, about 1940) is no longer in any obvious sense 'experimental'. Like most commonplaces, this one has a great deal of truth in it; but it might be a more useful commonplace, and we might be able to define more precisely than we usually do the degree of truth in it, if we could define more firmly than we usually do what we mean by 'experimental'.

It has not, in fact, seemed necessary to most critics to attempt to define the notion of 'experiment' in writing with any great abstract precision simply because we can, in practice, so easily recognize a piece of experimental writing when we see it. Here, for instance, is a fragment from a fine poem by Mr. Ezra Pound, written between forty and fifty years ago, which is obviously 'experimental':

> 'See, they return: ah, see the tentative
> Movements, and the slow feet,
> The trouble in the pace and the uncertain
> Wavering!
> See, they return, one, and by one,
> With fear, as half-awakened;
> As if the snow should hesitate
> And murmur in the wind,
>   and half turned back;
> These were the "Wing'd-with-Awe,"
>   Inviolable.'

Here, on the other hand, is a fragment from a good poem written the other day by Mr. Philip Larkin, which is

244

equally obviously *not* in that sense 'experimental', which is obviously in some broad sense 'traditional'. It is the first stanza of a three-stanza poem:

'Waiting for breakfast, while she brushed her hair,
I looked down at the empty hotel yard
Once meant for coaches. Cobblestones were wet,
But sent no light back to the loaded sky,
Sunk as it was with mist down to the roofs.
Drainpipes and fire-escapes climbed up
Past rooms still burning their electric light;
I thought: Featureless morning, featureless night.'

By comparing these two pieces of verse, both in their different ways so admirably assured, we may arrive at a clearer notion than we usually possess of what we mean by 'experimentalism' and what we mean by 'traditionalism' in poetry.

Mr. Larkin's passage is written in conversational iambic lines. He does not use rhyme till he wants to clinch an emotional point at the end of the stanza, but the punctuation, which does not allow the sense to flow very freely from one line to another (and, where there are no commas at the end of a line, creates isolated unrhymed couplets), is that of stanzaic poetry rather than, say, of Miltonic, Wordsworthian, or even Tennysonian blank verse. The metre is regular, but Mr. Larkin's lines are not so rigorously metrically strict as those of contemporaries of his like Mr. John Wain or Mr. Donald Davie who tend to model their individual lines on the couplet or quatrain lines of the eighteenth century: his lines do not go bang, bang, bang. He allows himself, for instance, pretty freely to substitute a trochee for an iambus in the middle of the line and to end an iambic line on a trailing syllable that does not invite rhetorical emphasis:

'I *looked*/*down* at/the *empt*/ў hŏt/el *yard*.'

There is no eighteenth-century pastiche there; the line has the prosaic and dragging quality which Lytton Strachey noted, for instance, in a line of Hardy's,

'And the daytime talk of the Roman investigations.'

But in both cases the prosaic, dragging quality is appropriate (Hardy has probably been an important influence on Mr. Larkin, as he has been on the recent poetry of Mr. C. Day Lewis). Yet though Mr. Larkin's 'handling' or what Saintsbury would call his 'fingering' is free, the liberties he takes with the strict iambic line are, after all, traditional ones.

Mr. Larkin's presentation, again, is perfectly unelliptical. He sets a scene for us. The 'I' of the poem has been spending a night with a young woman at a hotel. While she is tidying herself up in the morning, he waits for breakfast, and looks out of the window on dreary weather and a dreary scene which he describes, as Crabbe might have, in exact prosaic detail. The technique is that of the first paragraph of a good short story. The emotive punch of the stanza (with the rhyme to reinforce it), or the moral commentary, comes only in the last line:

'I thought: Featureless morning, featureless night.'

The whole stanza up to that line has, it might be said, no necessary *intrinsic* poetic value in itself. It is a build-up for the line; in Mr. Eliot's much-worn but still useful phrase, all the lines describing the dreary morning through the window are the 'objective correlative' of that controlled but violent emotive gesture, 'Featureless morning, featureless night'. That is not, of course, the final gesture of the poem. The girl herself is the one element of hope in the first stanza and in the second stanza we are told,

'Turning, I kissed her
Easily for joy tipping the balance to love.'

In the third stanza, the negative and positive elements of feeling in the poem are balanced up. The poet addresses his

Muse and wonders if the perhaps facile and escapist happiness the girl offers him will be disapproved of by his Muse. Is it only in a state of anxiety and deprivation that we can write poetry?

> 'Are you jealous of her?
> Will you refuse to come till I have sent
> Her terribly away, importantly live
> Part invalid, part baby, and part saint?'

What we should note specially about Mr. Larkin's method is that he is concerned not merely with the evocation, however vivid, of a mood but with presenting the logic and sequence of a series of moods and with relating that logic and sequence to a clearly, almost prosaically, presented 'situation': closeness to 'fact', real or imagined, gives such poetry its solidity; but such closeness also cuts out the possibility of a concentrated, direct, and elliptical attack by the poet on our emotions. Mr. Larkin's poem moves us as a complex whole, which we have followed in all its complexity, or it probably does not move us at all. There is nothing, or almost nothing, that we 'apprehend' in the poem before we have 'comprehended' it. There are no single lines and images that flash out at us. The rhythmical shape, regular, patient, not excessively neat, mirrors the patience of the poet's logical processes. The impact of the poem is almost exactly equivalent to what the poem is 'about'.

With Mr. Pound's passage, on the other hand, we might be very deeply moved before we had bothered to ask ourselves what Mr. Pound is talking about. The direct and immediate arousing of an emotional response is what Mr. Pound is most strongly concerned with; and in a sense we have our response, when we read his lines, before we quite know what the situation is that we are responding to; we know that his vaguely defined characters, his 'they', are returning, broken in body and spirit, before we know what they are returning from or who they are—before we realize that they are spiritually defeated warriors of some sort. Even when Mr. Pound does present his 'situation', he presents it cryptically and allusively. Mr. Larkin fills in, for us, all the connections we need; Mr. Pound leaves us, trusting to the evocative effect of his rhythms, to fill in most of the necessary connections ourselves. Rhythm, we should notice, in a sense 'makes' Mr. Pound's poem; it is only one subsidiary, though important, element in the success of Mr. Larkin's poem.

Mr. Pound's rhythmical form, unlike Mr. Larkin's, is very strictly what Sir Herbert Read calls 'organic form' as distinct from 'imposed form': it is also what the American critic, Mr. Yvor Winters, describes (and to me not convincingly condemns) as 'imitative form'. The hesitant, painfully lingering movement of the lines—the pause between the epithet at the end of one line and its noun at the beginning of the next, 'tentative/Movements', 'uncertain/ Wavering'—seems in itself to define the lagging return of heroes from a great combat as broken men. It is of the essence of this kind of poem that its subject-matter should not be, vague, but multiple. I used to associate this fine fragmentary poem with the First World War and shell-shock; in fact, it was written around 1911. The possibility of a great war breaking out may, nevertheless, have been in Pound's mind; but whatever contemporary applications he may have had, half prophetically, at the back of his mind, he describes, tenuously in themselves, but vividly as to their mood and movements, archaic warriors, say from a Greek frieze: and this 'distancing', of course, gives him half of his effect. We think not only of *Good-bye to All That* but of Thucydides. Mr. Pound seems to be saying not only that one war has broken up, or will break up, brave men, but that all wars do.

And war, itself, in Mr. Pound's mind might have been a metaphor for something else. There are many kinds of combat, many kinds of defeat. Mr. Pound might be thinking of the struggle of artists and poets of his own generation, himself, Mr. Eliot, Mr. Wyndham Lewis, among others, to revolutionize, to renew English art and poetry, and of the harsh discouragement they met with. He is making a very general statement, a statement about the nature of courage and failure, of attack and repulse, generally, with a range of disparate concrete instances in mind; and for all these he is evoking a drastically simplified fictive instance, or a symbol. This direct attack on the emotions, this daringly expressive use of rhythm, this elliptical effect of multiple reference, this central reliance on the image-symbol, are, it might seem, essential parts of what we mean by 'experimentalism', in the English poetry of this century. 'Experimental' poetry is poetry which, if it is successful, we 'apprehend' immediately, but which we may never, perhaps, fully intellectually 'comprehend'. And given that the experimental method is capable of such triumphs, the question we may have to ask ourselves is why, in the last ten years or so, so many good English poets of all generations have been so definitely in retreat from it.

There is, of course, one very simple but probably not adequate answer. The most notable experimental poems of this century, poems like *The Love Song of J. Alfred Prufrock*, *The Waste Land*, *Hugh Selwyn Mauberley*, or *The Cantos*, gained a great part of their immediate impact on their earliest readers from an effect of shock. They were not what people expected poetry to be. Now that they are part of the canon, the young poet who imitates their method cannot expect to obtain that effect of shock. 'Modernism' in poetry no longer rouses surprise or indignation; in an expressive Americanism, it is—not as an achievement, but as a fashion —'old hat'. When everybody takes it for granted that of course a contemporary poem must be obscure, the more original young poets will set out to show that it can be clear; when their respected elders, like Sir Herbert Read, preach to them on the advantages of free verse, they will be tempted to show off their paces in the *villanelle* and in *terza rima*; when there has been a great deal of emphasis by older poets on the elements of feeling, gesture, evocation, imagery, as being of primary importance in poetry, it is natural for the young to insist on the notion of a poem as a logical structure. In that sense, the reaction over the past ten years or so towards standards of clarity and correctness, towards the plain style, towards the sort of structural solidity which has been illustrated in Mr. Larkin's poem, could have been foreseen, before it happened, by any prescient critic.

The young are always in revolt against their elders, and there are times when what Dr. Donald Davie calls 'a rational conservatism' in aesthetics is itself the most appropriate of revolutionary attitudes. Again, Mr. Eliot once wisely remarked that the poet has two duties to language, which might appear at first sight contradictory; when the language of poetry seems to be growing stale, it needs an infusion of new blood from common speech; but when common speech itself seems to be in decay, it is the duty of the poet to attempt to preserve the traditional dignity of the language. In their attitude to diction, the best younger poets today do, certainly, seem to be Atticisers rather than Alexandrians. They shore no fragments of foreign speech against their ruins, as Mr. Eliot and Mr. Pound used to do. They do not, as Mr. Auden and Mr. MacNeice once did, snatch slangy and racy phrases from the air of current speech to vivify their poetry.

One reason for this new conservatism is, probably, that our current spoken idiom is rather obviously in decay: and, if this is so, there is obviously a great deal to be said for the young poet's setting out—whatever else he sets out to do— to be understood.

Yet when all has been said on behalf of the new conservatism in poetics, most lovers of poetry will find that they have still some reservations to make. We live, certainly, in a cramping and a damping time, a time that seems to demand from the man of letters, rather than any more exciting virtue, a cool common sense, a feeling for measure and balance. But are these virtues, admirable as they are, ever quite the central virtues of the poet? One of the main functions of poetry, as Arnold remarked, is certainly at all times to strengthen us; but are we always made stronger by playing safe? There has been a great reaction among poets of the new generation against the influence, for instance, of Dylan Thomas since his tragic death. Certainly, he did not play safe; certainly his poems are often hard to construe and almost impossible to paraphrase, and it may be that he sometimes did not care very much whether, at the level of a prosaic interpreter, they 'made sense'. These lines of his, for instance, might seem very intractable to exposition, though they can obviously be related vaguely to the bombing of London, to the deaths and dangers of that time. Yet they have a kind of poetic eloquence which even the most sympathetic of readers does not expect to find exemplified in the work of the younger generation, in the same degree:

> ' On almost the incendiary eve
>   Of several near deaths,
> When one at the great least of your best loved
>   And always known must leave
> Lions and fires of his flying breath,
>   Of your immortal friends
> Who'd raise the organs of the counted dust
>   To shoot and sing your praise,
> One who called deepest down shall hold his peace
>   That cannot sink or cease
>   Endlessly to his wound
> In many married London's estranging grief.'

Let us compare with that passage two fine stanzas by Mr. Donald Davie, which, for that matter, many readers may also find obscure; but their syntax is clear and their meaning is clear in its setting. Mr. Davie means that Cambridge, which is his topic, is a bad place to write poetry in because there is too much intellectual chatter, of a thin kind, in the university itself and because the rustic surroundings of the city are too flatly and cloddishly rustic. And he, also, is eloquent in his late Augustan way, though not so eloquent as Dylan Thomas in his obscure Pindaric way:

> 'I wonder still which of the hemispheres
> Infects the other, in this grassy globe;
> The chumbling moth of Madingley, that blears
> The labourer's lamp, destroys the scarlet robe.
>
> It was the Muse that could not make her home
> In that too thin and yet too sluggish air,
> Too volatile to live among the loam,
> Her sheaves too heavy for the talkers there.'

Taking greater risks, Thomas seems at last to reach at a greater prize; almost we grasp, when we read him, a grand statement about life, death, friendship, mourning, about the obscure interconnections of affection in a great city, about the intensification of our awareness of all these matters at a time when our own lives, and our friends' lives, hang in a balance. We almost grasp a grand universal statement. Mr. Davie's statement is about a particular place, certainly a very interesting place, and about its suitability as a background for poets. In the end, it is a specialized statement, for if the reader does not know Cambridge, and is not himself a poet, is he interested?

Perhaps the experimental mood may again revive in English poetry, as young poets a little relax their grip on safe particularizations—on 'facts', as that term was used in our remarks on Mr. Larkin—and reach out for the universal, even if across a gulf. There are, indeed, contemporary and fairly young poets, not belonging to any 'movement', who take this risk. Mr. W. S. Graham battles perpetually with the single universal problem of the dizzying flux of experience and its paradoxical relationship to the order that the poet makes out of words; he takes the risk of seeming often incomprehensible. Mr. David Gascoyne, with a tense, nervous spirituality, explores the 'bad lands' of the modern consciousness; he takes the risk of seeming often thin, and strained, and strident. The tentative achievements of such pioneers may, perhaps, matter more in the long run than the most gallant of concerted actions for control, for structure, for poetry as plain sense. The new rational conservative reaction was certainly called for; in Mr. Larkin at any rate—and there is at least remarkable promise in some of its other adherents—it has produced a poet of remarkable intelligence and sensitivity. Yet, though reason has its rights, the imagination, and the obscurer depths of our intuitive apprehension, these have their rights, too. In the end, there will always be experiment in poetry. The poet must always explore.

Contemporary Poetry and
the Anti-Romantic Idea

I

In the first essay in this book, I tended to accept the argument that a good deal of modern poetry, much of Mr. Eliot's and Mr. Pound's, for instance, which at one time was considered as marking a reaction against the romantic tradition, can be considered, in fact, as continuing and perhaps completing that tradition. Of the three arguments for this position, Sir Herbert Read's, Mr. John Bayley's, and Mr. Frank Kermode's, I was most impressed by Mr. Frank Kermode's. For him, the three essential qualities of the romantic attitude to poetry are, firstly, the emphasis on the image or symbol, what Professor Lehmann calls the 'aesthetic monad', as giving the poet insight into some realm of being which is out of the reach, for instance, of mere rational discourse; the notion of a poem as something that grows like a plant, not something that is built like a house; and the notion of the isolation of the poet (since he lives between necessarily intermittent, and uncertain, moments of revelation) and of the unhappy tension which is forced on him by the necessity of choice between what Yeats called 'perfection in the life' and 'perfection in the work'. There is a rival theory of poetry, which can be called the theory of poetry as a kind of moral discourse; and it is to this rival theory that, it seems to me, many of the younger poets of the 1950s consciously or unconsciously adhere. I want to say something about this theory.

The anti-romantic theory has been very clearly stated in

our own time by Professor Yvor Winters, the American critic. Where romantic criticism usually starts with putting a main emphasis on the notion of the image, anti-romantic criticism tends to start with the notion of the statement. For Professor Winters, a poem is primarily 'a statement in words', but a statement with 'a controlled content of feeling'. In this, it does not differ at all from many works written in prose but the use of verse permits at all times 'the expression of more powerful feeling' and of 'finer shades of feeling'. The words out of which poetic statements are made communicate concepts, as well as having associations of feeling. The relationships between concept and feeling are, for Professor Winters, roughly those of something determinant and that which is determined by it. Thus, it is just possible, for instance, that a Japanese poet might use the Japanese word for 'fire' as an equivalent for whatever is the Japanese word for 'plum-blossom'. Nevertheless, this will happen rarely and '*fire* will . . . have few opportunities to gather connotations from the concept, *plum-blossom*'. When a poet uses the word 'fire' the emotional effect of what he is saying, on us, will in fact have comparatively little to do, usually, with such remoter literary associations but much with whether the poet is talking about 'a fire on a hearth, in a furnace, or in a forest'. The rational statements which a poem makes, in fact, through referring to outward aspects of the world, through denoting things, are the 'motives', in Professor Winters's phrase, for the 'emotions' which poetry arouses in us. A poem, in fact, should present to us a situation of some sort, and a judgment on that situation, and we shall judge the judgment—and therefore judge the poem—rather as we should judge such a judgment on such a situation in 'real life'. 'The rational content', says Professor Winters, 'cannot be eliminated from words; consequently, the rational content cannot be eliminated from poetry. If it is unsatisfactory in itself, a part of the poem is unsatisfactory; the poem is damaged beyond argument. If we deny this, we must surely explain ourselves very fully.'

Professor Winters thus makes a distinction between what he calls 'rational progression' in a poem, a full structure of events or arguments motivating appropriate feelings, and what he thinks of as the modern decadent mode of 'qualitative progression', the presentation of a succession of not fully motivated feelings, linked only by some inner similarity. Two American critics, Mr. Wimsatt and Mr. Beardsley illustrate what Professor Winters is objecting to by quoting a comic poem by Mr. Morris Bishop:

'Moister than an oyster in its clammy cloister,
I'm bluer than a wooer who has slipped in a sewer,
Chiller than a killer in a cinema thriller,
Madder than an adder with a stone in the bladder.
If you want to know why, I cannot but reply:
  It is really no affair of yours.'

Wimsatt and Beardsley go on:
  'We offer the following crude example as a kind of skeleton figure to which we believe all the issues can be attached.

  1. X feels as angry as a hornet.
  2. X whose lunch has been stolen feels as angry as a hornet.

No. 1 is, we take it, the qualitative poem, the vehicle of a metaphor, an objective correlative—for nothing. No. 2 adds the tenor of the metaphor, the motive for feeling angry, and hence makes the feeling itself more specific. The total statement has a more complex and testable structure. The element of aptitude, or ineptitude, is more susceptible of discussion. "Light thickens and the crow makes wing to the rooky wood" might be a line from a poem about nothing, but initially owed much of its power, and we dare say still does, to the fact that it is spoken by a tormented murderer who, as night draws on, has sent his agents out to perform a further "deed of dreadful note".'

The younger English poets of the 1950s do not go in

much for poetical theorizing but one feels that if they did
their theories might not be unlike that of Professor Winters,
as glossed by Mr. Wimsatt and Mr. Beardsley. (One of
them, indeed, Mr. Thom Gunn, has worked with Professor
Winters in California.) The one newer English poet who
has written ambitiously about poetics, Dr. Donald Davie,
seems in what he has to say on behalf of an unelliptical,
explicit syntactical structure in poetry to be talking about
the same sort of thing, at least, as Professor Winters is talking about in his distinctions between 'rational progression'
and 'qualitative progression'. For all these writers, our
emotional response to a poem should be a response to how
the poem itself responds to a situation which we are able to
envisage with a considerable degree of definiteness and concreteness, *apart* from the poem. The final judgment, for
Professor Winters, on a poem is a moral judgment and
here Matthew Arnold, another notable anti-romantic
critic, might have agreed with him. Let me quote a famous
passage from one of Arnold's letters:

"They still think that the object of poetry is to produce
exquisite bits and images—such as Shelley's clouds *shep-
herded by the unwilling wind*, and Keats's *passim*: whereas
modern poetry can only subsist by its contents; by becoming a complete *magister vitae*, as the poetry of the ancients
did; by including, as theirs did, religion with poetry, instead
of existing as poetry only. . . . But the language, style, and
general proceedings of a poetry which has such an immense
task to perform must be very plain, direct, and severe; and
it must not lose itself in parts or ornamental work, but must
press forward to the whole. . . .'

I have been assuming, throughout this book, that the
language of poetry is a 'language by itself'; if Winters and
Arnold are right, it is not: the difference between, say
Arnold's *Literature and Dogma* and his *Rugby Chapel*, in so
far as both 'subsist by their contents' can merely be that
verse permits Arnold the expression of 'more powerful
feeling than is possible in prose' and also at all times 'the

expression of finer shades of feeling'. There is lots of prose which we ought to be able to condense into poetry; any good poem we ought to be able to expand into rational persuasive prose. We could gain power and discrimination doing the one, provided slower-witted readers with a useful crib doing the other. This leaves me unhappy. I remain obstinately convinced that the difference between, say, an eloquent paragraph of Ruskin's and a stanza of *In Memoriam* is a difference in kind. Real poems have been written in prose, very occasionally, as by Rimbaud and Baudelaire, but they are *tours de force*. I think one might express one main difference between poetry and prose, even prose full of colour and feeling, by speaking not, like Professor Winters, of poetic statements, but, like Professor R. P. Blackmur, of poetic gestures; by talking of not what a poem, in a possible prose paraphrase of its separable sense, *says*, but of what as a whole, sense, tone, feeling, intention, in my response to it, in so far as that is adequate, it *does*.

Dr. Edwin Muir, writing about Mr. Frank Wilson's recent book on Yeats and neo-Platonism, made a point like this. He said that, to be sure, the exposition of a neo-Platonic doctrine on the after-life might be part of the subject-matter of *Byzantium*, but that it was insensitive to take it as the *meaning* of that poem, the total meaning, the upshot, what one is left with. And this theory of poetry as a branch of moral eloquence (I am not, I hope, being unfair to Winters or to Arnold in describing it as that) falls down also, it seems to me, on simple psychological grounds. These: one does not sit down to write a poem with the idea in one's head of a separable prose content, edifying and coherent, which one will now put into verse: one discovers usually only after a great deal of groping the shape that the poem itself wanted to take. One does not even start with a notion, whether clear or vague, of a set of edifying attitudes to be 'put across'. On the contary, one starts with a set of inner tugs, or tensions, in painfully different directions, and the therapeutic value of completing the poem may lie either in the clarification of the nature of these tensions through a dramatic intensifying of them or in their at least symbolic resolution. Again, a critic who remains loyal to the romantic tradition, when Arnold talks contemptuously of 'exquisite bits and images', will reply that the image, as the great romantics understand it, is anything but an 'exquisite bit'. It is at once root and flower formative principle, and fulfilment in form. It is not an element *in* a poem, but a great poem, as a whole, is a single complex image, elemented out of other images. And one cannot take the images away and find a separable 'content', to be put into flat prose, by which the poem is to subsist:

> 'O chestnut tree, great-rooted blossomer,
> Are you the leaf, the blossom, or the bole?
> O body swayed to music, O brightening glance,
> How shall we know the dancer from the dance?'

That, at least, is the traditional romantic account of the matter. And it is against that that so many of our younger poets are in revolt.

II

One must not think of them, however, as simply going back consciously or unconsciously to what Arnold had to say. Many of them, of course, do believe in the importance of writing in a 'very plain, direct, and severe style', and the immediate reaction, there, of course, is against the style of, say, Dame Edith Sitwell, Mr. George Barker, Dylan Thomas. Severity, restraint, even dryness are prized as safeguards against some kind of overstrainings of the note, fakings, insincerities, and confusions. But where Arnold talks about the necessity of poetry 'becoming a complete *magister vitae*', of the necessity of poetry 'including religion . . . instead of existing as poetry only', do the young men there also agree with him.

One's first reaction would be to say no. Arnold, whatever his beliefs, had a Christian sensibility, which was the inescapable heritage of any Englishman of his education and class. I know very few English writers under forty who have got today what I would call a Christian sensibility, even where, as sometimes happens, they have as a matter of free intellectual choice assented to Christian belief. A liberal, empirical, sceptical, inquiring attitude, a suspiciousness towards all kinds of large or vague claims or statements, is the intellectual climate, in England if not elsewhere, of our age. There is not even today, among younger writers, that political idealism which in the 1930s gave some young poets a sense of shape and purpose in life not unakin to the sense of shape and purpose which Arnold's inherited Christian sensibility gave him. One thinks, for instance, of a certain plain directness, an honest simplicity of feeling, in this slight but very moving poem written shortly before his death in Spain by the young Communist, John Cornford:

> 'Heart of the heartless world,
> Dear heart, the thought of you,
> Is the pain at my side,
> The shadow that chills my view.
>
> The wind rises in the evening,
> Reminds that autumn is near.
> I am afraid to lose you,
> I am afraid of my fear.
>
> On the last mile to Huesca,
> The last fence for our pride,
> Think so kindly, dear, that I
> Sense you at my side.
>
> And if bad luck should lay my strength
> Into the shallow grave,
> Remember all the good you can;
> Don't forget my love.'

This is a poem written by a young man in love, who has a premonition that he is going to die in battle. and *sub specie aeternitatis* which side he is dying for, what set of hopes and illusions sustain him, does not matter much. But my point is that Cornford's sense of shape and purpose made possible the play between stoicism and pathos of

> 'I am afraid to lose you,
> I am afraid of my fear,'

or the moving ambiguity of the last two lines:

> 'Remember all the good you can,
> Don't forget my love.'

His love, when one read the poem first in the 1930s, didn't mean merely his romantic love for her, the 'dear heart' in the poem, but the generous love, for which he was dying for his fellow men. The modesty, the lack of ostentation of

> 'And if bad luck should lay my strength
> Into the shallow grave'

reminded one also that here was a romantically striking individuality subduing itself without fuss, but not without an acute awareness of what it was sacrificing, to a common purpose. And what might worry us about a lot of poetry of the 1950s in this same plain style is just, perhaps, the lack of these agreed, or these subconsciously absorbed and accepted, moral overtones.

Yet they are not wholly lacking. There is a poem by Mr. Philip Larkin, 'Church Going', which everyone who writes or lectures about the state of poetry in England in the 1950s finds himself bringing forward as the show-piece of the 'New Movement'. It is a poem on this whole subject of the break, in younger writers, with all sorts of aspects of the sense of tradition. And on the 'sense of tradition', when he writes about it in prose, Mr. Larkin is explicit enough:

'As a guiding principle I believe that every poem must be its own sole freshly-created universe, and therefore I have no belief in "tradition" or a common myth-kitty or casual allusions in poems to other poems or poets, which I find unpleasantly like the talk of literary understrappers letting you see they know the right people.'

And again, even more explicitly perhaps, Mr. Larkin writes:

'I find it hard to give any abstract views on poetry and its present condition as I find theorizing on the subject no help to me as a writer. In fact it would be true to say that I make a point of not knowing what poetry is or how to read a page or about the function of myth. It is fatal to decide, intellectually, what good poetry is because you are then in honour bound to try to write it, instead of the poems that only you can write.'

Now in view of these statements, what is interesting about 'Church Going' is that it works its way through from a toughly anti-traditional attitude, like that of these prose fragments, to a deep understanding of what, at one very important level at least, the tradition was about. The poet, on a bicycle trip, enters an empty church, inspired by some vague motive of half-irritated curiosity. He takes in the details of the interior in a quick, blank, bored way, but is also aware of something that could be called an atmosphere,

'. . . a tense, musty, unignorable silence.'

He takes off his bicycle clips from his trouser legs in a gesture of awkward respect (for what other people believe); he parodies the reading of the end of the lesson, in a gesture of equally awkward assertion (of what he himself believes, or disbelieves). He leaves an Irish sixpence. The place, he reflects, was not worth stopping for, but he did stop. Why? Partly a kind of nagging curiosity about what is going to happen to churches when nobody goes to church any more. Superstitious women may still haunt churchyards in the hope of seeing ghosts or picking magical herbs, but superstition will die as belief has died, disbelief itself will become insignificant, and will anything be left of churches but mere stone shells?

The church will be merely a building decaying. It may be visited by antiquaries and sentimentalists, both types whom the poet dislikes. Yet perhaps it will, after all, be visited most by people like himself who, without belief, without even an imaginative or sentimental sympathy with belief are drawn to churches because these were the places where the three great moments of human life, birth, marriage, death, were 'held unspilt', were 'robed as destinies', whereas in a purely secular society they tend to lose all dignity and coherence, to fall apart as mere natural 'compulsions'. The church is a serious place, and his serious moods draw even the unsympathetic agnostic, atheist, 'liberal humanist', plain man—however the poet would characterize himself—towards it. There is a traditional feeling that it is a proper place to grow wise in: if only because so many dead people lie around it in the churchyard and—this is implied rather than stated—the serious contemplation of death as the end of human life must teach us wisdom.

It is interesting that it is possible to suggest the impressiveness of this poem of Mr. Larkin's simply by giving an account, of this sort, of its 'rational progression': without quoting from it in any detail. It is, in fact, very well written, but, as in much of Mr. Larkin's work, there are few phrases, images, or even lines which are very striking out of their context. And yet the poem very subtly modulates from a rather uneasy jauntiness in the first stanza to, in the last, something that we can recognize as a quiet, a Wordsworthian or a Hardyesque version of the 'grand style'. The felicities are of a quiet, unobvious sort. The 'dubious women' who come to the graveyard to pick simples are dubious like dubious characters (they might be witches) and 'dubious', or sceptical, about whether the simples are likely to do any good. In a phrase like 'accoutred frowsty barn', the formality of 'accoutred' somehow checks, or cushions, the sneer of 'frowsty barn'. It is as if Mr. Larkin were saying: 'Though I sound contemptuous, I am not.' In the last stanza the phrase 'gravitating to this ground' suggests, without specifying, the graveyard and the pull of death. None of these felicities are grandiose or stagy, but they are inspired by a subtle tact. They may not seem memorable at a first reading, but in fact they stick in one's memory. One should also point out that the rhythm, which in the first stanza has an ambling pedestrian air, is flexible enough for such effects as this,

> 'But superstition, like belief, must die,
> And what remains when disbelief has gone?
> Grass, weedy pavement, brambles, buttress, sky,'

or of the very last two lines, one cut sharply into three members, the other an unbroken clinching condensation, of the poem:

> 'Which, he once heard, was proper to grow wise in,
> If only that so many dead lie round.'

And, if one keeps to Professor Winters's critical method, one's final judgment on the poet's judgment, one's criticism of his criticism of life, given that one accepts the starting point of his explorations, will be favourable. Starting where he did, he has arrived at where he ought to have arrived. For all those who are anxious to dismiss the school of poets to which Mr. Larkin belongs, the attitudes to poetry which he typifies, 'Church Going' is a stumbling-block. And it should be read alongside one of his own dignifiedly reticent remarks about his poetry:

'I write poems to preserve things I have seen/thought/felt . . . both for myself and for others, though I feel that my prime responsibility is to the experience itself, which I am trying to keep from oblivion for its own sake. Why I should do this I have no idea, but I think the impulse to preserve lies at the bottom of all art.'

III

I find Mr. Larkin, however, typical not only of what is best in his own school, but in his taste for 'rational progression' in a poem, and for subduedly sensitive rather than clamorously vibrant language, typical of much good work that is being done by young poets quite outside that school. Here, for instance, is a poem by Mr. Peter Redgrove, a poet in his twenties, who, as I happen to know from personal acquaintance with him, has at the most a grudging respect for Mr. Larkin and who abhors 'The Movement' and all its works:

BEDTIME STORY FOR MY SON

Where did the voice come from? I hunted through the
    rooms
For that small boy, that high, that head-voice,
The clatter at his heels caught on the door,
A shadow just caught moving through the door
Something like a school-satchel. My wife
Didn't seem afraid, even when it called for food
She smiled and turned her book and said:
'I couldn't go and love the empty air.'

We went to bed. Our dreams seemed full
Of boys in one or other guise, the paper-boy
Skidding along in grubby jeans, a music-lesson
She went out in the early afternoon to fetch a child
    from.
I pulled up from a pillow damp with heat
And saw her kissing hers, her legs were folded
Far away from mine. A pillow! It seemed
She couldn't love the empty air.

Perhaps, we thought, a child had come to grief
In some old room in the old house we kept,
And listened if the noises came from some especial room,
And then we'd take the boards up and discover
A pile of dusty bones like charcoal twigs and give
The tiny-sounding ghost a proper resting-place
So that it need not wander in the empty air.

No blood-stained attic harboured the floating sounds,
We found they came in rooms that we'd warmed with our
    life.
We traced the voice and found where it mostly came
From just underneath both our skins, and not only
In the night-time either, but at the height of noon
And when we sat at meals alone. Plainly, this is how we
    found
That love pines loudly to go out to where
It need not spend itself on fancy and the empty air.

This is not such an ambitious poem as Larkin's, of course,
and the word 'fancy' in the last line perhaps tactfully suggests how the poet wishes us to take it, as *a* fancy, 'something childish but very natural'. The tone, controlled by the
alternations of extreme formality and colloquial off-handed-
ness in rhythm and diction, by an ease that keeps us at a
certain distance, seems whimsical and detached, yet homely.
The starting point here is that the young couple whom the
poem is about do not have a child. The ghost or image
which haunts them, not really terrifyingly, is that not of a
dead child but of a child who wants to be born. The husband
lends himself to pretence, chasing something that is not
there, and the wife with a deeper understanding warns him
not to spend his feelings on fancy: 'I couldn't go and love
the empty air.' Even their dreams are haunted by little boys,
the husband wakes up to find his wife embracing a pillow,
as if it were a child or a cuddly toy, and mocks her, urbanely,
in return for her mockery:

> 'A pillow! It seemed
> She couldn't love the empty air.'

The third stanza, still unportentously, examines the possibility that they are really being haunted by something
sinister. But the tone, which suggests the giving of a mock
funeral to the bones say, of a tiny bird, robs the possibility
of even the shadow of real morbidity:

'. . . then we'd take up the boards and discover
A pile of dusty bones like charcoal twigs and give
The tiny-sounding ghost a proper resting-place
So that it need not wander in the empty air.'

The fourth stanza resolves the problem. The ghost came
from 'under their skins', from marriage demanding completion in new life, and the poet imagines himself telling his
small son that this is how he came to be born. It would, in
fact, be a fairy tale which would delicately expose the
essential urge that lies behind parenthood, without prema-
turely revealing 'the facts of life'. Summarizing this poem,
one becomes aware of how embarrassingly sentimental it
could have been and admires the coolness of tone which
keeps the humour and tenderness so firmly on this side of
sentiment. And, again, following Professor Winters's pre-
scriptions, we find ourselves morally approving the judgment, that married love in its fullness implies taking on the
risks and responsibilities of parenthood, and that fancy can
be guide to insight, which the poem unponderously implies. And, again, as in Mr. Larkin's poem, lines, phrases,
images are more impressive in their context than out of it;
we admire the little poem as a structure.

To concentrate on this notion of 'rational progression',
of a tight logical as well as formal structure in recent poetry
by young people, is, of course, probably unfairly to limit
my choices among poets to attend to. But this seems to me
a more obvious 'growing-point' in recent poetry than, for instance, the survival of the large, the sometimes vague romantic gesture. And in fact, this concern with tight coherence of
pattern is found also in poets who might call themselves romantic. Mr. Redgrove might. Mr. Martin Seymour-Smith,
who much admires Mr. Robert Graves, might call himself
romantic also, in so far as Mr. Graves might call himself that.
And perhaps this little poem of Mr. Seymour-Smith's might
count, for himself, not as poetry strictly, but might come
under Mr. Graves's category of 'satires and grotesques':

THE PUNISHMENT

Of all men living, who could be most wise
Insists that women may put out men's eyes;
Yet is himself protected from his ban
On love without obedience; he can
Inform the world that he's contented now
In a serene potency, and broadcast how
He lives happy in a woman's grip
Ignorant he holds the hand that holds the whip
Whose punishments therefore produce
Routine reports, no more, in Love's Official News.

Has cold theory caught this rebel up at last?
Are his days of fruitfulness all past
Now he guides her by whom he says he's led?
Or (though he's not yet blinded, sacrificed, or dead)
May not she (in fact) have sprung the last surprise,
Already used her cruelty (not his to subsidize)
To cut him, just a little, down to size,
By simply closing up, not putting out, his eyes?

Yet he's so restless on his tranquil rack
How harsh are we to wish such torments back
As would once more his whole frame wrench and
    crack?

Purely logically, that is the tightest of the three poems I
have so far considered in this essay. The effect of the metrical
and syntactical devices, the pauses, the jerks, the phrases cut
off by commas or enclosed in brackets is primarily to emphasize a series of logical paradoxes; and hence to criticize
ironically a 'romantic' attitude to poetry which, in his
straight poems, is very much Mr. Seymour-Smith's own
attitude. The satire is on the White Goddess, not taken
poetically, but taken all too prosaically, as a guide to everyday living. The idea is that here is a distinguished poet who

believes that good poetry comes out of letting oneself be tormented by women and never, in a horrible patriarchal way, demanding obedience from them. But, more patriarchal than he thinks he is, the poet has in fact a dutiful wife who only wants to obey him. She torments him, if at all, only because she is dutiful, because she thinks that is what he wants and needs to let him go on writing poetry. But, without knowing it, he holds the hand that holds the whip, and this mockery of torment produces only routine poems. Has, in fact, the poet's desperate and paradoxical theory proved true, and now he is happily domesticated is he also poetically sterile? Or, wait a moment: at a more obscure level, is the Threefold Goddess not still at work? Could there be a more humiliating punishment for this type of hero-poet than to be, not tortured but hoodwinked, scaled down to ordinary human size, reduced to comfortable, nodding somnolence? Yet even admitting that real intense torment might get first-rate poetry out of him, when he sees how restless he is even on his tranquil rack—perhaps Mr. Seymour-Smith had Pope's line in mind,

'Stretched on the rack of a too easy chair,'

would we, for the sake of any poems at all, wish him to undergo his former torment? Here again an exposition of the *sense* of the poem reveals much about its quality. It develops as an argument. And again it implies a moral judgment, with which we are forced to agree, on an element either of self-deception or of let's-pretend in a certain kind of romantic attitude; yet behind the satire there is an undertone, as in the first line,

'Of all men living, who could be most wise,'

of respect and sympathy.

Mr. Seymour-Smith is critically concerned in this poem, it seems to me, with the problem of poetic sincerity. And the main case *for* the anti-romantic attitude in many young poets in the 1950s is not a case against the romantic tradition in general, but a case against certain romantic attitudes, gestures, kinds of phrase, kinds of image, which in the climate of our day give the impression of pose, of stridency, of putting on the dog, of laying it on excessively thick. It is one of these sudden shifts of educated taste which leave certain poets of real talent and accomplishment for a time at least feeling high and dry. It is not they who have changed, it is the audience. What the younger reader especially tends to ask today about new poetry is: 'It sounds all right, but does it ring true?' A question very hard for the poet himself to answer when, because of this shift of taste in his readers, he has lost what used to be his sounding board.

I should like to quote finally a poem by a very young writer, indeed, Mr Jonathan Price, about this whole problem of sincerity, tone, the sounding board. In a sense it says more briefly and positively, more one-sidedly also, some things I have been saying in this essay. It is an apology, a rather pertly defiant one, for not being romantic:

MANNER OF SPEAKING

'Where are these poets' hearts?' a reader cries.
Not withered, but not worn upon the sleeve
Of singing robes. Some things they chose to leave
To bards who wield their pens beneath their thighs.

Acknowledged legislators, too, you find
Despairing over some poetic flower:
'So-and-so should be writing at this hour,
Mankind hath need of him.' He needs mankind.

When no great faith inspires a heaving breast
Even hot air is too much to expect.
Slogans deflated prompt the intellect
To check for faults by probing all the rest.

To make all fair in love that's fair in war
Detachment helps: as eyes grow dim and close
At an embrace, so lovers' nearness throws
Words out of focus. So with verse, but more.

Manner of speech depends in part on choice,
In part on circumstance: when values quake—
Black, white; right, wrong; on purpose, by mistake—
One shuns the shouting, trusts the speaking voice.

Some compare notes with an old writer's ghost;
But, by annihilating all that's made
With echoes of a literary shade,
Falsetto strains are all the song they boast.

Ventriloquism, like faked passion, shows.
Prospectors stake, then did beneath their claim
To riches; which suggests the poet's aim
Is writing to discover what he knows.

I do not think this is such a good poem as the other three
I have dealt with. A good poet should not bother about
slogans having been deflated, they should not have taken
him in in the first place. There is a kind of smartness in the
tone, and it is very pert to reproach other writers for 'comparing notes with an old writer's ghost', when you yourself
have just modelled three of your most effective lines,

'Manner of speech depends in part on choice,
In part on circumstance; when values quake—
Black, white; right, wrong; on purpose, by mistake—'

on some great lines by an older living writer, William
Empson, from *Arachne*:

"Twixt devil and deep sea, man hacks his caves;
Birth, death; one, many; what is true and seems;
Earth's vast hot iron, cold space's empty waves.'

These lines of Mr. Empson's not only 'ring true' but they 'sound all right' in a much more notable way, than any of the lines of the in many ways admirable younger poets whom I have been quoting. Their reverberance does suggest one reservation that one still has about this new anti-romantic poetry by young writers, this poetry of moral exploration, moral eloquence. One certainly wants poetry to hold together, to ring true, to relate to life, to contain a kind of judgment on life. One wants more than that, one wants the utterance of 'something above a mortal mouth': one does not want all poets 'cut . . . down to size'.

In the period we are living through, the 'accurate and sensitive' qualities of poetry by young writers (the phrase is Mr. Geoffrey Moore's, about Miss Elizabeth Jennings) are something to be grateful for, and as a cool emotional balance is the quality we most need in daily life, we should be grateful also to see it reflected in poetry. And it may be, as Mr. Donald Davie has suggested that the great romantic tradition has now at last run its course, and that we should take up the threads where the Augustans dropped them, think of the poet as the intelligent and sensitive critic of society, of the poem as a moral structure. I think the notion of *tone* as a critical touchstone—'It sounds all right, but does it ring true?'—which I know that I myself have come to rely on more and more over the years is basically an Augustan touchstone. I think that, like Dr. Johnson on Gray's *Odes* ('dull upon stilts; dull in a new way; dull in everything') that when we are bored we ought to have the right to say so, and should cheerfully take the risk of subsequent ages thinking us wrong. Nothing pleases me more in the work of critics of poetry younger than myself than their readiness to declare that the Emperor has no clothes. People of my generation used to lean over backwards to declare, 'There must be something in it!' Yet, with all that, when I had been reading through a great many poets of the 1950s as a prelude to writing this essay, I turned for relief to *Lycidas*:

> '. . . for what could that have done?
> What could the Muse herself that Orpheus bore,
> The Muse herself, for her enchanting son,
> Whom universal nature did lament,
> When, by the rout that made the hideous roar,
> His gory visage down the stream was sent,
> Down the swift Hebrus to the Lesbian shore.'

I thought, when I read that, that if Matthew Arnold believed poetry in our modern world 'can only subsist by its contents', he also believed in touchstones. And I wondered what are the 'contents' of this passage about Orpheus, which moves me almost to tears. For me, a strange joy in which the ideas of profound awe, intense terror and grief are somehow consumed. I am reading the passage after Frazer and after Freud. For Arnold what—graceful classical reminiscence? For Dr. Johnson what—stale pedantry, the stuff of schoolboys' Latin verses rehashed? It subsists, surely, by its *form*. Clay vessels can contain liquor as wholesome as brazen vessels; but it is we ourselves, as readers, from age to age, who put the new wine into the old vessels; my Milton is not Arnold's, not Johnson's. We bring our own 'ring of truth', but it is what 'sounds all right' that lasts for us to test it. And when, down the stream of time, the clay vessels clash with the brazen vessels, it is right and proper that they should crumble and sink.

Index

Index

Index

Index

Empson, William, 9, 65, 165–6, 170, 171, 179, 184, 193–201, 231, 235, 236, 271, 272; apparent casualness of, 193–4; as 'difficult' poet, 196–7; disciples of, 195–6; 'flat' and 'grand' manner of, 194–6; inner disturbance of, 194–5; and the metaphysical poets, 197; religion of, 197–200; as sceptic, 197–8; systems distrusted by, 197, 198; wide range of, 200–201

Enoch Arden (Tennyson), 172

Essays in Criticism (periodical), 107

Experimental poems of Eliot, Pound, 249; of later poets, 244 seqq.

Exploration, as poet's function, 253

'Extempore Effusion on the Death of James Hogg' (Wordsworth), 24

External objective phenomena, 17

'Faery Song, A' (Yeats), 47–8

'Fallacy of imitative form' (Winters), 177

'Familiar Letter to Siegfried Sassoon' (Graves), 140

'Fern Hill' (Dylan Thomas), 228, 229–30

'Fire Sermon' (Buddhist), Empson quotes, 198, 199

'Fisherman, The' (Yeats), 54

Fletcher, Iain, 9

'Force that through the green fuse, The' (Dylan Thomas), 218

Form and content, in romantic poem, 34–5; Valéry on, 31

Formal equivalence (symbol), 16, 18, 19

For the Time Being (Auden), 158, 161, 166

Four Quartets (Eliot), 119, 168

Frazer, Sir J., 110, 273

French, Mrs. (of Sir Jonah Barrington's *Memoirs*), 60

Freud, S., 156, 273

Frost, Robert, 127

'Funeral, The' (Spender), 205

'Furious Voyage, The' (Graves), 137

'Fusion of thought and feeling' (Eliot), 37

'Game of Chess, A' (Eliot), 107

Gascoyne, D., 168, 224, 253

Gentile, 182

Gnosticism, 139

Goethe, 32, 33

Gogarty, O. St. John, 54

Golden Bough, The (Frazer), 110

Goldsmith, Oliver, 161

Gonne, Maud, 38, 43, 46, 48, 50, 51, 59

Goodbye to All That (Graves), 145, 248

Gore-Booth, Eva, 62

Graham, W. S., 252

Grattan, H., 43, 53, 53 n.

Graves, Robert, 40, 47, 127, 135–48, 222, 239–40, 267; on Auden, 160; as anticipator of Auden, 143–4; dualistic theme of poetry of, 135 seqq.; early verse of, 139–43; *Poems, 1914–1926*, 143; *Poems, 1926–1930*, 143; politics of, 145, 147; vision of, 148

Gray, Thomas, 190; *Elegy* of, 13, 239; *Odes* of, 272

Gregory, Lady, 50, 51, 72

Grigson, Geoffrey, 217, 234

Groddeck, W., 150

Index

Index

Index

Index

Index

285